Conference of the North American Chapter of the Association for Computational Linguistics: Human Language Technologies 2016 (NAACL HLT 2016)

Demonstrations

San Diego, California, USA
12 – 17 June 2016

ISBN: 978-1-5108-2513-0

NAACL HLT 2016

The 2016 Conference of the North American Chapter of the Association for Computational Linguistics: Human Language Technologies

Proceedings of the Demonstrations Session

June 12-17, 2016
San Diego, California, USA

Introduction

iii

Welcome to the Demonstrations Session of NAACL HLT 2016 in San Diego.

The demonstrations session is an opportunity for researchers and developers to present their systems and programs related to natural language processing. We were fortunate to receive 32 outstanding papers, of which we accepted 20.

These systems will be displayed during the poster session on Monday and Tuesday of the conference.

Organizers:

John DeNero, University of California Berkeley
Mark Finlayson, Florida International University
Sravana Reddy, Wellesley College

Program Committee:

Željko Agić, University of Copenhagen
Omar Alonso, Microsoft Research
Tyler Baldwin, IBM Research
Keith Carlson, Dartmouth College
Jinho Choi, Emory University
Montse Cuadros Oller, Vicomtech-IK4
Thierry Declerck, German Research Center for Artificial Intelligence (DFK)
John DeNero, University of California Berkeley
Karthik Dinakar, MIT Media Lab
Mark Finlayson, Florida International University
Catherine Havasi, Luminoso
Brigitte Krenn, Austrian Research Institute for Artificial Intelligence (OFAI)
Finley Lacatusu, Language Computer Corporation
Changsong Liu, Michigan State University
Marie-Jean Meurs, University of Quebec in Montreal
Eni Mustafaraj, Wellesley College
Tsuyoshi Okita, Dublin City University
Petya Osenova, Sofia University
Arzucan Özgür, Bogazici University
Stelios Piperidis, Institute for Language and Speech Processing
Matt Post, Johns Hopkins University
Sravana Reddy, Wellesley College
Kirk Roberts, University of Texas at Dallas
Masoud Rouhizadeh, Oregon Health and Science University
Ivan Vladimir Meza Ruiz, National Autonomous University of Mexico
Irene Russo, Italian National Research Council
Sebastian Sulger, University of Konstanz
Le Sun, Chinese Academy of Sciences
Maarten van Gompel, Radboud University Nijmegen
Marc Vilain, MITRE
Xuchen Yao, kitt.ai
Liang-Chih Yu, Yuan Ze University

Table of Contents

Conference Program

June 13, 2016 (Monday)

rstWeb - A Browser-based Annotation Interface for Rhetorical Structure Theory and Discourse Relations
Amir Zeldes

Instant Feedback for Increasing the Presence of Solutions in Peer Reviews
Huy Nguyen, Wenting Xiong and Diane Litman

Farasa: A Fast and Furious Segmenter for Arabic
Ahmed Abdelali, Kareem Darwish, Nadir Durrani and Hamdy Mubarak

iAppraise: A Manual Machine Translation Evaluation Environment Supporting Eye-tracking
Ahmed Abdelali, Nadir Durrani and Francisco Guzmán

Linguistica 5: Unsupervised Learning of Linguistic Structure
Jackson Lee and John Goldsmith

TransRead: Designing a Bilingual Reading Experience with Machine Translation Technologies
François Yvon, Yong Xu, Marianna Apidianaki, Clément Pillias and Pierre Cubaud

New Dimensions in Testimony Demonstration
Ron Artstein, Alesia Gainer, Kallirroi Georgila, Anton Leuski, Ari Shapiro and David Traum

ArgRewrite: A Web-based Revision Assistant for Argumentative Writings
Fan Zhang, Rebecca Hwa, Diane Litman and Homa B. Hashemi

Scaling Up Word Clustering
Jon Dehdari, Liling Tan and Josef van Genabith

Task Completion Platform: A self-serve multi-domain goal oriented dialogue platform
Paul Crook, Alex Marin, Vipul Agarwal, Khushboo Aggarwal, Tasos Anastasakos, Ravi Bikkula, Daniel Boies, Asli Celikyilmaz, Senthilkumar Chandramohan, Zhaleh Feizollahi, Roman Holenstein, Minwoo Jeong, Omar Khan, Young-Bum Kim, Elizabeth Krawczyk, Xiaohu Liu, Danko Panic, Vasiliy Radostev, Nikhil Ramesh, Jean-Phillipe Robichaud, Alexandre Rochette, Logan Stromberg and Ruhi Sarikaya

rstWeb – A Browser-based Annotation Interface
for Rhetorical Structure Theory and Discourse Relations

Amir Zeldes

Department of Linguistics, Georgetown University
`amir.zeldes@georgetown.edu`

Abstract

This paper presents rstWeb, a new browser-based interface for Rhetorical Structure Theory and other discourse relation annotations. Expanding on previous tools for RST, rstWeb allows annotators to work online using only a browser. Project administrators can easily collect multiple annotations of the same documents on a central server, keep track of annotation processes and assign tasks and annotation schemes to users. A local version using an embedded web framework is also available, running offline on a desktop browser under the localhost.

1 Introduction

Since its introduction by Mann & Thompson (1988) Rhetorical Structure Theory has enjoyed continuing interest as a framework for the analysis of discourse relations, including the development of large scale corpora (especially the RST Discourse Treebank; RSTDT, Carlson et al. 2003) and automatic parsers (Joty et al. 2013, Surdeanu et al. 2015). However while the development of RST corpora and parsing has continued, there has been less progress in creating more up-to-date, collaborative and online interfaces for annotation, which would facilitate the development of new manually annotated data sets. Most work to date has used either the original RSTTool (O'Donnell 2000), a local desktop application written in Tcl/Tk, or its extension, the ISI RST Annotation Tool by Daniel Marcu (see: `http://www.isi.edu/~marcu/discourse/AnnotationSoftware.html`). Both tools are not being actively developed at pre-sent, and installing and running them across platforms can be challenging.

Meanwhile for other annotation tasks, online web interfaces have been developed which allow annotators to be trained and to work using only a browser, substantially facilitating the recruitment, curation and validation of data (e.g. Arborator, Gerdes 2013 for dependency syntax, or WebAnno, Yimam et al. 2013, for a variety of tasks). These server-based tools let project managers collect data centrally, without exchanging files with annotators, and track progress or log annotation processes automatically, while substantially reducing administration effort. The software presented here is meant to do the same for RST. Specifically it allows:

- Annotation using only a browser
- Import and export of RSTTool's .rs3 format
- Import of plain text (discourse unit per line)
- Support for multiple annotated versions of documents across users
- Enforcement of uniform annotation schemes across users
- Undo/redo functionality
- Logging of annotation steps
- Administration for user assignments, projects and guideline links
- Single mode for adding/deleting spans, multinuclear relations and satellite linking (no mode switching, see below)

The following section describes the technical infrastructure of rstWeb and the main requirements and workflows of the software. Section 3 briefly reports on a project employing rstWeb as an annota-

1

Proceedings of NAACL-HLT 2016 (Demonstrations), pages 1–5,
San Diego, California, June 12-17, 2016. ©2016 Association for Computational Linguistics

tion interface and estimates the reduction of user actions compared to previous tools based on annotation logs from RSTDT. Section 4 discusses some applications to discourse annotation outside RST. Section 5 ends with discussion for further work.

2 Software architecture

rstWeb[1] is written in Python with a SQLite backend, and these are required for the server running the software. In order to stay light-weight and responsive, JavaScript is used for the browser-based client, making the server-side demand almost no resources. jQuery and jsPlumb are used to render edges and animations. Following a static form-submit architecture (cf. Arborator, Gerdes 2013), no running services are used: Python scripts are exposed via a Web server (e.g. Apache), and calling them from a browser accesses the DB to serialize HTML for the client. For local machine use, a service script using the CherryPy framework can be used, requiring local users to install Python and CherryPy (`http://www.cherrypy.org/`). The software is platform independent, running on Mac, Linux and Windows platforms. Figure 1 gives a schematic overview of the system's architecture.

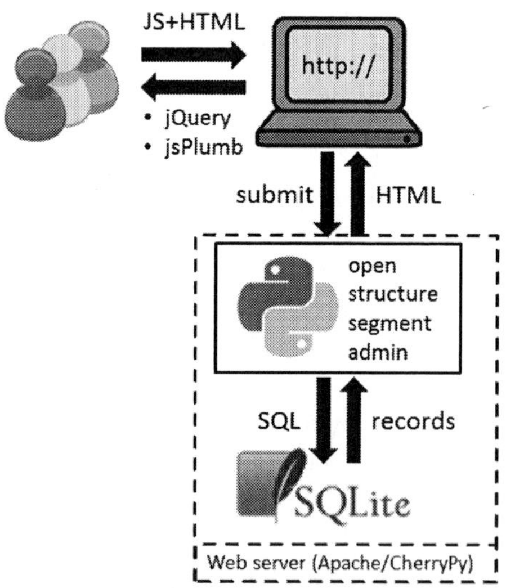

Figure 1: rstWeb schematic architecture.

Four scripts are exposed to the user, used to open and administrate projects ('open' and 'admin' scripts), and to annotate in two modes described below: 'segmentation' and 'structuring'.

[1] `http://corpling.uis.georgetown.edu/rstweb/info`

To annotate documents, users log in to the interface, where they can open any documents that have been assigned to them. Each user has their own copy of each assigned document, meaning that multiple users can annotate the same document in parallel for inter-annotator agreement experiments, though the tool does not support automatic calculation of agreement measures at present. Once a document has been opened, the user can move freely between two modes: segmentation of Elementary Discourse Units (EDUs), and structuring the units into an RST tree (see Figure 3 below).

In designing the annotation workflow, a central objective was to avoid constant switching between modes: in RSTTool, segmenting units, linking, unlinking, grouping them in spans or adding multinuclear relations, all required changing the 'mode' to do just that task; single clicks could then be used to carry out the action. This meant it was more convenient to complete multiple tasks of the same kind (e.g. spanning or unlinking) consecutively, which required some planning and reduced flexibility, or alternatively that frequent switching needed to be done. For rstWeb, the attempt was made to allow all operations on any node to be available simultaneously. This attempt has been successful for all tasks except for segmentation. An initial attempt to allow users to segment units within the RST diagram proved cumbersome, since reading EDUs in small boxes left-to-right is more difficult than reading the running text in one big box.

As a result, a dedicated segmentation mode was developed, the interface for which is shown in Figure 2. This interface closely resembles RSTTool's segmentation mode.

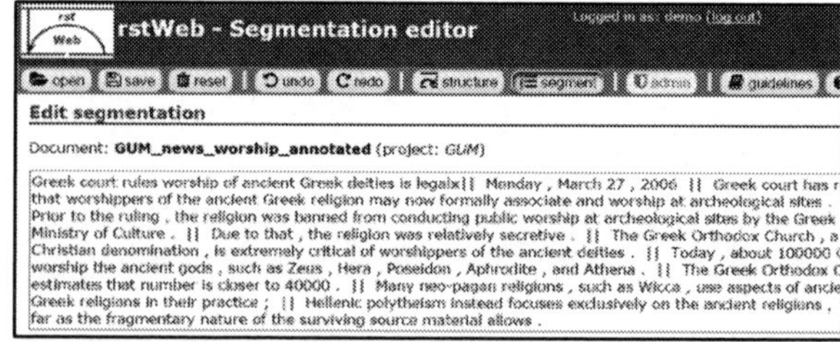

Figure 2: Discourse segmentation editor.

Users can move between modes and choose to re-segment while structuring: if a unit in a tree is segmented, the first portion of the divided segment retains the original function, and the second is created without attachment. Merging two units causes

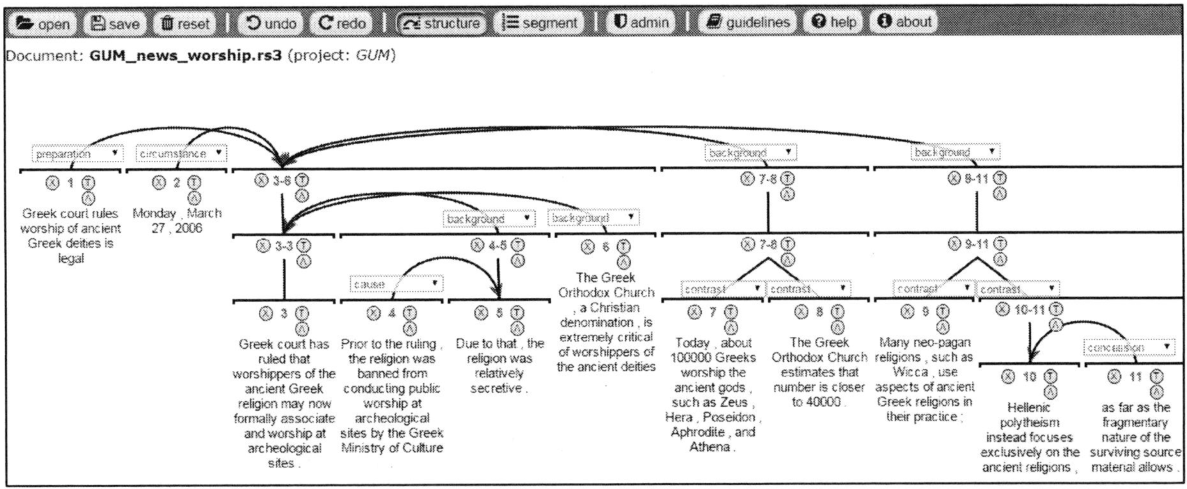

Figure 3: Structurer interface with an RST tree. The three buttons around each node allow users to unlink edges, create grouping spans or add multinuclear clusters above nodes, without switching annotation modes.

them to retain the attachment and label of the first unit. The tool has client-side undo/redo functionality, without submitting to the server, though undo/redo steps are logged as in the ISI tool.[2]

The other mode, structuring, is where the bulk of annotation work is done (see Figure 3). rstWeb supports the same tree structures as other tools, including crossing edges. However unlike earlier tools, there is no need to switch between annotation modes to connect or unlink nodes, add spans, or add multinuclear relations. These actions are handled by small buttons surrounding each node junction: X for unlinking, T for adding a span and ∧ for multinuclear nodes (see Figure 3). User reports suggest that this facilitates annotation substantially.

Finally, administrators can manage user assignments and import documents from plain text files (one EDU per line) or .rs3 files (RSTTool format), or export annotations in .rs3 format.[3] Documents can be grouped into projects, which can be given a guidelines URL for users to consult.

3   Annotating in rstWeb

rstWeb has been employed in the annotation of the GUM corpus (Zeldes 2016)[4], an open-access multilayer corpus including RST analyses, constructed via classroom annotation and extended yearly. The corpus contains texts from 4 genres: travel guides, how-to guides, online news and interviews. In the most recent round of data collection, encompassing 29 documents, RST annotation was done with rstWeb, instead of the previously used RSTTool. Documents were comparable in length (Ø 58.31 EDUs) with those in the RST Discourse Treebank with Ø 56.59 EDUs (Carlson et al. 2003). This suggests that the system can be used successfully for text sizes on par with the benchmark resource for RST. The amount of errors based on instructor corrections using rstWeb compared to RSTTool was very similar (see Zeldes 2016).

To give an idea of the mode changes required by a multi-mode workflow, switching between linking/unlinking/grouping and creating multinuclear clusters as in older tools, we can examine annotation step files from the RST Discourse Treebanks. Table 1 gives the necessary mode change rates per node (including non-terminals), and the proportion of changes per annotation step in 10 random Wall Street Journal documents from RSTDT (including undo actions, but excluding segmentation operations).

Although the tools are different and therefore hard to compare directly, rstWeb logs from the GUM data suggest a similar rate of Ø 0.43 action type changes per step, indicating that annotators generally use mode changes as needed in either environment, meaning the multimode interface should save a substantial amount of clicking.

---

[2] Step logging has been used in the evaluation of annotation methodology, for example in Marcu et al. (1999).

[3] This format can also be imported into corpus search tools supporting RST, such as ANNIS (Krause & Zeldes 2016).

[4] http://corpling.uis.georgetown.edu/gum

doc	cha	steps	nodes	cha/stp	cha/node
wsj_0602	74	143	128	0.5174	0.5781
wsj_0654	16	30	37	0.5333	0.4324
wsj_0667	18	25	33	0.72	0.5454
wsj_1146	207	546	636	0.3791	0.3254
wsj_1169	15	30	34	0.5	0.4411
wsj_1306	32	72	93	0.4444	0.3440
wsj_1387	113	209	271	0.5406	0.4169
wsj_2336	25	45	61	0.5555	0.4098
wsj_2373	12	39	58	0.3076	0.2068
wsj_2386	55	177	255	0.3107	0.2156
Ø	56.7	131.6	160.6	0.4809	0.3916

Table 1: Mode change proportions per step and node in 10 WSJ documents from the RST Discourse Treebank.

During a previous round of data collection for GUM, RST annotations for the same corpus with the same text types were created using RSTTool. Feedback from students who switched from working with RSTTool to rstWeb, as well as from instructors (including a trained teaching assistant), has been very positive.

4 Using rstWeb for other resources

Data has successfully been imported into rstWeb from several existing RST-annotated sources, including the RST Discourse Treebank (converted to .rs3) and the German Potsdam Commentary Corpus (Stede & Neumann 2014). Although the software has been designed specifically for RST annotation, it may be possible to use it for other types of annotation, especially those representing binary relations between clauses. In particular, it is possible to disable the buttons generating spans and/or multinuclear nodes: this could be useful for other (shallow) discourse parsing frameworks or subsets of these, in which annotators would not be allowed to create multinuclear nodes or possibly any form of hierarchy.

For some forms of annotation, and particularly for explicit connectives (e.g. marking up a word such as 'because') and gaps inside clauses (clause parts with no relations), as used e.g. in the Penn Discourse Treebank (Prasad et al. 2008), the interface is not suitable, since each unit of annotation must be broken off as a segment. For connectives, this could be a single word, which would be impractical to view in the RST style diagram. How-

ever for simple binary relation classification between clauses with similar schemas, the advantages of the online, browser-based interface may make it a useful option (cf. Figure 4, using the *Expansion.Conjunction* and *Expansion.Restatement* relations from PDTB; multinuclear buttons have been disabled, but hierarchies are still enabled).

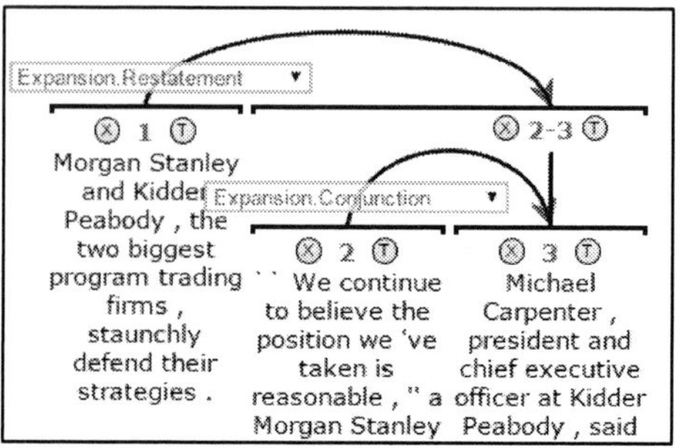

Figure 4: PDTB style hierarchical binary relations without connective annotation. Multinuclear buttons are disabled.

5 Conclusion

rstWeb offers a new, actively maintained tool for online, browser-based annotation of Rhetorical Structure Theory. The static script strategy of the backend means that server load when running rstWeb is negligible: it is not running at all unless a user has just submitted or requested data. Using CherryPy as a localhost container means that server code can be used offline or by single users who do not have access to a server – all code updates to the server version carry over to the local version. Using the browser as an interface means that users can work in a familiar environment, without installing software (at least for server based projects), that administrators do not need to exchange files with annotators, and that the system is cross-platform compatible without resorting to heavier Java based frameworks.

In future work, some additional features could be added to the software. In particular, it is currently not possible to edit the inventory of RST relations after the import of a document. Also, support for 'schemas', i.e. added span annotations to mark a unit as a 'title' etc., which was supported in previous tools, is not currently implemented, but is planned for an upcoming version. Finally, built in facilities for measuring inter-annotator agreement are interesting possible addition to the software.

References

Lynn Carlson, Daniel Marcu and Mary Ellen Oku-rowski. 2003. Building a Discourse-Tagged Corpus in the Framework of Rhetorical Structure Theory. In *Current and New Directions in Discourse and Dialogue*. (Text, Speech and Language Technology 22.) Kluwer, Dordrecht, 85–112.

Kim Gerdes. 2013. Collaborative Dependency Annotation. In *Proceedings of the Second International Conference on Dependency Linguistics (DepLing 2013)*. Prague, 88–97.

Shafiq Joty, Giuseppe Carenini, Raymond Ng, and Yashar Mehdad. 2013. Combining Intra- and Multi-Sentential Rhetorical Parsing for Document-Level Discourse Analysis. In *Proceedings of the 51st Annual Meeting of the Association for Computational Linguistics*. Sofia, Bulgaria, 486–496.

Thomas Krause and Amir Zeldes. 2016. ANNIS3: A New Architecture for Generic Corpus Query and Visualization. *Digital Scholarship in the Humanities* 31(1):118–139.

William C. Mann and Sandra A. Thompson. 1988. Rhetorical Structure Theory: Toward a Functional Theory of Text Organization. *Text* 8(3):243–281.

Daniel Marcu, Estibaliz Amorrortu, and Magdalena Romera. 1999. Experiments in Constructing a Corpus of Discourse Trees. In *Proceedings of the ACL Workshop Towards Standards and Tools for Discourse Tagging*. College Park, MD, 48–57.

Michael O'Donnell. 2000. RSTTool 2.4 - A Markup Tool for Rhetorical Structure Theory. In *Proceedings of the International Natural Language Generation Conference (INLG 2000)*. Mitzpe Ramon, Israel, 253–256.

Rashmi Prasad, Nikhil Dinesh, Alan Lee, Eleni Miltsakaki, Livio Robaldo, Aravind Joshi, and Bonnie Webber. 2008. The Penn Discourse Treebank 2.0. In *Proceedings of the 6th International Conference on Language Resources and Evaluation (LREC 2008)*. Marrakech, Morocco.

Manfred Stede and Arne Neumann. 2014. Potsdam Commentary Corpus 2.0: Annotation for Discourse Research. In *Proceedings of the Language Resources and Evaluation Conference (LREC 2014)*. Reykjavik, Iceland, 925–929.

Mihai Surdeanu, Thomas Hicks, and Marco A. Valenzuela-Escarcega. 2015. Two Practical Rhetorical Structure Theory Parsers. In *Proceedings of NAACL-HLT 2015*. Denver, CO, 1–5.

Seid Muhie Yimam, Iryna Gurevych, Richard Eckart de Castilho, and Chris Biemann. 2013. WebAnno: A Flexible, Web-based and Visually Supported System for Distributed Annotations. In *Proceedings of the 51st Annual Meeting of the Association for Computational Linguistics*. Sofia, Bulgaria, 1–6.

Amir Zeldes. 2016. The GUM Corpus: Creating Multilayer Resources in the Classroom. *Language Resources and Evaluation*. Available online at http://dx.doi.org/10.1007/s10579-016-9343-x.

Instant Feedback for Increasing the Presence of Solutions in Peer Reviews

Huy Nguyen[1] and **Wenting Xiong**[3] and **Diane Litman**[1,2]

[1]Computer Science Department, University of Pittsburgh, PA, USA
[2]Learning Research & Development Center, University of Pittsburgh, PA, USA
[3]IBM Watson Health, Yorktown Heights, NY, USA
E-mail: {hvn3,dlitman}@pitt.edu, wxiong@us.ibm.com

Abstract

We present the design and evaluation of a web-based peer review system that uses natural language processing to automatically evaluate and provide instant feedback regarding the presence of solutions in peer reviews. Student reviewers can then choose to either revise their reviews to address the system's feedback, or ignore the feedback and submit their original reviews. A system deployment in multiple high school classrooms shows that our solution prediction model triggers instant feedback with high precision, and that the feedback is successful in increasing the number of peer reviews with solutions.

1 Introduction

Peer review provides learning opportunities for students in their roles as both author and reviewer, and is a promising approach for helping students improve their writing (Lundstrom and Baker, 2009). However, one limitation of peer review is that student reviewers are generally novices in their disciplines and typically inexperienced in constructing helpful textual reviews (Cho and Schunn, 2007). Research in the learning sciences has identified properties of helpful comments in textual reviews, e.g., localizing where problems occur in a paper and suggesting solutions to problems (Nelson and Schunn, 2009), or providing review justifications such as explanations of judgments (Gielen et al., 2010). Research in computer science, in turn, has used natural language processing and machine learning to build models for automatically identifying helpful

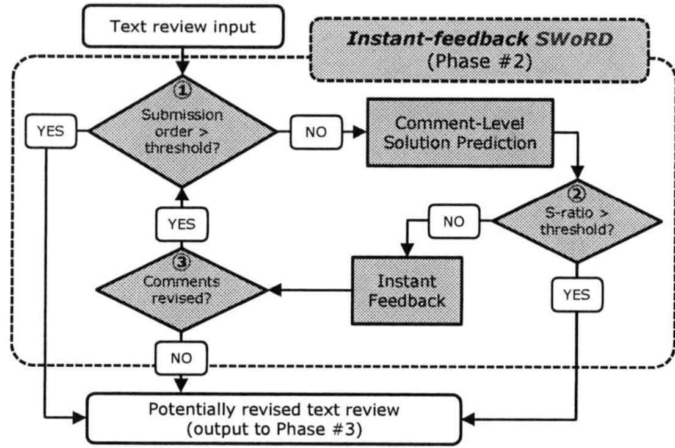

Figure 1: Architecture of Instant-feedback SWoRD.

review properties, including *localization* and *solution* (Xiong and Litman, 2010; Nguyen and Litman, 2013; Xiong et al., 2012; Nguyen and Litman, 2014), as well as *quality* and *tone* (Ramachandran and Gehringer, 2015). While such prediction models have been evaluated intrinsically (i.e., with respect to predicting gold-standard labels), few have actually been incorporated into working peer review systems and evaluated extrinsically (Ramachandran and Gehringer, 2013; Nguyen et al., 2014).

The SWoRD research project[1] involves different active research threads for improving the utility of an existing web-based peer review system. Our research in the SWoRD project aims at building instant feedback components for improving the quality of textual peer reviews. Our initial work focused on improving review localization (Nguyen et al., 2014). Here we focus on increasing the presence of solutions in reviews. When students submit reviews,

---

[1]*https://sites.google.com/site/swordlrdc/new-features*

6

Proceedings of NAACL-HLT 2016 (Demonstrations), pages 6–10,
San Diego, California, June 12-17, 2016. ©2016 Association for Computational Linguistics

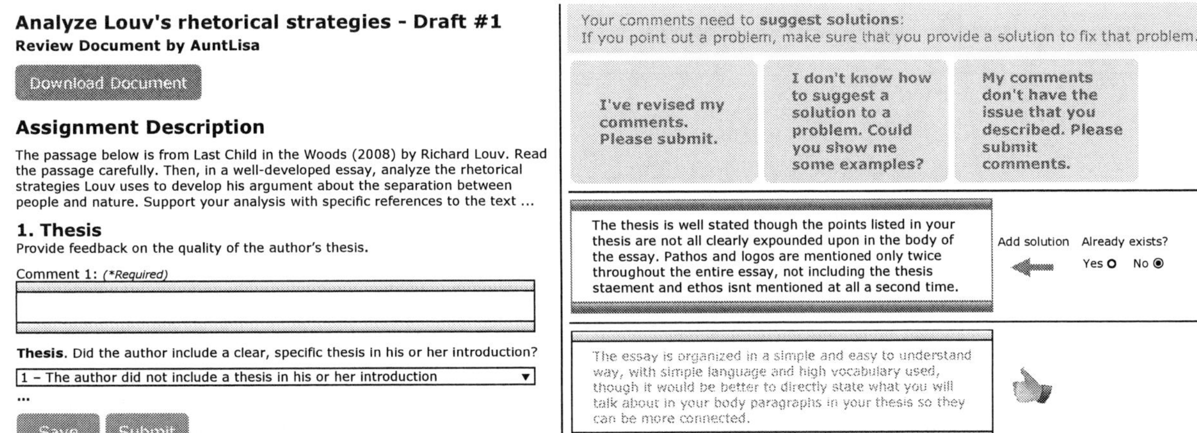

Figure 2: Screenshots of original **review interface** (left) and new **instant feedback interface** (right). For readability, the review interface shows only one comment prompt and its associated rating prompt. The instant feedback interface displays a solution feedback message and three possible reviewer reactions (top), and highlights *problem-only* (middle) and *solution* (bottom) comments.

natural language processing is used to automatically predict whether a solution is present in each peer review comment (Figure 1). If not enough critical comments are predicted to contain explicit solutions for how to make the paper better, students are taken from the original review interface to a new instant feedback interface which scaffolds them in productively revising the original peer reviews (Figure 2).

Sections 2 and 3 describe the Instant-feedback workflow, and the supporting natural language processing techniques. Section 4 demonstrates the promise of our system in supporting student review revision in a recent system deployment.

2   Instant-feedback SWoRD

SWoRD[2] was developed to support web-based reciprocal peer review, especially in large classes involving writing in the disciplines where writing and revision are hard to support due to lack of resources. A typical peer review exercise in SWoRD involves three main phases: (1) student authors submit papers to SWoRD, (2) student reviewers download papers assigned to them and submit peer reviews of the papers, and (3) student authors submit paper revisions that address the peer reviews they received. To further enhance the utility of SWoRD, we have developed *Instant-feedback SWoRD*, with the goal of helping student reviewers increase the presence of solutions in the peer review comments produced during Phase 2 of the typical peer review exercise.

Figures 2 and 1 illustrate technical details of Instant-feedback SWoRD. As in the original SWoRD, student reviewers create a new review session by opening the review interface (Figure 2, left). Now, however, whenever the SUBMIT button is clicked, the "text review input" is passed to the "Submission order check" (Figure 1, diamond #1). The submission order threshold[3] specifies how many times a review will be processed for instant feedback (e.g., 0 means no instant feedback, 1 means only the original comments are analyzed, 2 means revised comments are also analyzed, etc.). If the threshold is not reached, each comment in the review is analyzed by the "Comment-level Solution Prediction Component" (see Section 3) and classified as a *Solution*, *Problem-only*, or *Non-criticism*. *Problem-only* comments point out problems without providing solutions, while *Non-criticisms* such as summaries or praise do not require solutions. To measure how many problem comments have solutions, we define S-RATIO as number of *solution* comments over the sum of *solution* and *problem-only* comments. If the predicted S-RATIO is less than or equal to a threshold[4] (Figure 1, diamond #2), instant feedback is trig-

---

[2]SWoRD is now licensed by Panther Learning Systems Inc. – *www.peerceptiv.com*. A free version for users willing to trial instant feedback is available at *https://sword.lrdc.pitt.edu*.

[3]The deployment in Section 4 used a threshold of 1.

[4]For the deployment in Section 4, S-RATIO was tuned to 0.7

gered to scaffold students in revising *problem-only* comments. Otherwise the review is deemed acceptable and stored for later use by Phase 3.

When instant feedback is triggered, the instant feedback interface (Figure 2, right) displays a message at the top suggesting that comments may need to be revised to include solutions, followed by buttons representing the 3 possible reviewer responses: revise the review and resubmit (left), view some predefined example comments with solutions before responding (center), or submit the review without revision (right). To call the reviewer's attention to comments that might need revision, the interface turns text boxes around *predicted problem-only comments* to red (Figure 2, middle right). For these comments, the system also generates option buttons that ask reviewers to provide feedback on the prediction. We hypothesized that asking students to reason about the absence of solutions in their own comments would promote review revision. Their feedback on the system's predictions also provides new annotated examples for future re-training of the prediction model (described in Section 3). Conversely, the interface highlights *predicted solution comments* in green (Figure 2, bottom right) along with displaying a thumbs-up icon. This highlighting was designed to draw reviewer attention to examples of solutions in their own comments. Finally, for reviews that are revised and resubmitted, Instant-feedback SWoRD increases the submission order and re-checks the threshold (diamond #1 in Figure 1). Unrevised reviews are instead stored for Phase 3 of SWoRD.

3 Comment-level Solution Prediction

To support the instant feedback interface described in the prior section, we developed a 3-way classification model for predicting a review comment's feedback type: *Solution*, *Problem-only*, or *Non-criticism*. Challenges emerge from the fact that SWoRD serves a wide range of classes ranging from high school to graduate school and from STEM to language arts. Consequently, our prediction model has to process peer review comments that greatly differ in style and vocabulary. We thus focused on modeling how students suggested solutions by developing the following feature sets that abstracted

over specific lexicons and paper topics:

- *Simple*: word count and order of the comment.
- *Keywords*: we semi-automatically created 10 keyword sets to model different content patterns, extending prior work (Xiong et al., 2010): *Solution, Idea, Suggestion, Location, Connective, Positive, Negative, Summary, Error, Negation*. For each set, we count the total occurrences of its keywords in the comment.
- *Location phrases*: we observed in our training data that solution content usually co-occurs with location information in comments. Thus, we extracted words and phrases that signal positional localization in comments of training data. This feature set includes hand-crafted regular expressions of location patterns (e.g., *on page 5*) (Xiong et al., 2010), location seed words (manually collected, e.g., *page, thesis, conclusion*), and location bigrams (automatically extracted given the location seeds, e.g., *transition paragraph*). For each location seed, phrase or regular expression, we count its occurrences or matches in the comment.
- *Paper content*: motivated by topic word features in (Kim et al., 2006), this feature set was designed to model how much of a paper's content/topic was mentioned in the comment. We first extracted bigrams with TF-IDF above average in the training data, and collected unigrams that make-up these bigrams, e.g., 'civil' and 'war' in 'civil war'.[5] *Domain unigram* feature is the number of collected unigrams in the comment. *Window size* feature is the length of maximal common text span between the comment and the paper (Ernst-Gerlach and Crane, 2008). *Similarity* feature searches for the highest similarity score between paper sentence to the comment. We extract 5 paper sentences (1 covering the common span, 2 preceding, and 2 following). For each pair of paper sentence and the comment, we apply different similarity scores (e.g., Levenshtein, cosine) to 4 abstractions of the pair (sequence of tokens, sequence of part-of-speech, sequence of nouns, sequence of verbs), and return the pair's sum score. Feature value is the highest sum score over all pairs.

Our solution prediction model was trained with logistic regression using annotated peer review comments from two university classes (Computer Science, History) and a high-school class (Literature). During learning, we used a cost matrix to favor instant feedback precision over recall by penalizing relevant error types. We thought it would be better to miss some feedback opportunities than to incorrectly trigger instant feedback (e.g., asking students to revise reviews where all comments already con-

---

using development data from prior classes.

[5]Starting with unigrams gave us a noisy set and degraded model performance. We plan to apply LDA (Blei et al., 2003) for this task in future.

Model	Acc.	κ	F1:Sln	F1:Prb	F1:Non
BoW	0.50	0.24	0.40	0.51	0.57
SWoRD	**0.62**	**0.44**	**0.55**	**0.59**	**0.72**

Table 1: Comment-level solution prediction performance. Acc: Accuracy, F1 by class label is reported – Sln: Solution, Prb: Problem-only, Non: Non-criticism.

tained solutions) or to incorrectly display comments as red or green in the feedback interface.

4 Preliminary Evaluation

In Spring 2015, SWoRD with instant-feedback was deployed in 9 high-school Advanced Placement (AP) classes. We conducted preliminary evaluations to answer two research questions: (1) *How precisely does the system predict peer review solution and trigger the instant feedback?* (2) *How does the instant feedback impact review revisions?* We collected peer review submissions which were intervened by Instant-feedback SWoRD (i.e., triggered instant feedback), and their immediately subsequent resubmissions (if any), then had an expert manually code the collected comments for their feedback types: *solution, problem-only, non-criticism* (double-coded data had inter-rater κ 0.87).

Only intervened reviews were used to evaluate model performance because subsequent resubmissions were not predicted. In our deployment, 134 of 1428 reviews were intervened, containing 891 comments: 223 *Solution*, 340 *Problem-only*, and 328 *Non-criticism*. Table 1 shows that our deployed model outperforms a Bag-of-Words (BoW) baseline[6] in 3-way classification. Given that the AP data was never used for model training, the obtained performance is promising and encourages us to improve the model with more data.

Regarding instant feedback precision, we calculated the true S-RATIO for each intervened review (using gold standard labels). Table 2 shows that given the 0.7 threshold used for this deployment, Instant-feedback SWoRD incorrectly triggered instant feedback for 24 submissions (column 3) out of 134, yielding a precision 0.82. Because Instant-feedback SWoRD does not let student reviewers know the S-RATIO threshold, students should only think that the instant feedback was incorrect when

---

[6]Used 1,2,3-grams as features.

True S-RATIO	≤ 1.0	> 0.7	$= 1.0$
#intervened	134	24 (18%)	16 (12%)

Table 2: True S-RATIO of intervened submission

they provided solutions for all mentioned problems (true S-RATIO = 1). From this student perspective, Instant-feedback SWoRD had 16 incorrect triggers (column 4), achieving a precision 0.88.

Finally, to evaluate the impact of instant feedback on review revision, we considered the 74 subsequent resubmissions. We collected comments that were *revised* or *newly-added* to the resubmissions (no comment was deleted), and obtained 115 comments. Pairing 111 revised comments with their original versions, we observed that 73 (66%) comments were fixed from problem-only to solution, 3 (3%) from non-criticism to solution, only 1 comment (0.9%) was edited from solution to non-criticism, and none from solution to problem-only. All of the 4 newly-added comments mentioned problems and provided solutions. These results suggest that Instant-feedback SWoRD does indeed help reviewers revise their comments to include more solutions.

5 Conclusions and Future Work

This paper presented Instant-feedback SWoRD, which was designed to increase the presence of solutions in peer reviews. Evaluation results showed that Instant-feedback SWoRD achieved high performance in predicting solution in review comments and in triggering instant feedback. Moreover, for reviewers who revised their reviews after receiving instant feedback, the number of comments with solution increased. In future work, we plan to use more data from a wider range of classes to re-train the currently deployed prediction model. Also, a comprehensive comparison of our approach to studies of similar tasks would give us insight into features and algorithms for performance improvement.

Acknowledgments

This research is supported by NSF/1122504, and IES/R305A120370. The larger research project (co-led by Professors Kevin Ashley, Amanda Godley, Diane Litman and Chris Schunn) is a collaboration with the Learning Research & Development Center and the School of Education. We are grateful to our colleagues in the project.

References

David M Blei, Andrew Y Ng, and Michael I Jordan. 2003. Latent Dirichlet allocation. *The Journal of Machine Learning Research*, 3:993–1022.

Kwangsu Cho and Christian D. Schunn. 2007. Scaffolded Writing and Rewriting in the Discipline: A Web-based Reciprocal Peer Review System. *Computers & Education*, 48(3):409–426, April.

Andrea Ernst-Gerlach and Gregory Crane. 2008. Identifying Quotations in Reference Works and Primary Materials. In *Research and Advanced Technology for Digital Libraries*, volume 5173 of *Lecture Notes in Computer Science*, pages 78–87. Springer Berlin Heidelberg.

Sarah Gielen, Elien Peeters, Filip Dochy, Patrick Onghena, and Katrien Struyven. 2010. Improving the effectiveness of peer feedback for learning. *Learning and Instruction*, 20(4):304 – 315. Unravelling Peer Assessment.

Soo-Min Kim, Patrick Pantel, Tim Chklovski, and Marco Pennacchiotti. 2006. Automatically Assessing Review Helpfulness. In *Proceedings of the 2006 Conference on Empirical Methods in Natural Language Processing*, EMNLP '06, pages 423–430, Stroudsburg, PA, USA. Association for Computational Linguistics.

Kristi Lundstrom and Wendy Baker. 2009. To give is better than to receive: The benefits of peer review to the reviewer's own writing. *Journal of Second Language Writing*, 18(1):30–43, March.

Melissa Nelson and Christian Schunn. 2009. The nature of feedback: how different types of peer feedback affect writing performance. *Instructional Science*, 37(4):375–401.

Huy Nguyen and Diane Litman. 2013. Identifying Localization in Peer Reviews of Argument Diagrams. In *Artificial Intelligence in Education*, volume 7926 of *Lecture Notes in Computer Science*, pages 91–100. Springer Berlin Heidelberg.

Huy Nguyen and Diane Litman. 2014. Improving Peer Feedback Prediction: The Sentence Level is Right. In *Proceedings of the Ninth Workshop on Innovative Use of NLP for Building Educational Applications*, pages 99–108, Baltimore, Maryland, June. Association for Computational Linguistics.

Huy Nguyen, Wenting Xiong, and Diane Litman. 2014. Classroom Evaluation of a Scaffolding Intervention for Improving Peer Review Localization. In *Intelligent Tutoring Systems*, volume 8474 of *Lecture Notes in Computer Science*, pages 272–282. Springer International Publishing.

Lakshmi Ramachandran and Edward F. Gehringer. 2013. A User Study on the Automated Assessment of Reviews. In *Proceedings of the Workshops at the 16th International Conference on Artificial Intelligence in Education AIED 2013, Memphis, USA, July 9-13, 2013.*

Lakshmi Ramachandran and Edward F. Gehringer. 2015. Identifying Content Patterns in Peer Reviews Using Graph-based Cohesion. In *Proceedings of the Twenty-Eighth International Florida Artificial Intelligence Research Society Conference, FLAIRS 2015, Hollywood, Florida. May 18-20, 2015.*, pages 269–275.

Wenting Xiong and Diane Litman. 2010. Identifying Problem Localization in Peer-Review Feedback. In *Intelligent Tutoring Systems*, volume 6095 of *Lecture Notes in Computer Science*, pages 429–431. Springer Berlin Heidelberg.

Wenting Xiong, Diane J Litman, and Christian D Schunn. 2010. Assessing Reviewer's Performance Based on Mining Problem Localization in Peer-Review Data. ERIC.

Wenting Xiong, Diane Litman, and Christian Schunn. 2012. Natural Language Processing techniques for researching and improving peer feedback. *Journal of Writing Research*, 4(2):155–176. Query date: 2015-05-24.

Farasa: A Fast and Furious Segmenter for Arabic

Ahmed Abdelali   Kareem Darwish   Nadir Durrani   Hamdy Mubarak
Qatar Computing Research Institute
Hamad Bin Khalifa University
Doha, Qatar
`{aabdelali,kdarwish,ndurrani,hmubarak}@qf.org.qa`

Abstract

In this paper, we present Farasa, a fast and accurate Arabic segmenter. Our approach is based on SVM-rank using linear kernels. We measure the performance of the segmenter in terms of accuracy and efficiency, in two NLP tasks, namely Machine Translation (MT) and Information Retrieval (IR). Farasa outperforms or is at par with the state-of-the-art Arabic segmenters (Stanford and MADAMIRA), while being more than one order of magnitude faster.

1 Introduction

Word segmentation/tokenization is one of the most important pre-processing steps for many NLP task, particularly for a morphologically rich language such as Arabic. Arabic word segmentation involves breaking words into its constituent prefix(es), stem, and suffix(es). For example, the word "wktAbnA"[1] "وكتابنا" (gloss: "and our book") is composed of the prefix "w" "و" (and), stem "ktAb" "كتاب" (book), and a possessive pronoun "nA" "نا" (our). The task of the tokenizer is to segment the word into "w+ ktAb +nA" "و+ كتاب +نا". Segmentation has been shown to have significant impact on NLP applications such as MT and IR.

Many Arabic segmenters have been proposed in the past 20 years. These include rule based analyzers (Beesley et al., 1989; Beesley, 1996; Buckwalter, 2002; Khoja, 2001), light stemmers (Aljlayl and Frieder, 2002; Darwish and Oard, 2007), and statistical word segmenters (Darwish, 2002; Habash et al., 2009; Diab, 2009; Darwish et al., 2014). Statistical word segmenters are considered state-of-the-art with reported segmentation accuracy above 98%.

We introduce a new segmenter, Farasa ("insight" in Arabic), an SVM-based segmenter that uses a variety of features and lexicons to rank possible segmentations of a word. The features include: likelihoods of stems, prefixes, suffixes, their combinations; presence in lexicons containing valid stems or named entities; and underlying stem templates.

We carried out extensive tests comparing Farasa with two state-of-the-art segmenters: MADAMIRA (Pasha et al., 2014), and the Stanford Arabic segmenter (Monroe et al., 2014), on two standard NLP tasks namely MT and IR. The comparisons were done in terms of accuracy and efficiency. We trained Arabic↔English Statistical Machine Translation (SMT) systems using each of the three segmenters. Farasa performs clearly better than Stanford's segmenter and is at par with MADAMIRA, in terms of BLEU (Papineni et al., 2002). On the IR task, Farasa outperforms both with statistically significant improvements. Moreover, we observed Farasa to be at least an order of magnitude faster than both. Farasa also performs slightly better than the two in an intrinsic evaluation. Farasa has been made freely available.[2]

2 Farasa

Features: In this section we introduce the features and lexicons that we used for seg-

---

[1] Buckwalter encoding is used exclusively in this paper

[2] Tool available at: http://alt.qcri.org/tools/farasa/

Proceedings of NAACL-HLT 2016 (Demonstrations), pages 11–16,
San Diego, California, June 12-17, 2016. ©2016 Association for Computational Linguistics

mentation. For any given word (out of context), all possible character-level segmentations are found and ones leading to a sequence of $prefix_1+...+prefix_n+stem+suffix_1+...+suffix_m$, where: $prefix_{1..n}$ are valid prefixes; $suffix_{1..m}$ are valid suffixes; and prefix and suffix sequences are legal, are retained. Our valid prefixes are: f, w, l, b, k, Al, s. ف، و، ل، ب، ك، ال، س. Our valid suffixes are: A, p, t, k, n, w, y, At, An, wn, wA, yn, kmA, km, kn, h, hA, hmA, hm, hn, nA, tmA, tm, and tn ا، ة، ت، ك، ن، و، ي، ات، ان، ون، وا، ين، كما، كم، كن، ه، ها، هما، هم، هن، نا، تما، تم، تن. Using these prefixes and suffixes, we generated a list of valid prefix and suffix sequences. For example, sequences where a coordinating conjunction (w or f) precedes a preposition (b, l, k), which in turn precedes a determiner (Al), is legal, for example in the word fbAlktab فبالكتاب (gloss: "and in the book") which is segmented to (f+b+Al+ktAb ف+ ب+ ال+ كتاب). Conversely, a determiner is not allowed to precede any other prefix. We used the following features:

- Leading Prefixes: conditional probability that a leading character sequence is a prefix.

- Trailing Suffixes: conditional probability that a trailing character sequence is a suffix.

- LM Prob (Stem): unigram probability of stem based on a language model that we trained from a corpus containing over 12 years worth of articles of Aljazeera.net (from 2000 to 2011). The corpus is composed of 114,758 articles containing 94 million words.

- LM Prob: unigram probability of stem with first suffix.

- Prefix|Suffix: probability of prefix given suffix.

- Suffix|Prefix: probability of suffix given prefix.

- Stem Template: whether a valid stem template can be obtained from the stem. Stem templates are patterns that transform an Arabic root into a stem. For example, apply the template CCAC on the root "ktb" "كتب" produces the stem "ktAb" "كتاب" (meaning: book). To find stem templates, we used the module described in Darwish et al. (2014).

- Stem Lexicon: whether the stem appears in a lexicon of automatically generated stems. This can help identify valid stems. This list is generated by placing roots into stem templates to generate a stem, which is retained if it appears in the aforementioned Aljazeera corpus.

- Gazetteer Lexicon: whether the stem that has no trailing suffixes appears in a gazetteer of person and location names. The gazetteer was extracted from Arabic Wikipedia in the manner described by (Darwish et al., 2012) and we retained just word unigrams.

- Function Words: whether the stem is a function word such as "ElY" "علی" (on) and "mn" "من" (from).

- AraComLex: whether the stem appears in the AraComLex Arabic lexicon, which contains 31,753 stems of which 24,976 are nouns and 6,777 are verbs (Attia et al., 2011).

- Buckwalter Lexicon: whether the stem appears in the Buckwalter lexicon as extracted from the AraMorph package (Buckwalter, 2002).

- Length Difference: difference in length from the average stem length.

Learning: We constructed feature vectors for each possible segmentation and marked correct segmentation for each word. We then used SVM-Rank (Joachims, 2006) to learn feature weights. We used a linear kernel with a trade-off factor between training errors and margin (C) equal to 100, which is based on offline experiments done on a dev set. During test, all possible segmentations with valid prefix-suffix combinations are generated, and the different segmentations are scored using the classifier. We had two varieties of Farasa. In the first, $Farasa_{Base}$, the classifier is used to segment all words directly. It also uses a small lookup list of concatenated stop-words where the letter "n" "ن" is dropped such as "EmA" "عما" ("En+mA" "عن +ما"), and "mmA" "مما" ("mn+mA" "من +ما"). In the second, $Farasa_{Lookup}$, previously seen segmentations during training are cached, and classification is applied on words that were unseen during training. The cache includes words that have only one segmentation during training, or words appearing 5 or more times with one segmentation appearing more than 70% of times.

Training and Testing: For training, we used parts 1 (version 4.1), 2 (version 3.1), and 3 (version 2) of

	MADAMIRA	Farasa$_{base}$	Farasa$_{lookup}$
Accuracy	98.76%	98.76%	98.94%

Table 1: Segmentation Accuracy

Seg	iwslt$_{12}$	iwslt$_{13}$	Avg	Time
MADAMIRA	30.4	30.8	30.6	4074
Stanford	30.0	30.5	30.3	395
Farasa	30.2	30.8	30.5	80

Table 2: Arabic-to-English Machine Translation, BLEU scores and Time (in seconds)

the the Penn Arabic Treebank (ATB). Many of the current results reported in the literature are done on subsets of the Penn Arabic Treebank (ATB). Testing done on a subset of the ATB is problematic due to its limited lexical diversity, leading to artificially high results. We created a new test set composed of 70 WikiNews articles (from 2013 and 2014) that cover a variety of themes, namely: politics, economics, health, science and technology, sports, arts, and culture. The articles are evenly distributed among the different themes (10 per theme). The articles contain 18,271 words. Table 1 compares segmentation accuracy for both versions of Farasa with MADAMIRA, where both were configured to segment all possible affixes. We did not compare to Stanford, because it only segments based on the ATB segmentation scheme. Farasa$_{lookup}$ performs slightly better than MADAMIRA. From analyzing the errors in Farasa, we found that most of the errors were due to either: foreign named entities such as "lynks" "لينكس" (meaning: Linux) and "bAlysky" "باليسكي" (meaning: Palisky); or to long words with more than four segmentations such as "wlmfAj}thmA" "ولمفاجئتهما" ("w+l+mfAj}+t+hmA" "و + ل + مفاجئ + ت + هما") (meaning "and to surprise both of them"). Perhaps, adding larger gazetteers of foreign names would help reduce the first kind of errors. For the second type of errors, the classifier generates the correct segmentation, but it receives often a slightly lower score than the incorrect segmentation. Perhaps adding more features can help correct such errors.

3 Machine Translation

Setup: We trained Statistical Machine Translation (SMT) systems for Arabic↔English, to compare Farasa with Stanford and MADAMIRA[3]. The comparison was done in terms of BLEU (Papineni et al., 2002) and processing times. We used concatenation of IWSLT TED talks (Cettolo et al., 2014) (containing 183K Sentences) and NEWS corpus (containing 202K Sentences) to train phrase-based systems.

Systems: We used Moses (Koehn et al., 2007), a state-of-the-art toolkit with the the settings described in (Durrani et al., 2014a): these include a maximum sentence length of 80, Fast-Aligner for word-alignments (Dyer et al., 2013), an interpolated Kneser-Ney smoothed 5-gram language model with KenLM (Heafield, 2011), used at runtime, MBR decoding (Kumar and Byrne, 2004), Cube Pruning (Huang and Chiang, 2007) using a stack size of 1,000 during tuning and 5,000 during testing. We tuned with the k-best batch MIRA (Cherry and Foster, 2012). Among other features, we used lexicalized reordering model (Galley and Manning, 2008), a 5-gram Operation Sequence Model (Durrani et al., 2011), Class-based Models (Durrani et al., 2014b)[4] and other default parameters. We used an unsupervised transliteration model (Durrani et al., 2014c) to transliterate the OOV words. We used the standard tune and test set provided by the IWSLT shared task to evaluate the systems.

In each experiment, we simply changed the segmentation pipeline to try different segmentation. We used ATB scheme for MADAMIRA which has shown to outperform its alternatives (S2 and D3) previously (Sajjad et al., 2013).

Results: Table 2 compares the Arabic-to-English SMT systems using the three segmentation tools. Farasa performs better than Stanford's Arabic segmenter giving an improvement of +0.25, but slightly worse than MADAMIRA (-0.10). The differences are not statistically significant. For efficiency, Farasa is faster than Stanford and MADAMIRA by a factor of 5 and 50 respectively.[5] The run-time of MADAMIRA makes it cumbersome to run on bigger corpora like the multiUN (UN) (Eisele and

---

[3]Release-01292014-1.0 was used in the experiments

[4]We used mkcls to cluster the data into 50 clusters.

[5]Time is the average of 10 runs on a machine with 8 Intel i7-3770 cores, 16 GB RAM, and 7 Seagate disks in software RAID 5 running Linux 3.13.0-48

Seg	iwslt$_{12}$	iwslt$_{13}$	Avg	Time
MADAMIRA	19.6	19.1	19.4	1781
Stanford	17.4	17.2	17.3	692
Farasa	19.2	19.3	19.3	66

Table 3: English-to-Arabic Machine Translation, BLEU scores and Time (in seconds)

Chen, 2010) which contains roughly 4M sentences. This factor becomes even daunting when training a segmented target-side language model for English-to-Arabic system. Table 3 shows results from English-to-Arabic system. In this case, Stanford performs significantly worse than others. MADAMIRA performs slightly better than Farasa. However, as before, Farasa is more than multiple orders of magnitude faster.

4 Information Retrieval

Setup: We also used extrinsic IR evaluation to determine the quality of stemming compared to MADAMIRA and the Stanford segmenter. We performed experiments on the TREC 2001/2002 cross language track collection, which contains 383,872 Arabic newswire articles, containing 59.6 million words), and 75 topics with their relevance judgments (Oard and Gey, 2002). This is presently the best available large Arabic information retrieval test collection. We used Mean Average Precision (MAP) and precision at 10 (P@10) as the measures of goodness for this retrieval task. Going down from the top a retrieved ranked list, Average Precision (AP) is the average of precision values computed at every relevant document found. P@10 is the same as MAP, but the ranked list is restricted to 10 results. We used SOLR (ver. 5.6)[6] to perform all experimentation. SOLR uses a *tf-idf* ranking model. We used a paired 2-tailed t-test with p-value less than 0.05 to ascertain statistical significance. For experimental setups, we performed letter normalization, where we conflated: variants of "alef", "ta marbouta" and "ha", "alef maqsoura" and "ya", and the different forms of "hamza". Unlike MT, Arabic IR performs better with more elaborate segmentation which improves matching of core units of meaning, namely stems. For MADAMIRA, we used the D34MT scheme, where all affixes are segmented. Stanford tokenizer only provides the ATB tokenization scheme. Farasa

---

[6]http://lucene.apache.org/solr/

Stemming	MAP	P@10	Time
Words	0.20	0.34	-
MADAMIRA	0.26 ^{w,s}	0.39 ^{w}	21:27:21
Stanford	0.22 ^{w}	0.37	03:43:25
Farasa	0.28 ^{w,s,m}	0.43 ^{w,s,m}	00:15:26

Table 4: Retrieval Results in MAP and P@10 and Processing Time (in hh:mm:ss). For statistical significance, w = better than words, s = better than Stanford, and m = better than MADAMIRA

was used with the default scheme, where all affixes are segmented.

Results: Table 4 summarizes the retrieval results for using words without stemming and using MADAMIRA, Stanford, and Farasa for stemming. The table also indicates statistical significance and reports on the processing time that each of the segmenters took to process the entire document collection. As can be seen from the results, Farasa outperformed using words, MADAMIRA, and Stanford significantly. Farasa was an order of magnitude faster than Stanford and two orders of magnitude faster than MADAMIRA.

5 Analysis

The major advantage of using Farasa is speed, without loss in accuracy. This mainly results from optimization described earlier in the Section 2 which includes caching and limiting the context used for building the features vector. Stanford segmenter uses a third-order (i.e., 4-gram) Markov CRF model (Green and DeNero, 2012) to predict the correct segmentation. On the other hand, MADAMIRA bases its segmentation on the output of a morphological analyzer which provides a list of possible analyses (independent of context) for each word. Both text and analyses are passed to a feature modeling component, which applies SVM and language models to derive predictions for the word segmentation (Pasha et al., 2014). This hierarchy could explain the slowness of MADAMIRA versus other tokenizers.

6 Conclusion

In this paper we introduced Farasa, a new Arabic segmenter, which uses SVM for ranking. We compared our segmenter with state-of-the-art segmenters MADAMIRA and Stanford, on standard

MT and IR tasks and demonstrated Farasa to be significantly better (in terms of accuracy) than both on the IR tasks and at par with MADAMIRA on the MT tasks. We found Farasa by orders of magnitude faster than both. Farasa has been made available for use[7] and will be added to Moses for Arabic tokenization.

References

Mohammed Aljlayl and Ophir Frieder. 2002. On arabic search: improving the retrieval effectiveness via a light stemming approach. In *CIKM-2002*, pages 340–347.

Mohammed Attia, Pavel Pecina, Antonio Toral, Lamia Tounsi, and Josef van Genabith. 2011. An open-source finite state morphological transducer for modern standard arabic. In *Workshop on Finite State Methods and Natural Language Processing*, pages 125–133.

Kenneth Beesley, Tim Buckwalter, and Stuart Newton. 1989. Two-level finite-state analysis of arabic morphology. In *Proceedings of the Seminar on Bilingual Computing in Arabic and English*, pages 6–7.

Kenneth R Beesley. 1996. Arabic finite-state morphological analysis and generation. In *ACL*, pages 89–94.

Tim Buckwalter. 2002. Buckwalter {Arabic} morphological analyzer version 1.0.

Mauro Cettolo, Jan Niehues, Sebastian Stüker, Luisa Bentivogli, and Marcello Federico. 2014. Report on the 11th IWSLT Evaluation Campaign. *IWSLT-14*.

Colin Cherry and George Foster. 2012. Batch Tuning Strategies for Statistical Machine Translation. In *Proceedings of the 2012 Conference of the North American Chapter of the Association for Computational Linguistics: Human Language Technologies*, HLT-NAACL'12, pages 427–436, Montréal, Canada.

Kareem Darwish and Douglas W Oard. 2007. Adapting morphology for arabic information retrieval*. In *Arabic Computational Morphology*, pages 245–262.

Kareem Darwish, Walid Magdy, and Ahmed Mourad. 2012. Language processing for arabic microblog retrieval. In *ACM CIKM-2012*, pages 2427–2430.

Kareem Darwish, Ahmed Abdelali, and Hamdy Mubarak. 2014. Using stem-templates to improve arabic pos and gender/number tagging. In *LREC-2014*.

Kareem Darwish. 2002. Building a shallow arabic morphological analyzer in one day. In *Computational Approaches to Semitic Languages, ACL-2002*, pages 1–8.

Mona Diab. 2009. Second generation amira tools for arabic processing: Fast and robust tokenization, pos tagging, and base phrase chunking. In *Intl. Conference on Arabic Language Resources and Tools*.

Nadir Durrani, Helmut Schmid, and Alexander Fraser. 2011. A Joint Sequence Translation Model with Integrated Reordering. In *ACL'11*, pages 1045–1054, Portland, Oregon, USA, June.

Nadir Durrani, Barry Haddow, Philipp Koehn, and Kenneth Heafield. 2014a. Edinburgh's Phrase-based Machine Translation Systems for WMT-14. In *WMT'14*, pages 97–104, Baltimore, Maryland, USA.

Nadir Durrani, Philipp Koehn, Helmut Schmid, and Alexander Fraser. 2014b. Investigating the Usefulness of Generalized Word Representations in SMT. In *COLING'14*, pages 421–432, Dublin, Ireland.

Nadir Durrani, Hassan Sajjad, Hieu Hoang, and Philipp Koehn. 2014c. Integrating an Unsupervised Transliteration Model into Statistical Machine Translation. In *EACL'14*, pages 148–153, Gothenburg, Sweden.

Chris Dyer, Victor Chahuneau, and Noah A. Smith. 2013. A Simple, Fast, and Effective Reparameterization of IBM Model 2. In *Proceedings of NAACL'13*.

Andreas Eisele and Yu Chen. 2010. MultiUN: A Multilingual Corpus from United Nation Documents. In *LREC-2010*, Valleta, Malta, May.

Michel Galley and Christopher D. Manning. 2008. A Simple and Effective Hierarchical Phrase Reordering Model. In *EMNLP-2008*, pages 848–856, Honolulu, Hawaii, October.

Spence Green and John DeNero. 2012. A class-based agreement model for generating accurately inflected translations. In *ACL-2012*.

Nizar Habash, Owen Rambow, and Ryan Roth. 2009. Mada+ tokan: A toolkit for arabic tokenization, diacritization, morphological disambiguation, pos tagging, stemming and lemmatization. In *MEDAR*, pages 102–109.

Kenneth Heafield. 2011. KenLM: faster and smaller language model queries. In *Sixth Workshop on Statistical Machine Translation, EMNLP-2011*, pages 187–197, Edinburgh, Scotland, United Kingdom, July.

Liang Huang and David Chiang. 2007. Forest Rescoring: Faster Decoding with Integrated Language Models. In *Proceedings of the 45th Annual Meeting of the Association of Computational Linguistics*, ACL'07, pages 144–151, Prague, Czech Republic.

Thorsten Joachims. 2006. Training linear svms in linear time. In *ACM SIGKDD-2006*, pages 217–226. ACM.

Shereen Khoja. 2001. Apt: Arabic part-of-speech tagger. In *NAACL*, pages 20–25.

Philipp Koehn, Hieu Hoang, Alexandra Birch, Chris Callison-Burch, Marcello Federico, Nicola Bertoldi,

---

[7]http://alt.qcri.org/tools/farasa/

Brooke Cowan, Wade Shen, Christine Moran, Richard Zens, Chris Dyer, Ondrej Bojar, Alexandra Constantin, and Evan Herbst. 2007. Moses: Open source toolkit for statistical machine translation. In *ACL-2007*, Prague, Czech Republic.

Shankar Kumar and William J. Byrne. 2004. Minimum Bayes-Risk Decoding for Statistical Machine Translation. In *Proceedings of the North American Chapter of the Association for Computational Linguistics: Human Language Technologies*, HLT-NAACL'04, pages 169–176, Boston, Massachusetts, USA.

Will Monroe, Spence Green, and Christopher D Manning. 2014. Word segmentation of informal arabic with domain adaptation. *ACL, Short Papers*.

Kishore Papineni, Salim Roukos, Todd Ward, and Wei-Jing Zhu. 2002. BLEU: a method for automatic evaluation of machine translation. In *ACL-2002*, Philadelphia, PA, USA.

Arfath Pasha, Mohamed Al-Badrashiny, Mona Diab, Ahmed El Kholy, Ramy Eskander, Nizar Habash, Manoj Pooleery, Owen Rambow, and Ryan M Roth. 2014. Madamira: A fast, comprehensive tool for morphological analysis and disambiguation of arabic. In *LREC-2014*, Reykjavik, Iceland.

Hassan Sajjad, Francisco GuzmÃąn, Preslav Nakov, Ahmed Abdelali, Kenton Murray, Fahad Al Obaidli, and Stephan Vogel. 2013. QCRI at IWSLT 2013: Experiments in Arabic-English and English-Arabic spoken language translation. In *IWSLT-13*, December.

iAppraise: A Manual Machine Translation Evaluation Environment Supporting Eye-tracking

Ahmed Abdelali   Nadir Durrani   Francisco Guzmán

Qatar Computing Research Institute
Hamad Bin Khalifa University
Doha, Qatar
`{aabdelali,ndurrani,fguzman}@qf.org.qa`

Abstract

We present *iAppraise*: an open-source framework that enables the use of eye-tracking for MT evaluation. It connects Appraise, an open-source toolkit for MT evaluation, to a low-cost eye-tracking device, to make its usage accessible to a broader audience. It also provides a set of tools for extracting and exploiting gaze data, which facilitate eye-tracking analysis. In this paper, we describe different modules of the framework, and explain how the tool can be used in a MT evaluation scenario. During the demonstration, the users will be able to perform an evaluation task, observe their own reading behavior during a replay of the session, and export and extract features from the data.

1 Introduction

Evaluation is one of the difficult problems in Machine Translation (MT). Despite its clear drawbacks,[1] *human evaluation* remains the most reliable method to evaluate MT systems and track the advances in Machine Translation. Appraise is an open-source toolkit designed to facilitate the human evaluation of machine translation (Federmann, 2012). It has been adopted as the preferred tool in the WMT evaluation campaigns (Bojar et al., 2013), and thus, it is currently used by dozens of researchers.

According to the eye-mind hypothesis (Just and Carpenter, 1980) people cognitively process objects that are in front of their eyes. This has enabled researchers to analyze and understand how people perform certain tasks like reading (Rayner, 1998;

Garrod, 2006; Harley, 2013). In recent times, eye-tracking has also been used in Machine Translation to identify and classify translation errors (Stymne et al., 2012), to evaluate the usability of automatic translations (Doherty and O'Brien, 2014), and to improve the consistency of the human evaluation process (Guzmán et al., 2015), etc. Furthermore, tracking how evaluators consume MT output, can help to reduce human evaluation subjectivity, as we could use evidence of what people *do* (i.e. unbiased reading patterns) and not only what they *say* they *think* (i.e. user-biased evaluation scores). However, the main limitation for the adoption of eye-tracking research has been the steep learning curve that is associated with eye-tracking analysis and the high-cost of eye-tracking devices.

In this paper, we present *iAppraise*: an open-source framework that enables the use of eye-tracking for MT evaluation, and facilitates the replication and dissemination of eye-tracking research in MT. First, it is designed to work with the increasingly popular, low-cost[2] eye-tracker *eyeTribe*. Secondly, it provides a set of tools for extracting and exploiting gaze features, which facilitate eye-tracking analysis. Lastly, it integrates fully with the Appraise toolkit, making it accessible to a larger audience.

Our setup allows to track eye-movements during the MT evaluation process. The data generated can be used to visualize a re-enactment of the evaluation session in real-time, thus providing useful qualitative insights on the evaluation; or to extract features for further quantitative analysis.

---

[1] It is subjective, expensive, time-consuming, boring, etc.

[2] It costs less than a hundred US dollars, and provides capabilities on par with previous generation eye-trackers.

17

Proceedings of NAACL-HLT 2016 (Demonstrations), pages 17–21,
San Diego, California, June 12-17, 2016. ©2016 Association for Computational Linguistics

The applications for this toolkit are multiple. Using reading patterns from evaluators could be a useful tool for MT evaluation: (*i*) to shed light into the evaluation process: e.g. the general reading behavior that evaluators follow to complete their task; (*ii*) to understand which parts of a translation are more difficult for the annotator; and (*iii*) to develop automatic evaluation systems that use reading patterns to predict translation quality. In an effort carried using this framework, we proposed a model to predict the quality of the MT output. Our results showed that reading patterns obtained from the eye-movements of the evaluators can help to anticipate the evaluation scores to be given by them. We found that the features extracted from the eye-tracking data (discussed in Section 2.6) capture more than just the fluency of a translation. Details of findings are reported in (Sajjad et al., 2016). In this paper, we describe the overall architecture of *iAppraise*: the communication modules, the user interface, and the analysis package.

2 iAppraise: Eye Tracking for Appraise

Appraise (Federmann, 2012) is an open-source toolkit,[3] used for for manual evaluation of machine translation output. However, it also allows to collect human judgments on a number of annotation tasks (such as ranking, error classification, quality estimation and post-editing) and provides an environment to maintain and export the collected data. The toolkit is based on the Django web framework that supports database modeling and object-relational mapping, and uses Twitter's Bootstrap as a template for the interface design.

iAppraise consist of a series of modules that extend Appraise to integrate eye-tracking from the eyeTribe[4] into the translation evaluation tasks. Below we briefly describe the architecture of the toolkit.

2.1 Overall Architecture

In Figure 1 we present the overall architecture of our toolkit. First, the *iAppraise Adapter* communicates directly with the EyeTribe eye-tracker through its API and propagates the gaze events to the *iAppraise UI (User Interface)*.

---

[3]Available at: `github.com/cfedermann/Appraise`
[4]http://dev.theEyeTribe.com/api/

The *iAppraise UI* module takes the gaze events, and translates their coordinates into local browser coordinates. It also converts all the textual material in the display into *traceable* objects, that can detect *Gaze* when a user is looking at them. Additionally, the module contains a view-task whose layout is optimized for the recognition of gaze events.

When a traceable object in *iAppraise UI* detects that a user is looking at it, it stores this information, augmented with UI details from the gaze data. This data is later stored in *iAppraise Model/DB* at the end of each evaluation session. Finally, the *iAppraise Analysis* module is designed to extract useful eye-tracking features from the generated data. These can be used for modeling or analysis.

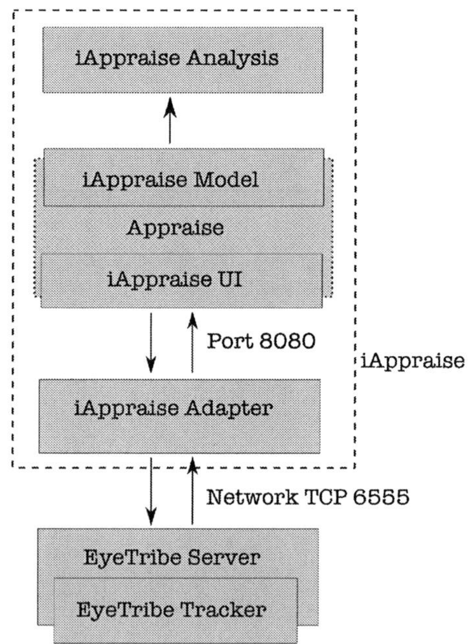

Figure 1: iAppraise architecture

2.2 iAppraise Communication Interfaces

The *EyeTribe* eye-tracker, running at 30Hz or 60Hz, broadcasts gaze data through a TCP port (EyeTribe default port 6555) using *JSON* (JavaScript Object Notation) formatted messages. The iAppraise Adapter employs two sockets, one that listens to the eye-tracker, and the other to pass the data to the *iAppraise* UI.

2.3 iAppraise User Interface

To facilitate the usage of eye-tracking data for machine translation evaluation, we added an evaluation task to the original Appraise.[5] This task has a layout and graphical elements, that have been optimized for the use of eye-tracking. The template has two main content regions: *Reference* and *Translation*. The task for this view requires to score the quality of a translation by comparing it to the provided reference. The annotator is required to use a slider (see Figure 2) to provide a score. In return, he/she gets feedback in the form of stars, that reflect how close his/her score is to an optional gold-standard score. In principle, the stars are part of a gamification strategy used to keep the evaluator engaged. If the gold standard scores are not be available this option can be turned off.

2.4 iAppraise Model/DB

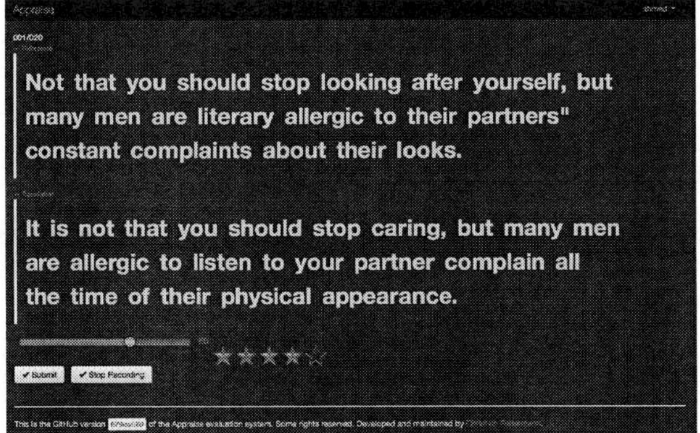

Figure 2: iAppraise Eye-Tracking Evaluation task layout with feedback. From top to bottom: Reference and Translation sentences, slider for scoring, and feedback in a form of stars.

To handle data flow and gather information resulted from the eye-tracking and user interaction, a new data model was added to Appraise. This data model stores the data received from the *iAppraise UI* into a database. Table 1 shows the different attributes and the description of the fields for the data recorded during an eye-tracking task.

---

[5] `appraise/templates/evaluation/`
`eyetracking.htm`

Attribute	Description
Task attributes	
pscore	Eye-tracker precision at the time of the recording. Computed as the number of words observed in a random sample of words.
score	Score given by the user
Gaze attributes	
region	Active region where the gaze landed
gazex	Actual coordinate x of the gaze
gazey	Actual coordinate y of the gaze
data	JSON EyeTribe message[6]
Environment attributes	
scaling	The ratio of the (vertical) size of one physical pixel on the current display to the size of one device independent pixels(dips)
zoom	Window zooming level
scrollx	Number of horizontal pixels the current document has been scrolled from the upper left corner of the window
scrolly	Number of vertical pixels the current document has been scrolled from the upper left corner of the window
clientWidth	Window width
div0Height	Window height
innerHeight	The inner height of the browser window
outerHeight	The outer height of the browser window

Table 1: Description of attributes stored in the database.

2.5 Eyetacking Replay

The eye-tracking data collected during the evaluation session can be visualized as a re-enactment or replay. This allows to analyze the evaluator during the task, or to perform some basic troubleshooting. The replay highlights the background of words in the sequence that they were observed (See Figure 3 for demonstration).

2.6 iAppraise Analysis

The *iAppraise Analysis* module extracts useful features from the *iAppraise DB* that can be used to analyze the evaluation process or a train a prediction model. It consists of several auxiliary scripts that parse the data and extract features described below:

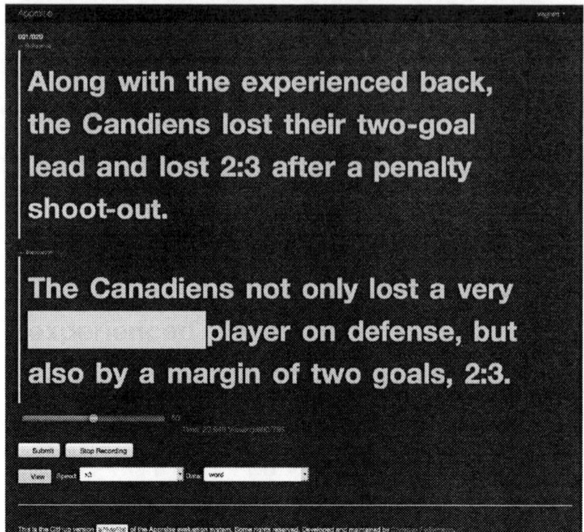

Figure 3: iAppraise Eye-Tracking task replay; words gets highlighted in the sequence that they were observed.

Jump features While reading text, the gaze of a person does not visit every single word, but advances in jumps called *saccades*. These jumps can go forward (*progressions*) or backward (*regressions*). We classify the word-transitions according to the direction of the jump and distance between the start and end words. For subsequent words n, $n + 1$, this would mean a forward jump of distance equal to 1. All jumps with distance greater than 4 are sorted into a 5+ bucket. Additionally, we separate the features for reference and translation jumps. We also count the total number of jumps.

Total jump distance We aggregate jump distances[7] to count the total distance covered while evaluating a sentence. We count reference and translation distance features separately. Such information is useful in analyzing the complexity and readability of the translation.

Inter-region jumps While reading a translation, evaluators can jump between the translation and a reference to compare them. Intuitively, more jumps of this type could signify that the translation is harder to evaluate. Here we count the number of reference↔translation transitions.

---

[7]Jump count and distance features have also shown to be useful in SMT decoders (Durrani et al., 2011).

Dwell time The amount of time a person fixates on a region is a crucial marker for processing difficulty in sentence comprehension (Clifton et al., 2007) and moderately correlates with the quality of a translation (Doherty et al., 2010). We count the time spent by the reader on each particular word. We separate reference and translation features.

Lexicalized features The features discussed above do not associate gaze movements with the words being read. We believe that this information can be critical to judge the overall difficulty of the reference sentence, and to evaluate which translation fragments are problematic to the reader. To compute the lexicalized features, we extract streams of reference and translation lexical sequences based on the gaze jumps, and score them using a tri-gram language model. Let $R_i = r_1, r_2, \ldots, r_m$ be a sub-sequence of gaze movement over reference and there are $R_1, R_2, \ldots, R_n$ sequences, the *lex* feature is computed as follows:

$$lex(R) = \sum_i^n \frac{\log p(R_i)}{|R_i|}$$

$$p(R_i) = \sum_j^m p(r_j | r_{j-1}, r_{j-2})$$

The normalization factor $|R_i|$ is used to make the probabilities comparable. We also use unnormalized scores as additional feature. A similar set of features $lex(T)$ is computed for the translations. All features are normalized by the length of the sentence.

In a related effort, we used the above features to predict the quality scores given by an evaluator. More details on the model and how effective each of the features were, please refer to Sajjad et al. (2016).

3 iAppraise Demonstration Script

iAppraise demonstration will allow the users to experiment with the tool and the eye tracking device. The users will be able to perform an evaluation task, observe a replay of their own eye movements, and to export their gaze data. We will also demonstrate the basic functioning for additional tools and scripts. This includes using the exported data to extract features and information about the evaluation task.

The iAppraise server is available as an open-source project, and can also be downloaded as an already-configured virtual machine that can be deployed on any environment.

4 Conclusion

In this paper, we presented *iAppraise*, a framework to provide eye-tracking capabilities to directly Appraise. Here we described the different components that make up the framework. The main goal of the framework is to provide a tool that lowers the entry-level bar to using eye-tracking in the MT community. *iAppraise* has several advantages: (*i*) it connects low-cost eye-trackers to an open-source MT analysis platform; and (*ii*) it provides a set of analysis tools that allow the use of the gaze information effortlessly. We expect that in the future, more researchers will adopt *iAppraise* to explore the human consumption of text in other NLP tasks.

References

Ondřej Bojar, Christian Buck, Chris Callison-Burch, Christian Federmann, Barry Haddow, Philipp Koehn, Christof Monz, Matt Post, Radu Soricut, and Lucia Specia. 2013. Findings of the 2013 Workshop on Statistical Machine Translation. In *Proceedings of the Eighth Workshop on Statistical Machine Translation*, pages 1–44, Sofia, Bulgaria, August. Association for Computational Linguistics.

Charles Clifton, Adrian Staub, and Keith Rayner. 2007. Eye movements in reading words and sentences. *Eye movements: A window on mind and brain*, pages 341–372.

Stephen Doherty and Sharon O'Brien. 2014. Assessing the usability of raw machine translated output: A user-centered study using eye tracking. *International Journal of Human-Computer Interaction*, 30(1):40–51.

Stephen Doherty, Sharon O?Brien, and Michael Carl. 2010. Eye tracking as an MT evaluation technique. *Machine translation*, 24(1):1–13.

Nadir Durrani, Helmut Schmid, and Alexander Fraser. 2011. A Joint Sequence Translation Model with Integrated Reordering. In *Proceedings of the Association for Computational Linguistics: Human Language Technologies (ACL-HLT'11)*, Portland, OR, USA.

Christian Federmann. 2012. Appraise: an open-source toolkit for manual evaluation of mt output. *The Prague Bulletin of Mathematical Linguistics*, 98:25–35.

Simon Garrod. 2006. Psycholinguistic research methods. *The encyclopedia of language and linguistics*, 2:251–257.

Francisco Guzmán, Ahmed Abdelali, Irina Temnikova, Hassan Sajjad, and Stephan Vogel. 2015. How do humans evaluate machine translation. In *Proceedings of the Tenth Workshop on Statistical Machine Translation*, pages 457–466, Lisbon, Portugal, September. Association for Computational Linguistics.

Trevor A Harley. 2013. *The psychology of language: From data to theory*. Psychology Press.

Marcel A Just and Patricia A Carpenter. 1980. A theory of reading: from eye fixations to comprehension. *Psychological review*, 87(4):329.

Keith Rayner. 1998. Eye movements in reading and information processing: 20 years of research. *Psychological bulletin*, 124(3):372.

Hassan Sajjad, Francisco Guzmán, Nadir Durrani, Ahmed Abdelali, Houda Bouamor, Irina Temnikova, and Stephan Vogel. 2016. Eyes Don't Lie: Predicting Machine Translation Quality Using Eye Movement. In *Proceedings of the 2016 Conference of the North American Chapter of the Association for Computational Linguistics: Human Language Technologies*, San Diego, California, June. Association for Computational Linguistics.

Sara Stymne, Henrik Danielsson, Sofia Bremin, Hongzhan Hu, Johanna Karlsson, Anna Prytz Lillkull, and Martin Wester. 2012. Eye tracking as a tool for machine translation error analysis. In *LREC*, pages 1121–1126.

Linguistica 5: Unsupervised Learning of Linguistic Structure

Jackson L. Lee
University of Chicago
1115 East 58th Street
Chicago, IL 60637, USA
jsllee@uchicago.edu

John A. Goldsmith
University of Chicago
1115 East 58th Street
Chicago, IL 60637, USA
goldsmith@uchicago.edu

Abstract

This paper introduces *Linguistica 5*, a software for unsupervised learning of linguistic structure. It is a descendant of Goldsmith's (2001, 2006) Linguistica. Open-source and written in Python, the new *Linguistica 5* is both a graphical user interface software and a Python library. While *Linguistica 5* inherits its predecessors' strength in unsupervised learning of natural language morphology, it incorporates significant improvements in multiple ways. Notable new features include tools for data visualization as well as straightforward extensions for both its components and embedding in other programs.

1 Introduction

The unsupervised learning of linguistic structure has been an important area of investigation in various disciplines. In natural language processing, unsupervised methods have the practical advantage over supervised ones that relatively less training data (which is time-consuming and costly to prepare) is required. In linguistics and cognitive science, a deeper understanding of how linguistic structure can be learned from unstructured data without supervision sheds light on human language acquisition. In this paper, we introduce *Linguistica 5*, a Python-based software for research on the unsupervised learning of linguistic structure. This software is a descendant of Linguistica 4 and its previous versions (Goldsmith, 2001; Goldsmith, 2006) dealing mainly with morphology.[1]

------

[1] http://linguistica.uchicago.edu/

In the following, we explain the axioms guiding the development of *Linguistica 5* in section 2. In section 3, the dual design of both a graphical user interface (GUI) and a Python library is introduced. Section 4 demonstrates data visualization using the GUI. Section 5 exemplifies how *Linguistica 5* can be used in conjunction with other computational tools in research. Section 6 concludes the paper.

2 Axioms

In the development of *Linguistica 5*, we adhere closely to the axioms of reproducible, accessible, and extensible research.

- **Reproducibility**: Research using *Linguistica 5* is reproducible, in the sense of Claerbout and Karrenbach (1992). *Linguistica 5* is open-source. The source code is publicly hosted at an online repository with detailed documentation (see footnote 1).

- **Accessibility**: Similar to all previous versions, *Linguistica 5* has a graphical user interface to make it accessible to a wide audience. However, *Linguistica 5* significantly departs from them by the introduction of data visualization tools. This is especially important for exploring potentially interesting patterns in large datasets; more on this in section 4.

- **Extensibility**: *Linguistica 5* facilitates extensible research in two ways. First, *Linguistica 5* is highly modular, which makes the addition of new components in further research straightforward. Second, apart from having a GUI, it

Proceedings of NAACL-HLT 2016 (Demonstrations), pages 22–26,
San Diego, California, June 12-17, 2016. ©2016 Association for Computational Linguistics

is also a Python library, which can be called in other Python programs for computational research. Section 5 provides an example.

3 Dual interface design: GUI and Python library

Previous versions of Linguistica are written in C++ and built in the Qt framework. These versions are designed to be GUI software out of the box. The major drawback is that the core backend is intimately tied with the GUI code, which makes further development and debugging difficult. To solve this problem, the new *Linguistica 5* takes a radically different approach.

First, we choose Python to be the new programming language for Linguistica, because it has been widely used in computational linguistics and natural language processing for its strengths in fast coding, strong library support for machine learning and other computational tools.

Second, the focus of the *Linguistica 5* development is its backend as a Python library, with a GUI wrapper written in PyQt. This new architecture has several advantages. In terms of the user interface, there are two independent choices. As in previous versions of Linguistica, the GUI allows convenient data analysis – and visualization, a new development in *Linguistica 5* (see section 4). Another novelty is that *Linguistica 5* is a Python library by design. Researchers are able to use *Linguistica 5* in a computationally dynamic and automatic fashion by calling it in their own programs for any research and computational work of their interest.

4 Data visualization

Research along the lines of Linguistica has focused on natural language morphology. Still within the realm of unsupervised learning of linguistic structure, *Linguistica 5* represents an important step forward by attempting to (i) induce structure that goes beyond morphology, and (ii) use it to improve results in morphological learning. Given large datasets, data visualization has become indispensable for both exploring new questions as well as uncovering unknown ones. The increased interest in visualization of linguistic data and resources is reflected by specialized research venues created recently, e.g., the Workshop on Visualization as Added Value in the Development, Use and Evaluation of Language Resources (VisLR) which debuted in 2014. Here we provide an example from our ongoing work.

The area of interest is unsupervised word category induction (see Christodoulopoulos et al. (2010) for a recent review), which potentially offers solutions to challenging problems in fully unsupervised morphological learning (e.g. is the induced morphological paradigm *walk-walks* a verbal or nominal paradigm? And how do we characterize its potential connection with other induced paradigms such as *jump-jumped-jumps*?).

Currently, we are exploring spectral approaches to the problem of unsupervised word category induction. A central component is to model syntactic neighborhood among words in a given dataset. The current model is implemented as a series of steps for word similarity computation. First, a graph of word similarity for all pairs of word types is computed based on the number of shared word ngram contexts. We compute the most significant eigenvectors of the normalized Laplacian of the graph. Each word is embedded in $\mathbb{R}^k$ based on the coordinates derived from the k eigenvectors. A new graph of word similarity is obtained based on the Euclidean distance of the word coordinates. Words in this resultant graph are connected to one another in such a way that corresponds to syntactic neighborhood. For instance, the word "the" likely has other articles or determiners such as "a" and "an" as syntactic neighbors that occur in syntactically similar positions. Using the Brown corpus (Kučera and Francis, 1967), several syntactic neighbors for the word types "the", "would", and "after" are in Table 1.

Word	Syntactic neighbors
the	a his their an its this my our that
would	could must will can should may might
after	before like during since without through

Table 1: Syntactic neighbors

Importantly, the syntactic neighbors of a given word are themselves word types in the given dataset. The interconnectedness of words in the syntactic neighborhood results calls for network visualization. This can be done in *Linguistica 5* as one of the key new features. Figure 1 shows a screenshot of

Linguistica 5 displaying the syntactic word neighborhood network for the most frequent 1,000 word types in the Brown corpus, as rendered by the force-directed graph layout in the JavaScript D3 library (Bostock et al., 2011). Figure 2 zooms in for the cluster of words that would be categorized as modal verbs such as "could", "would", and "must".

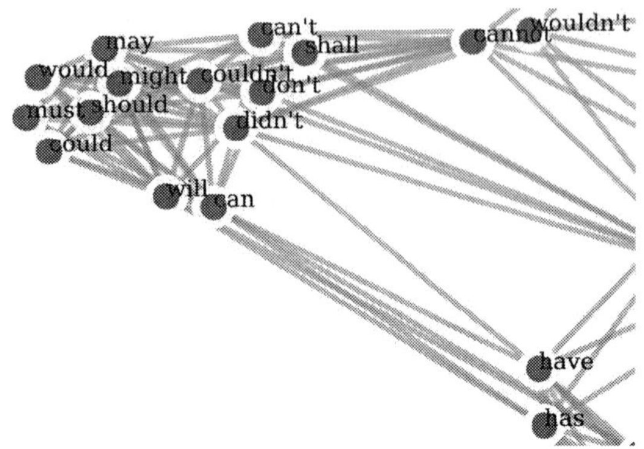

Figure 2: Zooming in Figure 1 for modal verbs

With induced knowledge analogous to word categories in natural language, results of unsupervised morphological learning could be improved. For instance, morphophonology could be learned. Induced morphological signatures (see section 5.1) such as $\{\emptyset, ed\}$ (*walk-walked*) and $\{\emptyset, d\}$ (*love-loved*) could be aligned for allomorphy across signatures (words with *ed* and *d* belonging to the same word category in this case). While this is work in progress, we have shown that data visualization tools in *Linguistica 5* as exemplified by syntactic neighborhood networks provide insights for new pursuits in research.

5 Embedding Linguistica 5 in other programs

Another new and powerful feature of *Linguistica 5* is that it is a Python library by design and is therefore callable in other Python-based programs. This is significant, because it is now possible to run the Linguistica algorithms dynamically for any data of interest from different sources (either from a local file or from an in-memory Python object).

We illustrate how *Linguistica 5* can be used as a Python library in conjunction with other tools with an example for computational modeling of human language acquisition, a growing field bringing linguistics, computer science, and cognitive science together (cf. Villavicencio et al. (2013)). We first provide the background on morphological signatures.

5.1 Morphological signatures

Unsupervised learning of morphology in Linguistica revolves around objects known as morphological signatures. A (morphological) signature, in the sense of Goldsmith (2001), is a morphological pattern associated with its stems as induced in some given data. For example, $\{\emptyset, s\}$ is a morphological signature very likely to be induced in any sizable English datasets, with possible associated stems such as *walk-, jump-* (which entails that the words *walk, walks, jump, jumps* occur in the data).

Using the Brown corpus (about 50,000 word types from one million word tokens) for written American English, *Linguistica 5* finds over 300 morphological signatures. Those with the most associated stems are shown in the screenshot in Figure 3; the signature $\{\emptyset, ed, ing, s\}$ is highlighted, with its associated stems displayed on the right.

	Signature	Stem count		NULL/ed/ing/s (number of stems: 151)			
1	NULL/s	2327		abound	administer	affirm	aff
2	's/NULL	813		appeal	arrest	assault	att
3	NULL/ly	587		awaken	award	beckon	be
4	NULL/d/s	346		bloom	bolt	broaden	bu
5	NULL/d	314		claw	click	climb	clu
6	ed/ing	197		coil	compound	concern	col
7	'/NULL	190		confront	contact	contrast	cra
8	's/NULL/s	181		crown	decay	deck	dia
9	d/s	175		display	drill	drown	du
10	ies/y	173		eschew	escort	exceed	exc
11	NULL/ed/ing/s	151		extend	filter	flounder	fro
12	NULL/ed	134		haunt	hoot	hover	ho

Figure 3: Signatures with the most stems in the Brown corpus

5.2 On human morphological acquisition

Given that *Linguistica 5* is designed to model unsupervised morphological learning as a major goal, we ask how it can be used to model human morphological learning using child-directed speech data. An important criterion is that for the model to be cognitively plausible, it has to simulate the incremental nature of the input data. This means that the Linguistica algorithm for morphological learning must be called and applied flexibly over some growing data.

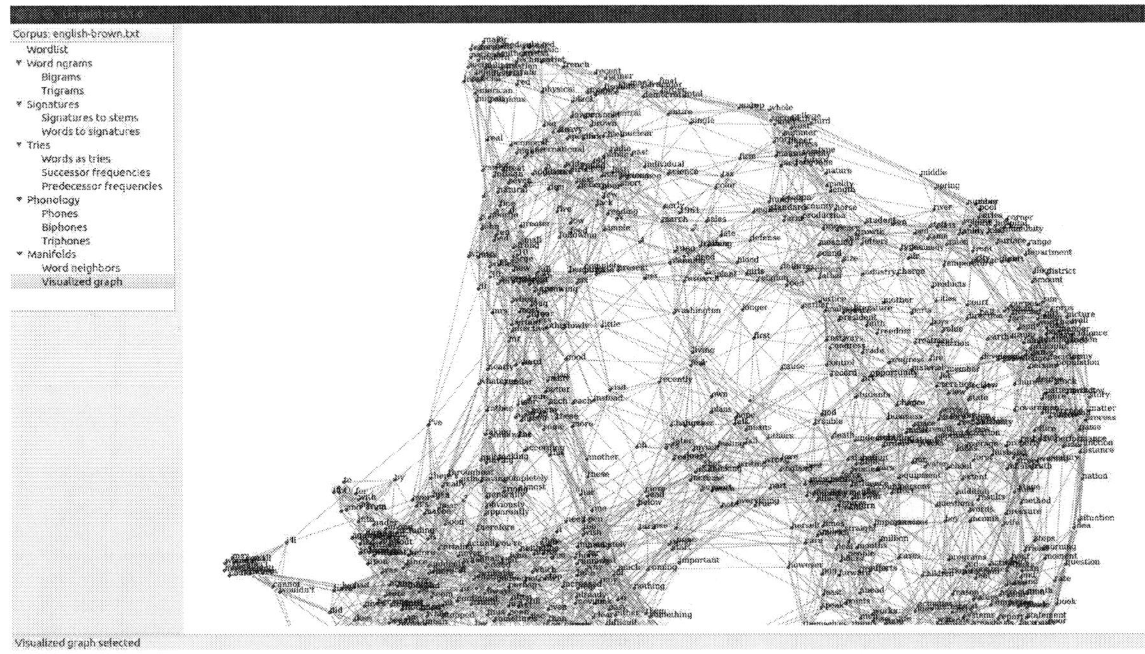

Figure 1: Syntactic word neighborhood network in *Linguistica 5*

Concretely, we tested *Linguistica 5* for its ability to model morphological acquisition using Eve's data in the Brown portion (Brown, 1973) of the CHILDES database (MacWhinney, 2000), an idea sketched in Lee (2015). The child-directed speech (CDS) at different ages of the target child in the data was extracted by the PyLangAcq library (Lee et al., 2016) and fed into *Linguistica 5*. Table 2 shows the results of morphological signature induction from growing word types up to the ages of 18, 21, and 24 months, respectively.

Age	# word types	Induced signatures
18 mths	610	{'s Ø}{Ø s}
21 mths	1,246	{'s Ø}{Ø s}{Ø ing}{ll s}
24 mths	1,601	{'s Ø}{Ø s}{Ø ing}{ll s}{'s Ø s}

Table 2: Morphological signatures from CDS to Eve

The classic study of first language acquisition by Brown (1973) reports that the first three morphological patterns acquired by English-speaking children are the third-person singular inflection {Ø, s}, the possessive {'s, Ø}, and the progressive {Ø, ing}. Table 2 shows these are patterns that *Linguistica 5* successfully discovers in Eve's child-directed speech. Other induced signatures are {ll, s} (as in *she'll-she's*) and {'s, Ø, s}, a more complex pattern found when more data becomes available to the learner. The results for modeling language acquisition here contrast sharply with those from the Brown corpus in section 5.1, for the much larger amount of input data and results in the latter. But of particular interest is the *incremental* nature of learning in the former case. The fact that *Linguistica 5* is a Python library makes it possible to devise tools embedding it for multiple learning iterations run automatically.

In this section, we have shown how *Linguistica 5* can be used jointly with other programs for highly dynamic computational research, which is complementary to its GUI counterpart for exploratory ground work.

6   Conclusions

Linguistica 5 opens new doors to reproducible, accessible, and extensible research in unsupervised learning of linguistic structure. Building on the strengths of its predecessors, *Linguistica 5* incorporates novel elements of data visualization as well as employs a flexible and modular architecture to allow its integration into other projects and to maximize continual research and development.

Acknowledgments

This work was completed in part with resources provided by the University of Chicago Research Computing Center and Big Ideas Generator. We would also like to thank the three anonymous reviewers for very helpful comments and suggestions.

References

Michael Bostock, Vadim Ogievetsky, and Jeffrey Heer. 2011. D^3 data-driven documents. *Visualization and Computer Graphics, IEEE Transactions on*, 17(12):2301–2309.

Roger Brown. 1973. *A first language: The early stages.* Harvard University Press.

Christos Christodoulopoulos, Sharon Goldwater, and Mark Steedman. 2010. Two decades of unsupervised pos induction: How far have we come? In *Proceedings of the Conference on Empirical Methods in Natural Language Processing*.

Jon Claerbout and Martin Karrenbach. 1992. Electronic documents give reproducible research a new meaning. In *Proc. 62nd Ann. Int. Meeting of the Soc. of Exploration Geophysics*, pages 601–604.

John A. Goldsmith. 2001. Unsupervised learning of the morphology of a natural language. *Computational Linguistics*, 27(2):153–198.

John A. Goldsmith. 2006. An algorithm for the unsupervised learning of morphology. *Natural Language Engineering*, 12(4):353–371.

Henry Kučera and W. Nelson Francis. 1967. *Computational Analysis of Present-Day American English.* Brown University Press, Providence.

Jackson L. Lee, Ross Burkholder, Gallagher B. Flinn, and Emily R. Coppess. 2016. Working with CHAT transcripts in Python. Technical Report TR-2016-02, Department of Computer Science, University of Chicago.

Jackson L. Lee. 2015. Morphological paradigms: Computational structure and unsupervised learning. In *Proceedings of NAACL HLT 2015 Student Research Workshop*.

Brian MacWhinney. 2000. *The CHILDES project: Tools for analyzing talk.* Lawrence Erlbaum Associates, Mahwah, NJ.

Aline Villavicencio, Thierry Poibeau, Anna Korhonen, and Afra Alishahi, editors. 2013. *Cognitive Aspects of Computational Language Acquisition.* Springer.

TRANSREAD: Designing a Bilingual Reading Experience with Machine Translation Technologies

François Yvon and **Yong Xu** and **Marianna Apidianaki**
LIMSI, CNRS, Université Paris-Saclay
91 403 Orsay
{yvon,yong,marianna}@limsi.fr

Clément Pillias and **Pierre Cubaud**
CEDRIC, CNAM
2 rue Conté, 75003 PARIS
{clement.pillias,cubaud}@cnam.fr

Abstract

In this paper, we use multilingual Natural Language Processing (NLP) tools to improve the reading experience of parallel texts on mobile devices. Such enterprise poses multiple challenging issues both from the NLP and from the Human Computer Interaction (HCI) perspectives. We discuss these problems, and report on our own solutions, now implemented in a full-fledged bilingual reading device.

1 Introduction

Owing to 15 years of advances in Statistical Machine Translation (SMT), automatically translated texts are nowadays of sufficiently high quality to serve the general public and the translation industry. Contrary to (S)MT which primarily targets readers without any assumed literacy in the source language, the TRANSREAD project studies applications targeting *partially bilingual users*, such as language learners, migrants settling in a new country, inhabitants of multilingual states, editors in the publishing industry and professional translators. Its main goal is to help such users to read texts in the original (source) language, even though a translation might be available in their mother tongue. Bitext processing techniques (Wu, 2010; Tiedemann, 2011) such as cross-lingual alignments at different levels or cross-lingual dictionary access, can facilitate and enrich the reading experience of texts in their original language. Such endeavour poses difficult challenges: it first requires to push existing MT technologies to the limit and to revisit assumptions that are rarely questioned, such as the need to deliver *fully aligned* bitexts, including many-to-many sentence links, and to output *high-precision word and phrase alignments*, even for rare words or gappy multi-word units.

A second challenge is visualisation and interaction design. In fact, most existing interfaces for bilingual reading/writing have targeted specialists of the MT industry, serving purposes such as manual alignment input and visualisation (Smith and Jahry, 2000; Germann, 2008; Gilmanov et al., 2014; Steele and Specia, 2015), MT tracing and debugging (DeNeefe et al., 2005; Weese and Callison-Burch, 2010), MT quality assessment (Federmann, 2012; Chatzitheodorou, 2013; Girardi et al., 2014) or MT post-edition (Aziz et al., 2012). By contrast, our aim is not just to visualize the translation or bilingual correspondences, but rather to enable a smooth and seamless reading experience for the general public. Ebook reading applications typically allow the reader to select a word and to access the corresponding dictionary entry, but applications that exploit the full translation context are much rarer. In *DoppelText*[1], *DuoLir*[2] and *Parallel Text Reader* on iOS, the selection is performed at the sentence level, using alignments. Whatever level is used, this kind of *switch-on-demand* interaction interrupts the flow of reading and can be a source of frustration. Another approach uses *synchronized views*, where the bitext is shown to the reader along with alignment links. In *ParallelBooks*[3], the bitext is synchronized by scrolling and the translation (at the paragraph level) only appears when the user taps

---

[1] http://www.doppeltext.com/
[2] http://www.duolir.com/
[3] http://www.parallelbooks.com/

Proceedings of NAACL-HLT 2016 (Demonstrations), pages 27–31,
San Diego, California, June 12-17, 2016. ©2016 Association for Computational Linguistics

the screen. Synchronized views have the potential to enable a seamless reading of the bitext (Pillias and Cubaud, 2015), at the cost however of a larger screen space. This paper discusses these various challenges and reports on the state of development of our main tool - the bilingual reader. Additional information, including resources and demos, can be found on the project website.[4]

2 Augmenting e-books with alignments

A major requirement of electronic reading devices is their ability to seamlessly reformat and adapt their typesetting, which does not only include the text itself but also other editorial (header, footer), typographic (bold, italic, font sizes and shapes) and dispositional information. An early design choice was to include alignment information as auxiliary source of information to the original electronic book(s). Each side of the bitext is thus stored in the EPUB format,[5] a de facto standard for electronic books, thereby enabling us to take advantage of its inherent ability to encode arbitrary documents and media files, as well as directives regarding their display.

Linguistic annotations are stored in an additional file to the EPUB archive and use an XML-based representation inspired by the XCES format,[6] already proposed in the early 2000s to represent alignment information. References to actual textual units (in the EPUB/html files) are maintained as the complete path from the root of the document to the node containing the unit. Our format for representing annotations is generic enough to represent alignment links at various levels of granularity, as well as other arbitrary information. It relies on two types of basic markups: `<link>` for binary relationships (bilingual links or monolingual co-references), and `<mark>` for unary information concerning one single unit (be it a paragraph, a sentence, a fragment or a word). In our sample file, these tags are used to encode part-of-speech as well as sense disambiguation information. However, only the information related to bilingual alignment links is currently displayed.

3 Challenges of bitext alignments

Our representation of alignment relationships accommodates alignment links at various levels of granularity. Our display currently exploits 5 such levels, based on sentential, sub-sentential and word alignments, which were computed for two short stories by S. Maugham.[7]

3.1 Sentence alignment

Sentence alignment in parallel texts (bitexts) is a well established problem in multilingual NLP (Brown et al., 1991; Gale and Church, 1991; Kay and Röscheisen, 1993), for which a wide array of methods exist (Tiedemann, 2011). The problem is however far from being solved, especially for literary texts where parallelism is less strict than for technical or legal documents (Yu et al., 2012). For this demo, alignments have been produced semi-automatically. The automatic part used techniques presented by (Xu et al., 2015), which implement a multi-pass, coarse-to-fine alignment strategy. The first pass uses very reliable 1:1 alignment links computed using the approach of (Moore, 2002), while the next stages complete this initial partial alignment by including additional correspondences, the probabilities of which are evaluated using a large-scale MaxEnt classifier embarking a very large number of features. Automatic alignments were then manually checked and fixed: for our simple bitexts they were mostly correct, with a link level F-score $\approx 97\%$.

3.2 Word alignments

For this demo, gold word alignments were collected as follows: automatic word alignments were first computed by running the MGiza (Gao and Vogel, 2008) implementation of IBM Model 4 (Brown et al., 1993) in both directions. Alignments in the intersection were checked and corrected following the recommandations of Och and Ney (2003). Even for such simple texts, alignment errors were numerous, with an AER close to 0.17 ('The Promise'), and to 0.19 ('The Verger'). This confirms the intuition that computing high quality word alignments for literary texts might be significantly more difficult than for other text genres. This also calls for improved

---

techniques for computing confidence measures for word alignments (Huang, 2009): depending on the intended reading context, it might be better to avoid displaying erroneous alignment links.

3.3 Subsentential alignments

The task of designing sound and tractable alignment models is notoriously much harder for groups of words than for words (Marcu and Wong, 2002; DeNero and Klein, 2008). Two main strategies have been explored in the literature: the most common, employed in most SMT systems (Koehn et al., 2007) starts with alignments for isolated words, which are incrementally grown subject to consistency constraints. The alternative way is to start with sentential alignments and adopt a divisive strategy, which yields progressive refinements of an initially holistic pairing; this can be performed exactly under ITG constraints (Wu, 1997); heuristic approaches, capable of handling alignments for arbitrarily long segments have also been proposed in (Lardilleux et al., 2012): both techniques require to evaluate the parallelism of arbitrary chunks. We follow the latter here, also using punctuation marks to select segmentation points. The resulting alignments are deliberately pretty coarse and primarily meant to be used in a contrastive condition for the human tests.

4 A Bilingual Reader

4.1 Design

The current version of the TRANSREAD bilingual reader displays paginated versions of the bitext in parallel views. In Figure 1, the source text is displayed on the right side of the screen and its translation on the left. The user has selected a word in the source version. Touching a word highlights its context on both sides, exploiting the alignment structure in a hierarchical way. Highlighting can be triggered from both versions of the text. The different levels are depicted using bounding boxes, which are pre-computed using the alignment and the HTML graphs. Bounding boxes are not always rectangular, because of word hyphenation for text justification. We have tried to minimize visual overload by simplifying the resulting geometry of the boxes and using a colour scale as background. We use the "natural" theme from (Krause, 2010).

The display size for the bitext can be modified dynamically. When the application starts, the text versions are given an equal space, but the translation on the left can be shrunk so that the reader can concentrate on the original text. Structural highlighting is still functional in this mode, but when the translated text is shrunk to its minimum size, it can only be used as a visual hint.

Our reader is targeted for use on a tablet device. Interactions with the tactile screen of the tablet cause the well-known problem of fingers occluding the touched item. To avoid this issue, a pointer is displayed 1.3cm above the touch position sensed by the system, and its position determines what elements are selected. This *picking* is done by recursively searching the textual elements whose precomputed bounding boxes contain the pointer's position. When this process selects two sibling elements (e.g. two sentences in a paragraph), the system only keeps the one for which the distance from the pointer to the closest bounding box border is greatest. The pointer shape is an upward triangle. When a word is selected, we also display a downward triangle above it attached to the line of text, but following the pointer horizontally. These two triangles enclose the selected word without occluding it.

4.2 Implementation

As readers, we benefit from centuries of high quality printed typesetting. A poor digital typesetting would therefore lower the user experience of our bilingual reader, no matter how rich the interaction may be. But automated typesetting is a complex task, often under-estimated. For instance, justification on small columns, as those produced by bitext presentation, can exhibit "rivers" of white space that are difficult to handle automatically. Our first goal for the implementation was then to select a programming framework that would help for these questions. The Knuth-Plass algorithm[8] was used for justification, along with LaTeX rules[9] for hyphenation. Another important issue was to build a fully reconfigurable software in order to investigate a large design space of interaction for tablets. We have selected the Kivy framework for Python, which en-

---

[8] As described in `http://defoe.sourceforge.net/folio/knuth-plass.html`

[9] Provided by `http://tug.org/tex-hyphen/`

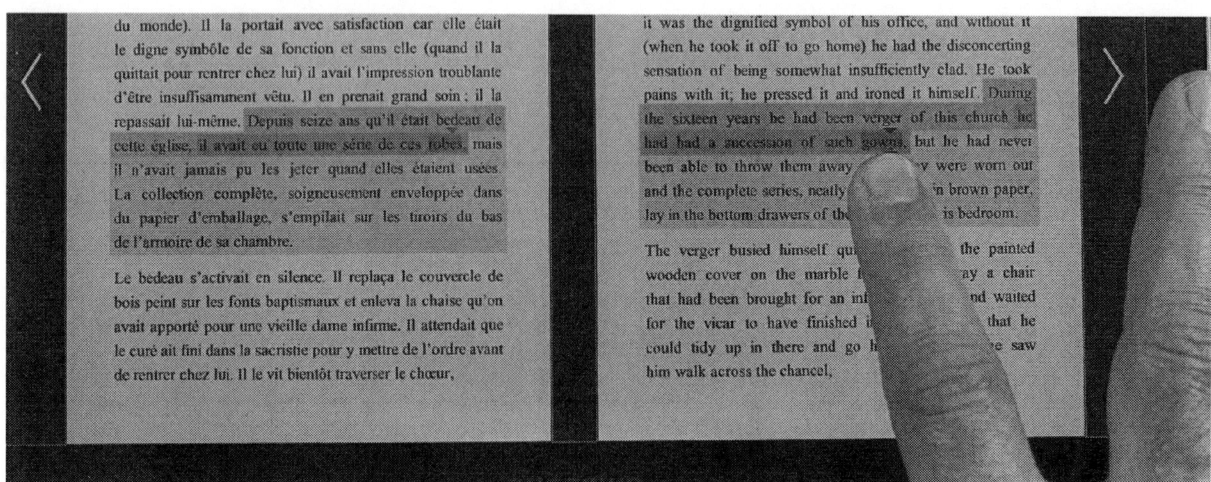

Figure 1: The TRANSREAD bilingual reader application running on tablet

ables cross-platform development for Android or iOS, and GPU-based graphics with OpenGL ES.

5 Perspectives

As reflected in this paper, a top priority is to pursue our efforts towards high-precision alignments, an application where supervised learning techniques could help (Moore, 2005). Additional functionalities in reading are also envisioned, such as an enhanced and non-distracting access to dictionary information for difficult words. Currently, Web Readers and mobile reading devices offer such functionality through a pop-up window presenting the complete dictionary entry. No assistance is however offered to access the right sense in context, which would be especially helpful for polysemous words or when language proficiency is low. In TRANSREAD, we propose to perform this selection automatically. Our word sense disambiguation (WSD) method (Apidianaki and Gong, 2015) exploits word-level alignments to annotate words on both sides of the bitext with the correct senses extracted from BabelNet (Navigli and Ponzetto, 2012). By integrating WSD information in the reader, we will be able to propose definitions, usage examples and Wikipedia entries, as well as synonymous words and semantically correct translations. Our WSD system embeds an alignment-based multi-word expression (MWE) identification mechanism (Marie and Apidianaki, 2015). Such information will serve as part

of a smart selection mechanism (Pantel et al., 2014), enabling the system to select appropriate spans and dictionary entries for MWEs found in texts.

An experimental evaluation of the interface general design is currently being conducted. We study, notably, the effect of the depth of the alignment structure on human readers behavior. As short term future work, we shall also investigate other interaction techniques for focus management, such as distortion and 3D views for page turning (Cubaud, 2008). The graphic composition engine developed for the current application already allows such effects. A research agenda should also include long term experiments with real-life reading sessions for a wide range of languages and text difficulties.

6 Conclusion

We have presented a first version of a bilingual reader using NLP and HCI technologies to enhance the reading experience. On our way, some tough challenges had to be overcome, an unexpected issue being the processing of typeset documents which is hardly addressed in the NLP literature. This venture has provided a context where such issues matter, illustrating the benefits of cross-domain research.

Acknowledgments

This work was partly funded by the French "National Research Agency" under project ANR-12-CORD-0015.

References

M. Apidianaki and L. Gong. 2015. LIMSI: Translations as Source of Indirect Supervision for Multilingual All-Words Sense Disambiguation and Entity Linking. In *Proc. SemEval*.

W. Aziz, S. C. M. De Sousa, and L. Specia. 2012. PET: a tool for post-editing and assessing machine translation. In *Proc. LREC*.

P. F. Brown, J. C. Lai, and R. L. Mercer. 1991. Aligning sentences in parallel corpora. In *Proc. ACL*.

P. F. Brown, S. A. Della Pietra, V. J. Della Pietra, and R. L. Mercer. 1993. The Mathematics of Statistical Machine Translation: Parameter Estimation. *Computational Linguistics*, 19(2):263–311.

K. Chatzitheodorou. 2013. COSTA MT Evaluation Tool: An open toolkit for human machine translation evaluation. *The Prague Bulletin of Mathematical Linguistics*, 100.

P. Cubaud, 2008. *Digital Libraries*, chapter 3D interaction for digital libraries.

S. DeNeefe, K. Knight, and H. H. Chan. 2005. Interactively Exploring a Machine Translation Model. In *Proc. ACL*.

J. DeNero and D. Klein. 2008. The Complexity of Phrase Alignment Problems. In *Proc. ACL-08:HLT*.

C. Federmann. 2012. Appraise: an Open-Source Toolkit for Manual Evaluation of MT output. *The Prague Bulletin of Mathematical Linguistics*, 98.

W. A. Gale and K. W. Church. 1991. A program for aligning sentences in bilingual corpora. In *Proc. ACL*.

Q. Gao and S. Vogel. 2008. Parallel Implementations of Word Alignment Tool. In *Software Engineering, Testing, and Quality Assurance for Natural Language Processing*.

U. Germann. 2008. Yawat: Yet Another Word Alignment Tool. In *Proc. ACL-08:HLT (demo)*.

T. Gilmanov, O. Scrivner, and S. Kübler. 2014. SWIFT Aligner, A Multifunctional Tool for Parallel Corpora: Visualization, Word Alignment, and (Morpho)-Syntactic Cross-Language Transfer. In *Proc. LREC*.

C. Girardi, L. Bentivogli, M. A. Farajian, and M. Federico. 2014. MT-EQuAl: a Toolkit for Human Assessment of Machine Translation Output. In *Proc. COLING*.

F. Huang. 2009. Confidence Measure for Word Alignment. In *Proc. ACL-AFNLP*.

M. Kay and M. Röscheisen. 1993. Text-Translation Alignement. *Computational Linguistics*, 19(1).

P. Koehn, H. Hoang, A. Birch, C. Callison-Burch, M. Federico, N. Bertoldi, B. Cowan, W. Shen, C. Moran, R. Zens, C. Dyer, O. Bojar, A. Constantin, and E. Herbst. 2007. Moses: Open Source Toolkit for Statistical Machine Translation. In *Proc. ACL (demo)*.

J. Krause, 2010. *Color Index - Revised Edition*.

A. Lardilleux, F. Yvon, and Y. Lepage. 2012. Hierarchical sub-sentential alignment with Anymalign. In *Proc. EAMT*.

D. Marcu and D. Wong. 2002. A Phrase-Based, Joint Probability Model for Statistical Machine Translation. In *Proc. EMNLP*.

B. Marie and M. Apidianaki. 2015. Alignment-based sense selection in METEOR and the RATATOUILLE recipe. In *Proc. WMT*.

R. C. Moore. 2002. Fast and Accurate Sentence Alignment of Bilingual Corpora. In *Proc. of AMTA*, Lecture Notes in Computer Science 2499.

R. C. Moore. 2005. A discriminative framework for bilingual word alignment. In *Proc. EMNLP:HLT*.

R. Navigli and S. P. Ponzetto. 2012. BabelNet: The Automatic Construction, Evaluation and Application of a Wide-Coverage Multilingual Semantic Network. *Artificial Intelligence*, 193.

F. J. Och and H. Ney. 2003. A Systematic Comparison of Various Statistical Alignment Models. *Computational Linguistics*, 29(1).

P. Pantel, M. Gamon, and A. Fuxman. 2014. Smart Selection. In *Proc. ACL*.

C. Pillias and P. Cubaud. 2015. Bilingual Reading Experiences: What They Could Be and How To Design for Them. In *Proc. IFIP Interact*.

N. A. Smith and M. E. Jahry. 2000. Cairo: An alignment visualization tool. In *Proc. LREC*.

D. Steele and L. Specia. 2015. WA-Continuum: Visualising Word Alignments across Multiple Parallel Sentences Simultaneously. In *Proc. ACL-IJCNLP*.

J. Tiedemann. 2011. *Bitext Alignment*. Number 14 in Synthesis Lectures on Human Language Technologies. Morgan and Claypool publishers.

J. Weese and C. Callison-Burch. 2010. Visualizing Data Structures in Parsing-Based Machine Translation. *The Prague Bulletin of Mathematical Linguistics*, 93.

D. Wu. 1997. Stochastic Inversion Transduction Grammar and Bilingual Parsing of Parallel Corpora. *Computational Linguistics*, 23(3).

D. Wu. 2010. Alignment. In *CRC Handbook of Natural Language Processsing*, number 16.

Y. Xu, A. Max, and F. Yvon. 2015. Sentence alignment for literary texts. *Linguistic Issues in Language Technology*, 12(6).

Q. Yu, A. Max, and F. Yvon. 2012. Aligning Bilingual Literary Works: a Pilot Study. In *Proc. NAACL-HLT Workshop on Computational Linguistics for Literature*.

New Dimensions in Testimony Demonstration

Ron Artstein and **Alesia Gainer** and **Kallirroi Georgila**
Anton Leuski and **Ari Shapiro** and **David Traum**
University of Southern California Institute for Creative Technologies
12015 Waterfront Drive, Playa Vista CA 90094, USA
`{artstein|gainer|kgeorgila|leuski|shapiro|traum}@ict.usc.edu`

Abstract

New Dimensions in Testimony is a prototype dialogue system that allows users to conduct a conversation with a real person who is not available for conversation in real time. Users talk to a persistent representation of Holocaust survivor Pinchas Gutter on a screen, while a dialogue agent selects appropriate responses to user utterances from a set of pre-recorded video statements, simulating a live conversation. The technology is similar to existing conversational agents, but to our knowledge this is the first system to portray a real person. The demonstration will show the system on a range of screens (from mobile phones to large TVs), and allow users to have individual conversations with Mr. Gutter.

1 Introduction

This demonstration presents *New Dimensions in Testimony*, the first dialogue system prototype to enable a conversation with a real person who is not available for conversation in real time. Technology such as the telegraph, telephone and videoconferencing allowed people to communicate with each other across long distances with increasing fidelity, but required that the participants make themselves available for conversation at the same time. Other technologies such as writing, audio recording and video recording allowed people to send messages across time, but did not allow synchronous conversation. In the past two decades, embodied conversational agents – that is, artificial characters controlled by computer programs – have been able to converse with users with increased complexity and naturalness. Our system demonstrates how conversational agent technology can be used with recorded video statements from a real person to create a conversation that is offset in time: the speaker recorded his statements in the past as a message to the future, and users now can interact with him and hold a conversation as if the speaker were present.

The *New Dimensions in Testimony* prototype is intended to emulate a conversation with Holocaust survivor Pinchas Gutter. Holocaust education today relies to a great extent on survivors talking to audiences in museums and classrooms, relating their experiences directly and creating an intimate connection with their audiences (Bar-On, 2003). However, the youngest survivors are in their seventies today, and in a few years there will be no more survivors left to tell the story in person. The prototype will afford future generations the opportunity to engage in such conversation, talking to Pinchas Gutter and asking him questions about his life before, during and after the Holocaust. What makes our project unique is the ability to connect on a personal level with a survivor, and the history, even when that survivor is not present.

The technology can have a wide range of applications, such as preserving the memory of a person for the future (historical figures as well as ordinary people); enabling conversation with family and friends who are temporarily unavailable (traveling, deployed overseas, or incarcerated); allowing popular speakers (leaders, celebrities) to engage with multiple people at the same time; and enabling access to expert knowledge and customer service.

Proceedings of NAACL-HLT 2016 (Demonstrations), pages 32–36,
San Diego, California, June 12-17, 2016. ©2016 Association for Computational Linguistics

2 Technical details

In the *New Dimensions in Testimony* prototype, users talk to a persistent representation of a Holocaust survivor presented on a video screen, and a computer algorithm selects and plays individual video clips of the survivor in response to user utterances. The result is much like an ordinary conversation between the user and the survivor. The system has been described in detail in previous publications, covering the proof of concept (Artstein et al., 2014), the content elicitation process (Artstein et al., 2015), the language processing (Traum et al., 2015a), the full prototype (Traum et al., 2015b), and ethical considerations (Artstein and Silver, 2016). Here we give a brief description of the language processing technology and the system's runtime components.

2.1 Language processing

At the heart of the runtime computer system is a response classifier and dialogue management component called NPCEditor (Leuski and Traum, 2011), which selects a response to each user utterance. NPCEditor combines the functions of Natural Language Understanding (NLU) and Dialogue Management – understanding the utterance text and selecting an appropriate response. The NLU functionality is a classifier trained on linked question-response pairs, which identifies the most appropriate response to new (unseen) user input. The dialogue management logic is designed to deal with instances where the classifier cannot identify a good direct response. During training, NPCEditor calculates a response threshold based on the classifier's confidence in the appropriateness of selected responses; at runtime, if the confidence for a selected response falls below the predetermined threshold, that response is replaced with an "off-topic" utterance that asks the user to repeat the question or takes initiative and changes the topic (Leuski et al., 2006); such failure to return a direct response, also called non-understanding (Bohus and Rudnicky, 2005), is usually preferred over returning an inappropriate one (misunderstanding). The current system uses a five-stage off-topic selection algorithm which is an extension of that presented in Artstein et al. (2009). Figure 1 shows a sample dialogue illustrating the handling of non-understanding.

> **User** Hello Pinchas, how are you?
> *Las Vegas how are you*
> **Pinchas** Can you just repeat that?
> **User** Hello Pinchas, can you hear me?
> *how thick is can you hear me*
> **Pinchas** I can hear you, yeah.
> **User** Pinchas, can you tell me how old you are?
> *Vegas can you tell me how old you are*
> **Pinchas** I was born in nineteen thirty two and we are now in two thousand and fourteen and you can make your own reckoning.
> **User** Can you tell me a little bit about your childhood?
> **Pinchas** My life before the war, I was born in Lodz in Poland, and I was eight years old when the war started. So the first eight years I lived in a home, a very religious one, a Hasidic home. I had a twin sister, my. . .
> **User** Have you ever met Hitler?
> *mermaid Hitler*
> **Pinchas** Please repeat that.
> **User** Did you ever meet Hitler?
> **Pinchas** Did I ever meet Hitler? Well, Hitler was a Führer of Germany and I was born in Poland and I was a little Jewish boy, so the chances of somebody like me meeting Hitler was impossible, because Hitler was. . .
> **User** What would you do if you met Hitler?
> **Pinchas** Geyn drerd arein, that's Yiddish and what it means go and bury yourself.

Figure 1: Sample dialogue from system testing, illustrating correct responses to noisy speech input as well as the handling of non-understanding using off-topic responses. Speech recognition output is shown in italics when it departs substantially from the spoken text. The final utterance was originally recorded as a response to the question "If you could ask one question or say anything to Adolf Hitler, what would that be?"

The system has over 1700 recorded responses (a total of almost 18 hours of video), allowing it to give appropriate direct responses to about 64% of the user questions, with 20% off-topic responses and the remaining 16% being errors. This is sufficient to enable a reasonable conversation flow (Traum et al., 2015a). Between responses the system loops through short videos of idle behavior by the survivor, giving the feeling of live presence. When the user starts speaking, this changes to concentrated listening behavior, adding to the feeling of engagement.

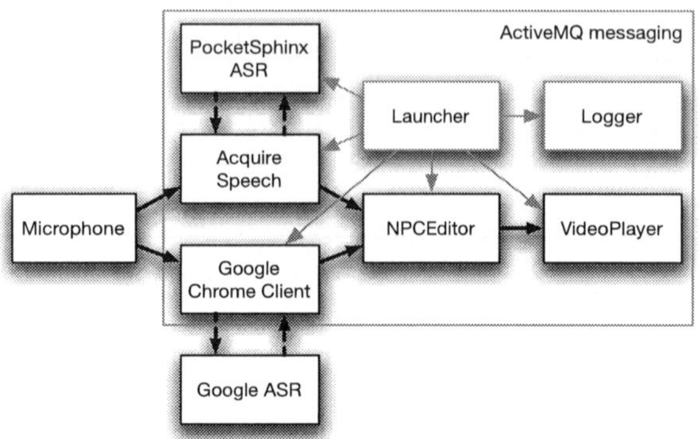

Figure 2: System architecture: Black lines show the data flow through the system, while gray arrows indicate the control messages from the Launcher interface. Solid arrows represent messages passed via ActiveMQ, and dotted lines represent data going over TCP/IP.

2.2 Software components

The system is built on top of the components from the USC ICT Virtual Human Toolkit, which is publicly available (Hartholt et al., 2013).[1] Specifically, we use the AcquireSpeech tool for capturing the user's speech, CMU PocketSphinx[2] and Google Chrome ASR[3] tools for speech recognition, NPCEditor (Leuski and Traum, 2011) for classifying the utterance text and selecting the appropriate response, and a video player to deliver the selected video response. The individual components run as separate applications and are linked together by VHMsg[4] messaging over ActiveMQ: each component connects to the broker server and sends and receives messages to other components via the broker. The system setup also uses the JLogger tool for recording the messages, and the Launcher tool that controls starting and stopping of individual tools. Figure 2 shows the overall system architecture. A typical session on a Mac is shown in Figure 3.

2.3 System hardware

A typical installation is run on a 15-inch MacBook Pro with Retina display, connected via HDMI to an external monitor or television. We have used displays ranging from a basic 22-inch desktop mon-

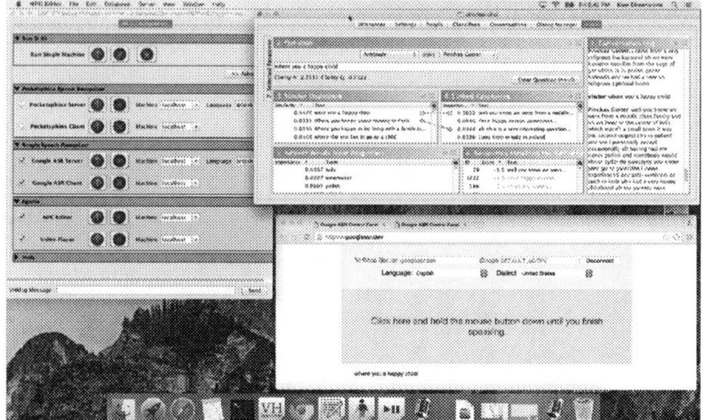

Figure 3: A typical desktop runtime environment: Launcher on the left, NPCEditor top right, Google Chrome ASR bottom right. Video player is displayed (maximized) on an external screen, and JLogger is minimized.

Figure 4: User talking to Mr. Gutter on a large TV.

itor for personal interaction to a large theatre projector screen, though our preferred display is an 80-inch high definition television in vertical orientation (Figure 4). This allows showing the speaker at approximately life size, making it appropriate for one-on-one and small group interaction, as well as large group interaction in a theatre setting.

For small, informal demonstrations in a quiet setting, we have had good results using the MacBook Pro's built-in microphone for audio capture, and the built-in trackpad as a push-to-talk button. In more challenging environments we use a Sennheiser HSP-4 headworn microphone, which works well to isolate the user's speech from the background noise. The microphone is connected to a wireless transmitter-receiver pair and sent to the computer through a Focusrite Scarlett 2i2 USB recording audio interface. Push-to-talk functionality is provided

---

[1] http://vhtoolkit.ict.usc.edu
[2] http://cmusphinx.sourceforge.net
[3] https://www.google.com/intl/en/chrome/demos/speech.html
[4] https://sourceforge.net/projects/vhmsg/

Figure 5: User talking to Mr. Gutter on a mobile phone.

by a wireless mouse, removing any physical connection with the computer and allowing the user full freedom of movement. The speaker's audio is normally transmitted over HDMI together with the video, but can be routed through the Focusrite interface to external speakers when needed.

2.4 Mobile version

The mobile version (Figure 5) is built using an Android-based virtual human software platform (Feng et al., 2015). This platform allows script-based access to speech recognition, video playback, and dialogue management services via Jerome, an implementation of the NPCEditor algorithm.

In order to accommodate the smaller display and mobile nature of a handheld device, the videos were reduced from 1080×1920 to 270×480, effectively reducing the size of the videos by a factor of 16. This results in a change in video file size from approximately 1.7 gb per hour (28 mb per minute) of content to 110 mb per hour (1.75 mb per minute) of content. Frequently used videos, such as those for listening and off-topic responses are stored locally on the mobile device, while the rest are stored on a video-streaming cloud service and are retrieved on demand. Streaming videos of such size via wifi connection yields similar response times to playing the videos locally on the device, and greatly reduces the size of the mobile app. An additional button on the app allows the user to indicate explicitly that a given response is inappropriate to the question asked; this information is used for future classifier training.

The classification algorithm and data are processed locally on the device. Speech recognition is handled via the Android's interface to Google ASR. Thus, there are three network messages for each user utterance: one to obtain the results of the ASR, another to retrieve the desired video if found, and a third to store the recognized question and response in a cloud-based database, for later analysis. The classifier data can be replaced through an update to the mobile app, thus allowing for easy propagation of improvements in the question/answer interaction as larger amounts of data are captured and analyzed.

3 Demonstration outline

The demonstration will feature a live interaction between participants and Pinchas Gutter, on both desktop and mobile platforms. Depending on the participant's preference, interaction will be either moderated (speech relayed by a demonstrator) or direct (participant operating the push-to-talk and talking into the microphone). The live conversations will highlight Mr. Gutter's understanding, his ability to deal with non-understanding of user utterances, and the overall coherence of the conversation. It will also showcase many of Mr. Gutter's moving personal stories, and illustrate the sense of closeness and bonding that can form when talking to a person through a system of time-offset interaction.

Acknowledgments

The New Dimensions in Testimony prototype is a collaboration between the USC Institute for Creative Technologies, the USC Shoah Foundation, and Conscience Display. It was made possible by generous donations from private foundations and individuals. We are extremely grateful to The Pears Foundation, Louis F. Smith, and two anonymous donors for their support. The Los Angeles Museum of the Holocaust, the Museum of Tolerance, New Roads School in Santa Monica, and the Illinois Holocaust Museum and Education Center offered their facilities for data collection and testing. We owe special thanks to Pinchas Gutter for sharing his story, and for his tireless efforts to educate the world about the Holocaust.

This work was supported in part by the U.S. Army; statements and opinions expressed do not necessarily reflect the position or the policy of the United States Government, and no official endorsement should be inferred.

References

Ron Artstein and Kenneth Silver. 2016. Ethics for a combined human-machine dialogue agent. In *AAAI Spring Symposium SS-16-04: Ethical and Moral Considerations in Non-Human Agents*, pages 184–189, Stanford, California, March. AAAI Press.

Ron Artstein, Sudeep Gandhe, Jillian Gerten, Anton Leuski, and David Traum. 2009. Semi-formal evaluation of conversational characters. In Orna Grumberg, Michael Kaminski, Shmuel Katz, and Shuly Wintner, editors, *Languages: From Formal to Natural. Essays Dedicated to Nissim Francez on the Occasion of His 65th Birthday*, volume 5533 of *Lecture Notes in Computer Science*, pages 22–35. Springer, Heidelberg, May.

Ron Artstein, David Traum, Oleg Alexander, Anton Leuski, Andrew Jones, Kallirroi Georgila, Paul Debevec, William Swartout, Heather Maio, and Stephen Smith. 2014. Time-offset interaction with a Holocaust survivor. In *Proceedings of IUI*, pages 163–168, Haifa, Israel, February.

Ron Artstein, Anton Leuski, Heather Maio, Tomer Mor-Barak, Carla Gordon, and David Traum. 2015. How many utterances are needed to support time-offset interaction? In *Proceedings of FLAIRS-28*, pages 144–149, Hollywood, Florida, May.

Dan Bar-On. 2003. Importance of testimonies in Holocaust education. *Dimensions Online: A Journal of Holocaust Studies*, 17(1).

Dan Bohus and Alexander I. Rudnicky. 2005. Sorry, I didn't catch that! – An investigation of non-understanding errors and recovery strategies. In *Proceedings of SIGDIAL*, pages 128–143, Lisbon, Portugal, September.

Andrew W. Feng, Anton Leuski, Stacy Marsella, Dan Casas, Sin-Hwa Kang, and Ari Shapiro. 2015. A platform for building mobile virtual humans. In Willem-Paul Brinkman, Joost Broekens, and Dirk Heylen, editors, *Intelligent Virtual Agents: 15th International Conference, IVA 2015, Delft, The Netherlands, August 26–28, 2015 Proceedings*, volume 9238 of *Lecture Notes in Computer Science*, pages 310–319. Springer, August.

Arno Hartholt, David Traum, Stacy C. Marsella, Ari Shapiro, Giota Stratou, Anton Leuski, Louis-Philippe Morency, and Jonathan Gratch. 2013. All together now: Introducing the virtual human toolkit. In Ruth Aylett, Brigitte Krenn, Catherine Pelachaud, and Hiroshi Shimodaira, editors, *Intelligent Virtual Agents: 13th International Conference, IVA 2013, Edinburgh, UK, August 29–31, 2013 Proceedings*, volume 8108 of *Lecture Notes in Computer Science*, pages 368–381. Springer, August.

Anton Leuski and David Traum. 2011. NPCEditor: Creating virtual human dialogue using information retrieval techniques. *AI Magazine*, 32(2):42–56.

Anton Leuski, Ronakkumar Patel, David Traum, and Brandon Kennedy. 2006. Building effective question answering characters. In *Proceedings of SIGDIAL*, Sydney, Australia, July.

David Traum, Kallirroi Georgila, Ron Artstein, and Anton Leuski. 2015a. Evaluating spoken dialogue processing for time-offset interaction. In *Proceedings of SIGDIAL*, pages 199–208, Prague, Czech Republic, September.

David Traum, Andrew Jones, Kia Hays, Heather Maio, Oleg Alexander, Ron Artstein, Paul Debevec, Alesia Gainer, Kallirroi Georgila, Kathleen Haase, Karen Jungblut, Anton Leuski, Stephen Smith, and William Swartout. 2015b. New Dimensions in Testimony: Digitally preserving a Holocaust survivor's interactive storytelling. In *Interactive Storytelling: 8th International Conference on Interactive Digital Storytelling, ICIDS 2015, Copenhagen, Denmark, November 30 – December 4, 2015 Proceedings*, volume 9445 of *Lecture Notes in Computer Science*, pages 269–281. Springer, December.

ArgRewrite: A Web-based Revision Assistant for Argumentative Writings

Fan Zhang **Rebecca Hwa** **Diane Litman** **Homa B. Hashemi**

University of Pittsburgh
Pittsburgh, PA, 15260
`{zhangfan,hwa,litman,hashemi}@cs.pitt.edu`

Abstract

While intelligent writing assistants have become more common, they typically have little support for revision behavior. We present ArgRewrite, a novel web-based revision assistant that focus on rewriting analysis. The system supports two major functionalities: 1) to assist students as they revise, the system automatically extracts and analyzes revisions; 2) to assist teachers, the system provides an overview of students' revisions and allows teachers to correct the automatically analyzed results, ensuring that students get the correct feedback.

1 Introduction

Making revisions is central to improving a student's writings, especially when there is a helpful instructor to offer detailed feedback between drafts. However, it is not practical for instructors to provide feedback on every change every time. While multiple intelligent writing assistants have been developed (Writelab, 2015; Draft, 2015; Turnitin, 2016), they typically focus on the quality of the current essay instead of the revisions that have been made. For example, Turnitin identifies weak points of the essay and gives suggestions on how to improve them; it also assigns an overall score to the essay so students can get a coarse-grained feedback on whether they are making progress in their revisions. However, without explicit feedback on each change, students may inefficiently search for a way to optimize the automatic score rather than actively making the existing revisions "better". Moreover, because students are the target users of these systems, instructors typically can neither correct the errors made by

the automatic analysis nor observe/assess the students' revision efforts.

We argue that an intelligent writing assistant ought to be aware of the revision process; it should: 1) identify all significant changes made by a writer between the essay drafts, 2) automatically determine the purposes of these changes, 3) provide the writer the means to compare between drafts in an easy to understand visualization, and 4) support instructor monitoring and corrections in the revision process as well. In our previous work (Zhang and Litman, 2014; Zhang and Litman, 2015), we focused on 1) and 2), the automatic extraction and classification of revisions for argumentative writings. In this work, we extend our framework to integrate the automatic analyzer with a web-based interface to support *student argumentative writings*. The purpose of each change between revisions is demonstrated to the writer as a kind of feedback. If the author's revision purpose is not correctly recognized, it indicates that the effect of the writer's change might have not met the writer's expectation, which suggests that the writer should revise their revisions. The framework also connects the automatic analyzer with an interface for the instructor to manually correct the analysis results. As a side benefit, it also sets up an annotation pipeline to collect further data to improve the underlying automatic analyzer.

2 System Overview

The design of ArgRewrite aims to encourage students to concentrate on revision improvement: to iteratively refine the essay based on the feedback of the automatic system or the writing instructor.

37

Proceedings of NAACL-HLT 2016 (Demonstrations), pages 37–41,
San Diego, California, June 12-17, 2016. ©2016 Association for Computational Linguistics

Our framework consists of three components, arranged in a server client model. On the server side, the **automatic analysis** component extracts revision changes by aligning sentences across drafts and infers the purposes of the extracted revisions; this may reduce the writing instructor's workload. On the client side, a web-based **rewriting assistant interface**[1] allows the student to retrieve the feedback to their revisions from the server, make changes to the essay and submit the modified essay to the server for another round of analysis. The interface is also accessible to the writing instructor and allows the instructor to have a quick overview of the students' revision efforts. Another client side interface is a Java-based **revision correction** component[2], which allows the writing instructors to override the results of the automatic analysis and upload the corrected feedback to the server.

As demonstrated in Figure 1, the complete process of the student's writing using our system starts with the student's rewriting and submission of the essay. The student writes the first draft of the essay before using our system and then modifies the original draft in our rewriting assistant interface. The submitted writings are automatically analyzed immediately after the receipt of the student's submission. Afterwards the instructor can manually correct the analysis results if necessary. The student can choose to view the analysis results immediately after the completion of automatic revision analysis or wait until the analysis results were corrected by the instructor. After receiving the analysis feedback, the student can choose to continue with the cycle of essay revising until the revisions are satisfactory.

3 Design of Components

3.1 Automatic analysis

Revision extraction. Following our prior work, we extracted revisions at the level of sentences by aligning sentences across drafts. An added sentence or a deleted sentence is treated as aligned to null. The

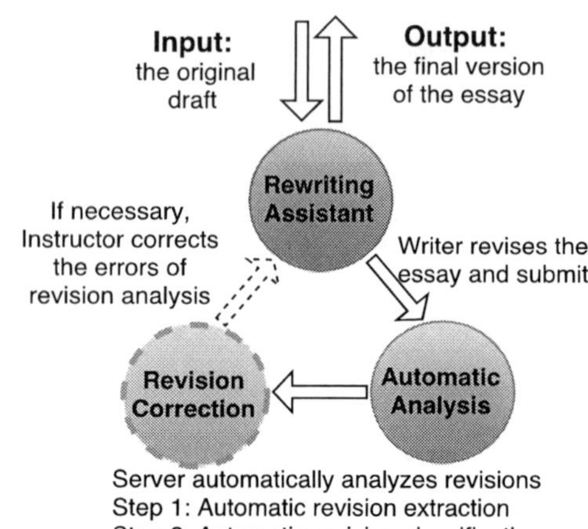

Figure 1: System structure of our rewriting assistance system.

aligned pairs where the sentences in the pair are not identical are extracted as revisions. We first use the Stanford Parser (Klein and Manning, 2003) to break the original text into sentences and then align the sentences using the algorithm in our prior work (Zhang and Litman, 2014) which considers both sentence similarity (calculated using TF*IDF score) and the global context of sentences.

Revision classification. Following the argumentative revision definition in our prior work (Zhang and Litman, 2015), revisions are first categorized to *Content* (*Text-based*) and *Surface*[3] according to whether the revision changed the meaning of the essay or not. The *Text-based* revisions include *Thesis/Ideas* (*Claim*), *Rebuttal*, *Reasoning* (*Warrant*), *Evidence*, and *Other content changes* (*General Content*). The *Surface* revisions include *Fluency* (*Word-usage/Clarity*), *Reordering* (*Organization*) and *Errors* (*Conventions/Grammar/Spelling*). On the basis of later work, the system includes the two new categories *Precision*[4] and *Unknown*[5]. Using the corpora and features defined in our prior work, a multi-class Random Forest classifier was trained to automatically predict the revision purpose type for each extracted revision.

---

[1]rewriting assistant interface: `www.cs.pitt.edu/~zhangfan/argrewrite` now supported on chrome and firefox browser only

[2]revision correction component: `www.cs.pitt.edu/~zhangfan/revisionCorrection.jar`. Tutorial to the web and java interface: `www.cs.pitt.edu/~zhangfan/argrewrite/tutorial.pdf`

[3]The two types are defined in (Faigley and Witte, 1981).

[4]Revisions that make the essay more precise/accurate, e.g. "In the past" modified to "In the past 5 years".

[5]For cases where the purpose of the revision is unrecognizable to the instructor, used when the instructor disagrees with the prediction of the automatic analysis component but cannot categorize the purpose to existing categories.

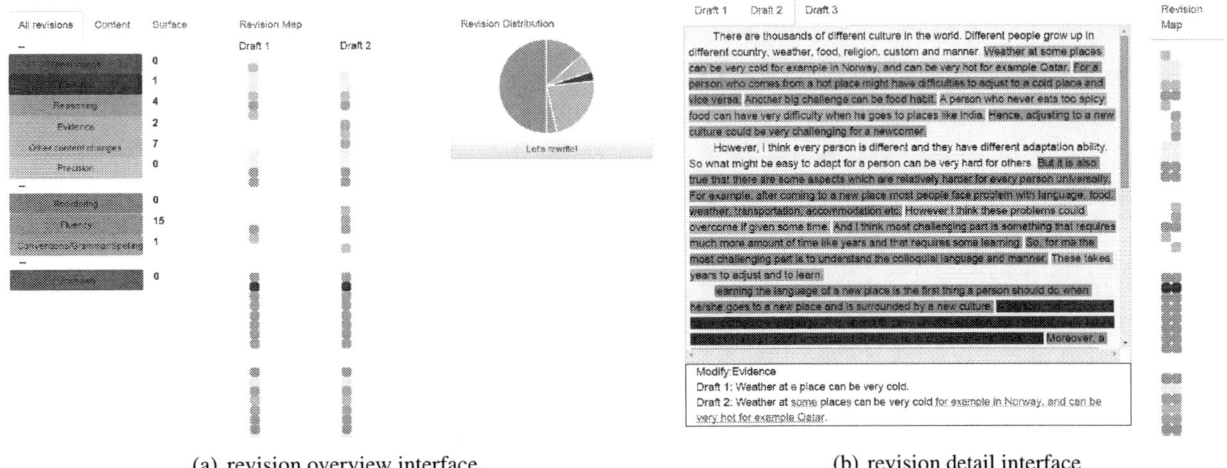

(a) revision overview interface   (b) revision detail interface

Figure 2: Screenshot of the web interface, which includes (a) the *revision overview* interface with the *revision statistics* (the numbers indicate the numbers of specified revision purposes) region, the *revision map* region and the *revision distribution* region, (b) the *revision detail* interface with the *revision text area* region and the *revision map* region (from left to right).

3.2 Rewriting assistant interface

Our rewriting assistant interface is designed with several principles in mind. 1) Because the revision classification taxonomy goes beyond the binary textual versus surface distinction, we want to make sure that users don't get lost distinguishing different categories; 2) We want to encourage users to think about their revisions holistically, not always just focusing on low-level details; 3) We want to encourage users to continuously re-evaluate whether they succeeded in making changes between drafts (rather than focusing on generating new contents). Thus, we have designed an interface that offers multiple views of the revision changes. As demonstrated in Figure 2, the interface includes a *revision overview* interface for the overview of the authors' revisions and a *revision detail* interface that allows the author to access the details of their essays and revisions.

Inspired by works on learning analytics (Liu et al., 2013; Verbert et al., 2013), we design the *revision overview* interface which displays the statistics of the revisions. Following design principle #1, the revision purposes are color coded and each purpose corresponds to a specific color. Our prior work (Zhang and Litman, 2015) demonstrates that only *Text-based* revisions are significantly correlated with the writing improvement. To inspire the writers to focus more on the important *Text-based* revisions, cold colors are chosen for the *Surface* revisions and

warm colors are chosen for the *Text-based* revisions. The statistics and the pie chart provide a quantitative summary of the writer's revision efforts. For example, in Figure 2, the writer makes many changes on the *Fluency* (15) of sentences but makes no change on the *Thesis/Ideas* (0). To allow the users to concentrate on improving one revision type at a time, the interface allows the user to click on a single revision purpose type and view only the specified revisions.

Following our design principle #2, the *revision map* in both interfaces presents an at-a-glance visual representation of the revision. This design is inspired by (Southavilay et al., 2013). Each sentence is represented as a square in the map. The left column of the map represents the sentences in the first draft and the right column represents the sentences in the second draft. The paragraphs within one draft are segmented by blanks in the map. The aligned sentences appear in the same row. The added/deleted sentences would be aligned to blank in the map. The revision map allows a user (either an instructor or a student) to view the structure of the essay and identify the locations of all the changes at once. For example, in Figure 2, the user can quickly identify that the writer aims at improving the clarity and soundness of the third paragraph by making a *Rebuttal* modification on the second sentence and *Fluency* modifications on all other sentences. The

39

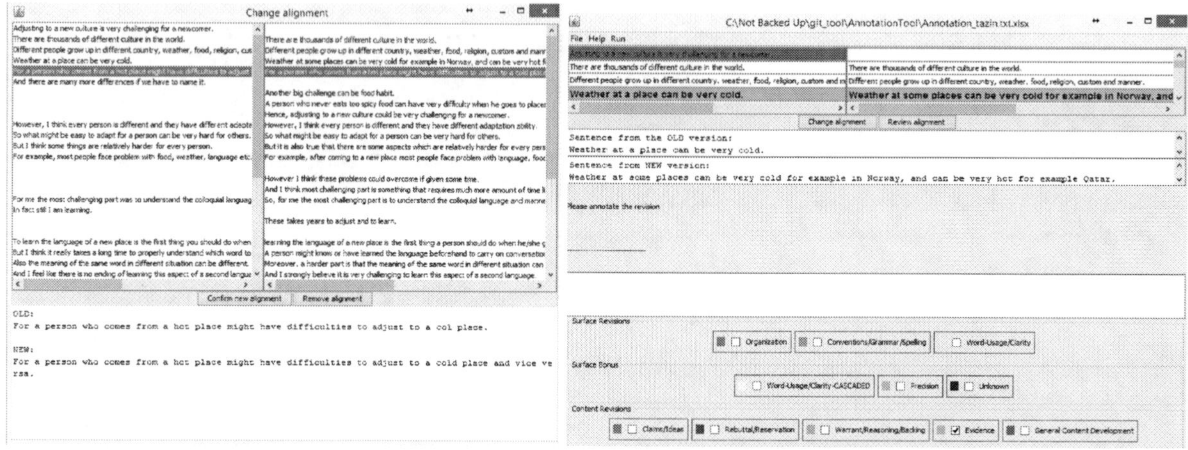

(a) sentence alignment correction   (b) revision purpose correction

Figure 3: Screenshot of the correction interface, including the sentence alignment correction and revision purpose correction.

user can also click on the square to view the details of the revision in the *revision text area* region of the *revision detail interface*.

To encourage students to make revisions (design principle #3), in the *revision detail* interface the *revision text area* region highlights the revisions (color-coded by the revision categories) in the essay and allows the writer to modify it directly. The writer clicks on the text to read the revision and examine whether the revision purpose is recognized by the instructor/system. A character-level diff[6] is done on the aligned sentences to help the writer identify the differences between two drafts. In the example the writer can see that their "Evidence" change is recognized, indicating that the revision effort is clear and effective. If the writer finds out that their real revision purpose is not recognized, they can modify the essay in the textbox directly and submit the essay to the server when all the edits are done.

3.3 Revision correction

The revision correction tool is developed for instructors only. The instructor loads the revision annotation files from the server, corrects the analysis results and uploads the corrections to the server. As demonstrated in Figure 3, the tool includes a *sentence alignment correction* interface and a *revision purpose correction* interface. The instructor first corrects the sentence alignment errors and then se-

lects the revision purposes for the re-aligned or mis-labeled sentence pairs. The correction actions of the instructors will be recorded and used to improve the analysis accuracy of the automatic analysis module.

4 Conclusion and Future Work

In this work we demonstrate a novel revision assistant for argumentative writings. Comparing to other assistants, the system focuses on inspiring writers to improve existing revisions instead of making new revisions. The system takes the writer's drafts as the input and presents the revision purposes (analyzed manually or automatically) as the feedback. The writer revises iteratively until the purposes of the revisions are clear enough to be recognized.

In the future we plan to develop and incorporate the function of revision quality analysis, which not only recognizes the revision purpose, but also evaluates the quality of the revision (whether the revision weakly/strongly improves the essay). We are also about to begin a user study to evaluate the system.

Acknowledgments

We want to thank the members of the SWoRD and ITSPOKE groups for their helpful feedback and all the anonymous reviewers for their suggestions.

This research is funded by NSF Award #1550635 and the Learning Research and Development Center of the University of Pittsburgh.

---

[6]google diff match: `https://code.google.com/archive/p/google-diff-match-patch/`

References

Draft. 2015. Draft. https://draftin.com/. [Online; accessed 10-03-2015].

Lester Faigley and Stephen Witte. 1981. Analyzing revision. *College composition and communication*, pages 400–414.

Dan Klein and Christopher D Manning. 2003. Accurate unlexicalized parsing. In *Proceedings of the 41st Annual Meeting on Association for Computational Linguistics-Volume 1*, pages 423–430. Association for Computational Linguistics.

Ming Liu, Rafael A Calvo, and Abelardo Pardo. 2013. Tracer: A tool to measure and visualize student engagement in writing activities. In *Advanced Learning Technologies (ICALT), 2013 IEEE 13th International Conference on*, pages 421–425. IEEE.

Vilaythong Southavilay, Kalina Yacef, Peter Reimann, and Rafael A Calvo. 2013. Analysis of collaborative writing processes using revision maps and probabilistic topic models. In *Proceedings of the Third International Conference on Learning Analytics and Knowledge*, pages 38–47. ACM.

Turnitin. 2016. Turnitin. http://turnitin.com/en_us/what-we-offer/revision-assistant. [Online; accessed 01-22-2016].

Katrien Verbert, Erik Duval, Joris Klerkx, Sten Govaerts, and José Luis Santos. 2013. Learning analytics dashboard applications. *American Behavioral Scientist*, pages 1500–1509.

Writelab. 2015. WriteLab. http://home.writelab.com/. [Online; accessed 10-03-2015].

Fan Zhang and Diane Litman. 2014. Sentence-level rewriting detection. In *Proceedings of the Ninth Workshop on Innovative Use of NLP for Building Educational Applications*, pages 149–154, Baltimore, Maryland, June. Association for Computational Linguistics.

Fan Zhang and Diane Litman. 2015. Annotation and classification of argumentative writing revisions. In *Proceedings of the Tenth Workshop on Innovative Use of NLP for Building Educational Applications*, pages 133–143, Denver, Colorado, June. Association for Computational Linguistics.

Scaling Up Word Clustering

Jon Dehdari[1,2] and **Liling Tan**[2] and **Josef van Genabith**[1,2]
[1]DFKI, Saarbrücken, Germany
{jon.dehdari,josef.van_genabith}@dfki.de
[2]University of Saarland, Saarbrücken, Germany
liling.tan@uni-saarland.de

Abstract

Word clusters improve performance in many NLP tasks including training neural network language models, but current increases in datasets are outpacing the ability of word clusterers to handle them. In this paper we present a novel bidirectional, interpolated, refining, and alternating (BIRA) predictive exchange algorithm and introduce ClusterCat, a clusterer based on this algorithm. We show that ClusterCat is 3–85 times faster than four other well-known clusterers, while also improving upon the predictive exchange algorithm's perplexity by up to 18%. Notably, ClusterCat clusters a 2.5 billion token English News Crawl corpus in 3 hours. We also evaluate in a machine translation setting, resulting in shorter training times achieving the same translation quality measured in BLEU scores. ClusterCat is portable and freely available.

1 Introduction

Words can be grouped into equivalence classes to reduce data sparsity and generalize data. Word clusters are useful in many NLP applications. Within machine translation, word classes are used in word alignment (Brown et al., 1993; Och and Ney, 2000), translation models (Koehn and Hoang, 2007; Wuebker et al., 2013), reordering (Cherry, 2013), preordering (Stymne, 2012), SAMT (Zollmann and Vogel, 2011), and OSM (Durrani et al., 2014).

Word clusterings have also found utility in parsing (Koo et al., 2008; Candito and Seddah, 2010; Kong et al., 2014), chunking (Turian et al., 2010), and NER (Miller et al., 2004; Liang, 2005; Turian et al., 2010; Ritter et al., 2011), among many others.

Word clusters also speed up normalization in training neural network and MaxEnt language models, via class-based decomposition (Goodman, 2001b). This reduces the normalization time from $\mathcal{O}(|V|)$ (the vocabulary size) to $\approx \mathcal{O}(\sqrt{|V|})$.

2 Exchange-Based Clustering

The **exchange algorithm** (Kneser and Ney, 1993) uses an unlexicalized (two-sided) model: $P(w_i|w_{i-1}) = P(w_i|c_i)P(c_i|c_{i-1})$ where the class c_i of the predicted word w_i is conditioned on the class c_{i-1} of the previous word w_{i-1}. Goodman (2001a) altered this model so that c_i is conditioned directly upon w_{i-1}: $P(w_i|w_{i-1}) = P(w_i|c_i)P(c_i|w_{i-1})$. This fractionates the history more, but it greatly speeds up hypothesizing an exchange since the history doesn't change. The resulting partially lexicalized (one-sided) model gives the accompanying **predictive exchange algorithm** (Uszkoreit and Brants, 2008) a time complexity of $\mathcal{O}((B + |V|) \times |C| \times I)$ where B is the number of unique bigrams, $|C|$ is the number of classes, and I is the number of training iterations, usually <20.

3 ClusterCat

ClusterCat is word clustering software designed to be fast and scalable, while also improving upon the predictive exchange algorithm. We describe in this section improvements in the model, the algorithm, as well as in the implementation.

Proceedings of NAACL-HLT 2016 (Demonstrations), pages 42–46,
San Diego, California, June 12-17, 2016. ©2016 Association for Computational Linguistics

3.1 Model and Algorithm

We developed a *bidirectional, interpolated, refining, and alternating* (BIRA) predictive exchange algorithm. The goal of BIRA is to produce better clusters by using multiple, changing models to escape local optima. This uses both forward and reversed bigram class models in order to improve cluster quality by evaluating log-likelihood on two different models. Unlike using trigrams, bidirectional bigram models only linearly increase time and memory requirements, and in fact some data structures can be shared. The two directions are interpolated to allow softer integration of these two models: $P(w_i|w_{i-1}, w_{i+1}) \triangleq P(w_i|c_i) \cdot (\lambda P(c_i|w_{i-1}) + (1-\lambda)P(c_i|w_{i+1}))$. Furthermore, the interpolation weight λ for the forward direction alternates to $1-\lambda$ every a iterations i to help escape local optima. The time complexity is $\mathcal{O}(2 \times (B + |V|) \times |C| \times I)$. The original predictive exchange algorithm can be obtained by setting $\lambda = 1$ and $a = 0$.

Cluster refinement improves both cluster quality *and* speed. The vocabulary is initially clustered into $|G|$ sets, where $|G| \ll |C|$, typically 2–10. This groups words into broad classes, like nouns, verbs, etc. After a few iterations (i) of this, the full partitioning C_f is explored. Clustering G converges very quickly, typically requiring no more than 3 iterations. In contrast to divisive hierarchical clustering and coarse-to-fine methods (Petrov, 2009), after the initial iterations, any word can still move to any cluster—there is no hard constraint that the more refined partitions be subsets of the initial coarser partitions. This gives more flexibility in optimizing on log-likelihood, especially given the noise that naturally arises from coarser clusterings. We explored cluster refinement over more stages than just two, successively increasing the number of clusters. We observed no improvement over the two-stage method described above.

The contributions of each of these, relative to the original predictive exchange algorithm, are shown in Figure 1. The data and configurations are discussed in more detail in Section 4. The greatest improvement is due to using lambda inversion (+Rev), followed by cluster refinement (+Refine), then interpolating the bidirectional models (+BiDi), with robust improvements by using all three of these—an

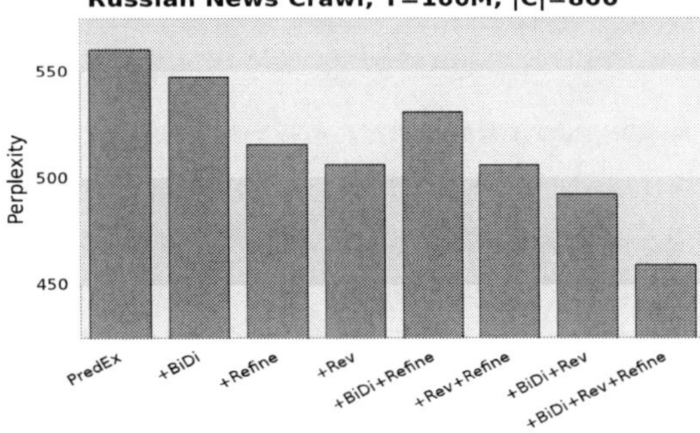

Figure 1: Dev set PP of combinations of improvements to the predictive exchange algorithm (cf. §3.1), using 100M tokens of the Russian News Crawl, with 800 word classes.

18% reduction in perplexity over the predictive exchange algorithm. We have found that both lambda inversion and cluster refinement prevent early convergence at local optima, while bidirectional models give immediate and consistent training set PP improvements, but this is attenuated in a unidirectional evaluation.

3.2 Implementation

We represent the set of bigrams B as an array of records that track the number of predecessors, as well as having a pointer to an array of the predecessors' IDs. This allows for easy prefetching to reduce memory latency, while also keeping memory overhead low. We dispense with the predictive exchange `RemoveWord` procedure for tentative steps, since this does not change the final clustering.

Most of the computation for the predictive exchange algorithm is spent on the logarithm function in $\delta \leftarrow \delta - N(w, c) \cdot \log N(w, c)$.[1] Since the codomain of $N(w, c)$ is $\mathbb{N}_0$, and due to the power law distribution of the algorithm's access to these entropy terms, we precompute $\lceil N \cdot \log N \rceil$ up to, say 10e+7, with minimal memory requirements.[2] This results in a considerable speedup of around 40%.

4 Experiments

We evaluate ClusterCat on training time, two-sided class-based language model (LM) perplexity

---

[1] δ is the change in log-likelihood, and $N(w, c)$ is the count of a given word followed by a given class.

[2] This was independently discovered in Botros et al. (2015).

(cf. Brown et al., 1992; Uszkoreit and Brants, 2008), and BLEU scores in phrase-based MT.

4.1 Intrinsic Evaluation

For the two-sided class-based LM task we used 800 and 1200 classes for English, and 800 classes for Russian. The clusterers (cf. Sec. 2) are Brown-cluster (Liang, 2005), ClusterCat (introduced in Section 3), `mkcls` (Och, 1995), Phrasal's clusterer (Green et al., 2014), and word2vec's clustering feature (Mikolov et al., 2013).

The data comes from the 2011–2013 News Crawl monolingual data of the WMT task.[3] For these experiments the data was deduplicated, shuffled, tokenized, digit-conflated, and lowercased. In order to have a large test set, one line per 100 of the resulting corpus was separated into the test set.[4] For English this gave 1B training tokens, 2M training types, and 12M test tokens. For Russian, 550M training tokens, 2.7M training types, and 6M test tokens.

All clusterers had a minimum count threshold of 3 occurrences in the training set. All used 12 threads and 15 iterations, except single-threaded `mkcls` which used the default one iteration. Clusterings were performed on a 2.4 GHz Opteron 8378 machine featuring 16 threads and 64 GB of RAM.

Table 1 presents wall clock times. The predictive exchange-based clusterers (ClusterCat and Phrasal) exhibit slow time growth as $|C|$ increases, while the other three (Brown, `mkcls`, and word2vec) are much more sensitive to $|C|$. ClusterCat is three times faster than Phrasal for all sets. For both English and Russian we observe prohibitive growth for `mkcls`, with the full Russian training set taking over 3 days, compared to 1.5 hours for ClusterCat.

Training Set	Brown	CC	mkcls	Phrasal	w2v
EN, $|C| = 800$	12.5	1.4	48.8	5.1	20.6
EN, $|C| = 1200$	25.5	1.7	68.8	6.2	33.7
RU, $|C| = 800$	14.6	1.5	75.0	5.5	12.0

Table 1: Clustering times (hours) of full training sets. For English, $T = 10^9$; for Russian, $T = 10^{8.74}$.

We performed an additional experiment on ClusterCat, adding more training data.[5] *ClusterCat took*

---

[3]`http://bit.ly/1SAjeIx`

[4]We provide a script to replicate the data setup at `http://www.dfki.de/~jode03/naacl2016.sh`.

[5]Adding years 2008–2010 and 2014 to the existing English

Training Set	Brown	CC	mkcls	Phrasal	w2v
EN, $|C| = 800$	160.2	158.1	155.0	178.3	383.4
EN, $|C| = 1200$	141.5	140.4	138.4	157.6	330.7
RU, $|C| = 800$	350.4	340.7	322.4	389.3	560.9

Table 2: 5-gram two-sided class-based LM PP using 10^9 English training tokens or $10^{8.74}$ Russian training tokens.

3.0 hours to cluster 2.5 billion training tokens, using 40 GB of memory for $|C| = 800$. When the number of clusters was tripled to $|C| = 2400$, the same 2.5B corpus was clustered in under 8 hours.

The clusterings are also evaluated on the perplexity (PP) of an external 5-gram two-sided class-based LM. Botros et al. (2015) found that the two-sided model (which `mkcls` uses) tends to give better PP in two-sided class-based LM experiments, but the one-sided model of the predictive exchange that we employed produces better PP for training LSTM LMs.

Table 2 shows perplexity results using a varying number of classes. As word2vec is the only clusterer not optimized on log-likelihood, its perplexity is quite high, and remains high as more training data is added.[6] On the other hand, `mkcls` gives the lowest perplexity, although this is an artefact of the two-sided evaluation. ClusterCat gives lower perplexity than the original predictive exchange algorithm (in Phrasal) and Brown clustering. The Russian experiments yielded higher PP for all clusterings, but otherwise the same comparative results. The metaheuristic techniques used in `mkcls` can be applied to other exchange-based clusterers—including ours—for further improvements.

It is also interesting to look at time-sensitive clustering. Figure 2 shows what perplexity can be obtained within a given training time frame. For each clusterer, each successive rightward point in the figure represents an order of magnitude more training data, from 10^6 to 10^9 tokens. *ClusterCat can train on 10 times more data than either `mkcls` or Brown-cluster and produces better perplexity than either, within a given amount of time.*

News Crawl training data. This training set was too large for the external class-based LM to fit into memory, so no perplexity evaluation of this clustering was possible.

[6]The skip-gram model within word2vec resulted in even higher PP at almost three times the clustering time, relative to the CBOW model that we used. Using hierarchical softmax with a window of one word on either side gave no appreciable difference in perplexity, while also increasing training time.

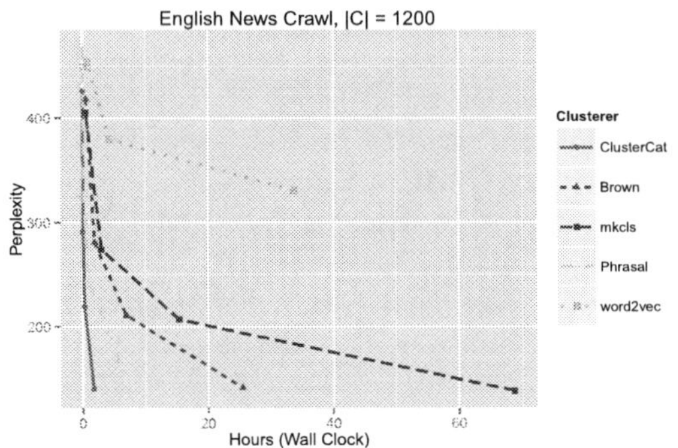

Figure 2: Relationship between two-sided class-based LM PP and the time needed to produce clusters ($|C| = 1200$). Points in the lower-left corner are best.

	$|C|$=50	100	200	500	1000
EN-RU	+0.2*	+0.7	−0.2	0	+0.2
RU-EN	−0.2	−0.1	+0.1	+0.1*	+0.1**

Table 3: BLEU score changes and significance across varying cluster sizes. Positive values indicate ClusterCat BLEU > mkcls BLEU.

4.2 Extrinsic Evaluation

We also evaluated mkcls and ClusterCat extrinsically in machine translation, for word alignment. As training sets get larger every year, mkcls struggles to keep pace, and is a substantial time bottleneck in MT pipelines. We compare time and BLEU scores of using either mkcls or ClusterCat for Russian↔English translation.

The parallel data comes from the WMT-2015 Common Crawl Corpus, News Commentary, Yandex 1M Corpus, and the Wiki Headlines Corpus.[7] The monolingual data consists of 2007–2014 News Commentary and News Crawl articles. The dev and test sets contain 3000 sentences from EN→RU manually translated news articles. We used standard configurations, like truecasing, MGIZA alignment, GDFA phrase extraction, phrase-based Moses, quantized KenLM 5-gram MKN LMs, and MERT tuning.

Table 3 presents the BLEU score changes across varying cluster sizes.[8] The BLEU score differences between using mkcls and ClusterCat are minimal but there are a few statistically significant changes, using bootstrap resampling (Koehn, 2004).

---

[7] http://bit.ly/1SAjeIx

[8] *: p-value < 0.05, **: p-value < 0.01. More results are presented in Dehdari et al. (2016).

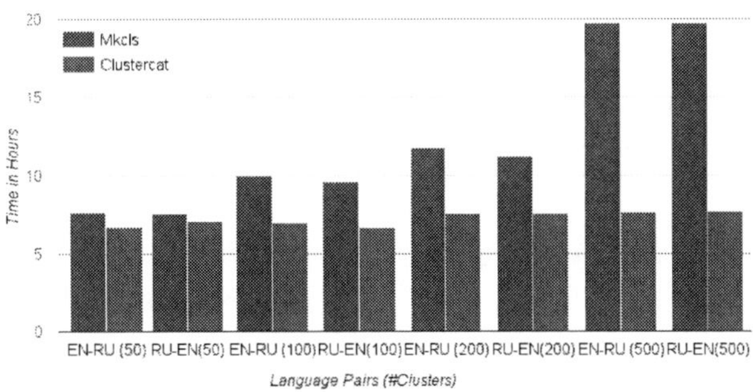

Figure 3: End-to-end translation model training times for English-Russian and Russian-English for various cluster sizes using mkcls and ClusterCat.

Figure 3 shows translation model training times, before MERT. Using ClusterCat reduces the translation model training time with 500 clusters from 20 hours using mkcls (of which 60% of the time is spent on clustering) to just 8 hours (of which 5% is spent on clustering).

5 Conclusion

In this article we have presented improvements to the predictive exchange algorithm that address longstanding drawbacks of the original algorithm compared to other clustering algorithms. Bidirectional models, lambda inversion, and cluster refinement produce better word clusters, as we showed in several two-sided class-based LM experiments. On these large datasets the quality of the resulting clusters is better than predictive exchange clusters and Brown clusters, and approaches the stochastic exchange clusters produced by mkcls, which takes 35–85 times longer.

We also improved upon the speed of the algorithm by cluster refinement and entropy term precalculation. MT experiments showed that word alignment models using ClusterCat fully match those using mkcls in BLEU scores, with time savings found by using ClusterCat. The software, as well as additional compatibility and visualization scripts, are available under a Free license at https://github.com/jonsafari/clustercat.

Acknowledgements

We would like to thank Hermann Ney, Kazuki Irie, and the reviewers. This work was supported by the QT21 project (Horizon 2020 No. 645452).

References

R. Botros, K. Irie, M. Sundermeyer, and H. Ney. 2015. On Efficient Training of Word Classes and Their Application to Recurrent Neural Network Language Models. In *Proc. INTERSPEECH*, pages 1443–1447.

P. Brown, P. deSouza, R. Mercer, V. Della Pietra, and J. Lai. 1992. Class-Based n-gram Models of Natural Language. *Comp. Ling.*, 18(4):467–479.

P. Brown, S. Della Pietra, V. Della Pietra, and R. Mercer. 1993. The Mathematics of Statistical Machine Translation: Parameter Estimation. *Comp. Ling.*, 19(2):263–311.

M. Candito and D. Seddah. 2010. Parsing Word Clusters. In *Proc. of the Workshop on SPMRL*, pages 76–84.

C. Cherry. 2013. Improved Reordering for Phrase-Based Translation using Sparse Features. In *Proc. NAACL-HLT 2013*, pages 22–31.

J. Dehdari, L. Tan, and J. van Genabith. 2016. BIRA: Improved Predictive Exchange Word Clustering. In *Proc. NAACL*, San Diego, CA, USA.

N. Durrani, P. Koehn, H. Schmid, and A. Fraser. 2014. Investigating the Usefulness of Generalized Word Representations in SMT. In *Proc. of Coling 2014*, pages 421–432.

J. Goodman. 2001a. A Bit of Progress in Language Modeling, Extended Version. Technical Report MSR-TR-2001-72, Microsoft Research.

J. Goodman. 2001b. Classes for Fast Maximum Entropy Training. In *Proc. of ICASSP*, pages 561–564.

S. Green, D. Cer, and C. Manning. 2014. An Empirical Comparison of Features and Tuning for Phrase-based Machine Translation. In *Proc. WMT*, pages 466–476.

R. Kneser and H. Ney. 1993. Improved clustering techniques for class-based statistical language modelling. In *Proc. EUROSPEECH*, pages 973–976.

P. Koehn and H. Hoang. 2007. Factored Translation Models. In *Proc. EMNLP-CoNLL*, pages 868–876.

P. Koehn. 2004. Statistical significance tests for machine translation evaluation. In *Proc. EMNLP*, pages 388–395.

L. Kong, N. Schneider, S. Swayamdipta, A. Bhatia, C. Dyer, and N. Smith. 2014. A Dependency Parser for Tweets. In *Proc. EMNLP*, pages 1001–1012.

T. Koo, X. Carreras, and M. Collins. 2008. Simple Semi-supervised Dependency Parsing. In *Proc. ACL: HLT*, pages 595–603.

P. Liang. 2005. Semi-Supervised Learning for Natural Language. Master's thesis, MIT.

T. Mikolov, K. Chen, G. Corrado, and J. Dean. 2013. Efficient Estimation of Word Representations in Vector Space. In *Proc. ICLR*.

S. Miller, J. Guinness, and A. Zamanian. 2004. Name Tagging with Word Clusters and Discriminative Training. In Susan Dumais, Daniel Marcu, and Salim Roukos, editors, *Proc. HLT-NAACL*, pages 337–342.

F. Och and H. Ney. 2000. A Comparison of Alignment Models for Statistical Machine Translation. In *Proc. Coling*, pages 1086–1090.

F. Och. 1995. Maximum-Likelihood-Schätzung von Wortkategorien mit Verfahren der kombinatorischen Optimierung. Bachelor's thesis (Studienarbeit), Universität Erlangen-Nürnburg.

S. Petrov. 2009. *Coarse-to-Fine Natural Language Processing*. Ph.D. thesis, UC-Berkeley.

A. Ritter, S. Clark, Mausam, and O. Etzioni. 2011. Named Entity Recognition in Tweets: An Experimental Study. In *Proc. EMNLP*, pages 1524–1534.

S. Stymne. 2012. Clustered Word Classes for Preordering in Statistical Machine Translation. In *Proc. of the Joint Workshop on Unsupervised and Semi-Supervised Learning in NLP*, pages 28–34.

J. Turian, L. Ratinov, and Y. Bengio. 2010. Word Representations: A Simple and General Method for Semi-Supervised Learning. In *Proc. ACL*, pages 384–394.

J. Uszkoreit and T. Brants. 2008. Distributed Word Clustering for Large Scale Class-Based Language Modeling in Machine Translation. In *Proc. ACL: HLT*, pages 755–762.

J. Wuebker, S. Peitz, F. Rietig, and H. Ney. 2013. Improving Statistical Machine Translation with Word Class Models. In *Proc. EMNLP*, pages 1377–1381.

A. Zollmann and S. Vogel. 2011. A Word-Class Approach to Labeling PSCFG Rules for Machine Translation. In *Proc. ACL-HLT*, pages 1–11.

Task Completion Platform: A self-serve multi-domain goal oriented dialogue platform

P. A. Crook, A. Marin, V. Agarwal, K. Aggarwal, T. Anastasakos, R. Bikkula, D. Boies, A. Celikyilmaz, S. Chandramohan, Z. Feizollahi, R. Holenstein, M. Jeong, O. Z. Khan, Y.-B. Kim, E. Krawczyk, X. Liu, D. Panic, V. Radostev, N. Ramesh, J.-P. Robichaud, A. Rochette, L. Stromberg and **R. Sarikaya**

Microsoft Corporation, One Microsoft Way, Redmond, WA 98052, USA

Abstract

We demonstrate the Task Completion Platform (TCP); a multi-domain dialogue platform that can host and execute large numbers of goal-orientated dialogue tasks. The platform features a task configuration language, TaskForm, that allows the definition of each individual task to be decoupled from the overarching dialogue policy used by the platform to complete those tasks. This separation allows for simple and rapid authoring of new tasks, while dialogue policy and platform functionality evolve independent of the tasks. The current platform includes machine learnt models that provide contextual slot carry-over, flexible item selection, and task selection/switching. Any new task immediately gains the benefit of these pieces of built-in platform functionality. The platform is used to power many of the multi-turn dialogues supported by the Cortana personal assistant.

1 Introduction

The aim of the Task Completion Platform (TCP) is to support the rapid development of large numbers of goal-orientated, multi-turn dialogues by simplifying the process of specifying a new task. To achieve this, the definition of individual tasks is separated from the mechanics and policy required to conduct a natural language, goal-orientated dialogue. TCP provides the functionality required to manage dialogues with users, leaving a task author to specify only the information to collect from the user and the interfaces to resources such as data hosted in external services and applications that will execute actions on behalf of the user. The platform is used to power many multi-turn dialogue interactions as part of the Cortana personal assistant.

2 Background

VoiceXML (VoiceXML, 2000) is a industry standard tool used to build dialogue systems. It is typically used to design system-directed dialogues, where the understanding of user input is constrained at each turn, and there is no opportunity for user initiative. Such dialogues are common in call centre interactive voice response systems, but are of limited utility when more natural interactions are desired, such as personal assistant dialogues supported by TCP.

A more flexible dialogue management platform is RavenClaw (Bohus and Rudnicky, 2009). RavenClaw systems are composed of a tree structure of agents, with the system at each turn deciding on an execution plan that allows a maximum number of agents to finish their processing. However, most systems built using RavenClaw require custom-built agents; it is difficult to integrate additional tasks into an existing system without having to rebuild the entire tree of agents. In contrast, TCP allows the addition of new experiences with only a configuration file change (as discussed in section 4).

Most similar is ClippyScript (Seide and McDirmid, 2012) which like TCP uses a hierarchical data flow to drive processing (akin to a functional language) as opposed to directed dialogue flow. A key difference is that, in defining tasks in ClippyScript, a dialog act is explicitly tied to a task condition by a rule. Thus, ClippyScript developers directly specify a rule based dialogue policy on a per task basis. In a TaskForm (TCP task

Proceedings of NAACL-HLT 2016 (Demonstrations), pages 47–51,
San Diego, California, June 12-17, 2016. ©2016 Association for Computational Linguistics

definition) dialog acts are declared in *association* with parameters but when to execute them is not explicitly encoded. This allows for separation of tasks and dialogue policies in TCP.

Work also exists on dialogue policy transfer (*e.g.* Wang et al. (2015)) but such work has typically not focused on easy and rapid definition of a diverse set of tasks, as we did in developing TCP.

The main contributions of our work on TCP include: strong separation between task definition and the shared dialogue policy; rapid new task authoring, with the platform providing key machine learning (ML) driven dialogue capabilities such as state tracking, dialogue policy learning, flexible selection, and LU model reuse, which significantly reduces the burden on individual task developers; and benefits to users by offering many multi-turn, mix-initiative dialogue tasks simultaneously.

3 Architectural Overview

The TCP platform supports execution of a variable number of goal-orientated tasks, which can be modified and improved without changing the core platform. The platform has a modular architecture, with the dialogue management process separated into discrete units which can also be independently updated and improved. Figure 1 presents the core platform modules, loosely grouped as: initial processing of input, dialogue state updates, and policy execution. Alternative interpretations of input and dialogue state are preserved in parallel for each step of the pipeline, with a final ranking step to select the optimal hypothesis and associated dialogue act.

The input to the system is either typed text or transcripts from an Automatic Speech Recognition (ASR) system, in the form of N-best hypotheses or confusion networks. The input is processed by a Natural Language Understanding (NLU) module. Several alternate NLU modules can be used in the platform, *e.g.* Deoras and Sarikaya (2013). A typical arrangement is described in Robichaud et al. (2014). To support multiple tasks across multiple domains, a collection of NLU models are executed in parallel, each determining the most likely *intent* and set of *slots* within their domain. An NLU slot is defined as a container that can hold a sequence of words from the user input, with the label indicating the role played by that text in a task or set of tasks. Together,

the detected intent and slots form the *semantic frame* for that domain. NLU models are contextual (Bhargava et al., 2013; Liu et al., 2015), taking into account the state of any task currently in progress.

On each turn, the dialogue state is updated taking into consideration the multiple NLU results. *Slot Carry Over (SCO)* (Boies et al., 2016) does contextual carry-over of slots from previous turns, using a combination of rules and ML models with lexical and structural features from the current and previous turn utterances. *Flexible Item Selection* uses task-independent ML models (Celikyilmaz et al., 2014; Celikyilmaz et al., 2015) to handle disambiguation turns where the user is asked to select between a number of possible items. The *Task Updates* module is responsible for applying both task-independent and task-specific dialogue state updates. The task-specific processing is driven by a set of configuration files in a new configuration language, Task-Form, with each form encapsulating the definition of one task. Using the TaskForm files, this module initiates new tasks, retrieves information from knowledge sources and applies data transformations (*e.g.* canonicalization). Data transformations and knowledge source look ups are performed using *Resolvers*, as discussed in section 4.

Dialogue policy execution is split into task-depenent and global policy. The *Per Task Policy* consists of analysing the state of each task currently in progress, and suggesting a dialog act to execute. The output of the module is a set of dialogue hypotheses representing alternative states or dialog actions for each task in progress. The number of hypotheses does not grow uncontrollably; depending on the state of the dialogue during the previous turn and the current input, only a small proportion of all the defined tasks will be active in any one turn.

The output dialog hypotheses are ranked using *Hypothesis Ranking (HR)* (Robichaud et al., 2014; Khan et al., 2015; Crook et al., 2015), which generates a ranked order and score for each hypothesis. This acts as a pseudo-belief distribution over the possible dialogue/task states. *Hypothesis Selection (HS)* policy selects a hypothesis based on contextual signals, such as the previous turn task, as well as the rank order and scores. The HS policy may select a meta-task dialog act, such as asking the user to specifically select a task when two or more tasks are

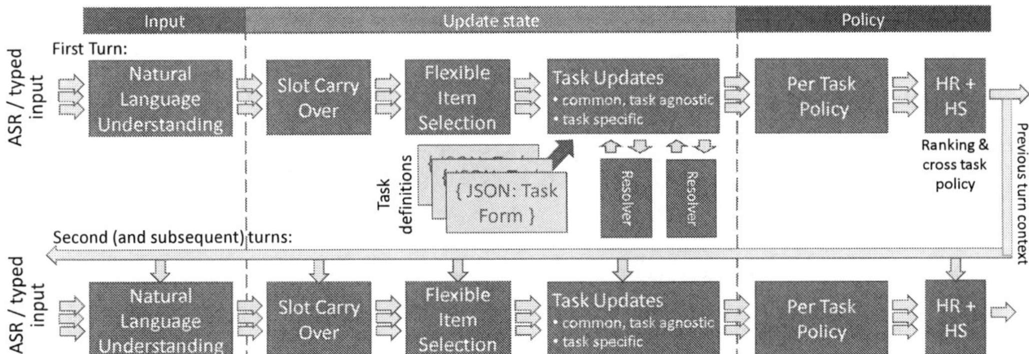

Figure 1: Functional modules of the TCP architecture

```
{"TriggerName": "PizzaOrdering",
 "Intent": "order_pizza",
 "TriggerOnlyOnTriggerQueries": false,
 "TriggerQueries":
 ["i wanna order a pizza",
  "i want to order a pizza",
  "order domino's pizza",
  "hey cortana, get me a pizza",
  ... ]}
```

Figure 2: An example definition of a task trigger.

highly ranked, or adding an implicit confirmation when the top hypothesis has low confidence. The selected dialog act is rendered to the user and the associated dialog hypothesis informs the next turn.

4 TaskForm Language Definition

The TaskForm language allows for defining tasks independently of the dialogue policy executed by the platform. Each task is represented as a set of independent triggers defining under what conditions task execution should begin, a set of parameters defining what information should be collected during the dialogue, and a set of dialog acts defining what is presented to the user. Additional structural information about a task can be captured through the use of validation conditions (not shown here).

A *task trigger* defines under what conditions a task may begin executing. These conditions are represented in terms of NLU results: combinations of domains, intents, and slots (presence or absence). Each trigger may also specify a list of must-trigger utterances, as shown in figure 2. At least one trigger must be satisfied for the task to begin execution.

We define a *task parameter* as a container that holds knowledge items required to complete a task. Each parameter definition specifies how the knowl-

edge items (*i.e.* its *value*) should be produced and what dialog acts are used to solicit relevant information. An example of a task parameter is shown in figure 3.

The knowledge items that are stored in a parameter can be: concrete entities *e.g.* a particular restaurant in a city; canonicalized attributes of an item, *e.g.* 'small', 'middle' or 'large'; concepts, 'delivery' or 'take-out'; or labels that index another knowledge source. Knowledge items can be retrieved from some knowledge source, *e.g.* a database or knowledge graph, or captured directly in code.

The value of a parameter is provided by an associated piece of code, a *resolver* implemented outside the TaskForm. In the TaskForm, a resolver definition (optional for platform-provided resolvers) contains only a reference to the code assembly, class name, and a list of NLU slot tags and input parameters which it can process. The parameter definition contains a resolver invocation block which lists a subset of slot tags and input parameters that should actually be used as input to the resolver during the task execution; this allows resolvers to be generic and reusable across multiple parameters and tasks. A platform-provided HTTP resolver allows for easy integration with third party APIs; each HTTP resolver definition need specify only a mapping between task parameters and API parameters, and a JPATH expression for interpreting the results.

There is a many-to-many relationship between NLU slots and the knowledge items (values) that fill a parameter. Dependent on the run-time results of resolution, additional dialog acts may be required to obtain further user input and refine the resolution. *E.g.* if the NLU slots **[place_name:Marriott]**

```
{ "ParameterName": "DeliveryAddress",
  "Description": "delivery address",
  "Type": "Location",
  "ResolverInvocation":
  {"Resolver": "Platform.PlacesResolver",
   "ResolverSlotTags": [ "absolute_location", "place_name", "place_type" ],
   "ResolverOutputParameterName": "PlaceParameter" },
  "DialogActs": {
  { "MissingValue": "DeliveryAddressMissingValueDialogAct",
    "Disambiguation": "DeliveryAddressDisambiguationDialogAct" } },
```

Figure 3: An example definition of a parameter.

```
{ "DialogActName": "DeliveryAddressMissingValueDialogAct",
  "Response":
  { "Prompts":
   [ "Where do you want the pizza delivered?",
     "Where do you want it delivered?",
     "Where should I send your pizza?" ],
   "SpokenPrompts":
   [ "Now, where do you want your pizza delivered?",
     "Okay, where do you want it delivered?",
     "Now tell me, where should I send your pizza?", ] } }
```

Figure 4: An example definition of a dialog act.

and [**absolute_location:Bellevue**] are used to index a knowledge source and extract values to fill the task parameter **DeliveryAddress**, the result may be a *list* of Marriott hotel locations in Bellevue. If the parameter specifies that it must hold a single value, further dialog acts will be used to narrow the results. These dialogue policy decisions could not be made by examining the slots in isolation of the resolved values.

As part of the execution of a task, the system may take one or more dialog acts before the value of a parameter is considered "filled". Allowed acts include:

- **MissingValue** - ask the user for input required to populate the parameter (plus a variation that presents suggested values to the user);
- **NoResultsFollowup** - prompt to change information as no results were found (plus a variation that presents suggestions);
- **Disambiguation** - ask the user to select the parameter value from a list;
- **ImplicitConfirmation** - implicitly confirm the newly filled parameter as part of the next turn;
- **Confirmation** - ask the user to confirm the parameter value the system computed;
- **ConfirmationFailure** - ask the user to provide new input if they rejected a confirmation act.

A *dialog act definition* captures the information that should be presented to the user when that dialog act is taken by the system. This information includes: a prompt to be read out, a list of strings to be shown on the screen, as well as hints to prime the NLU during the next turn of the conversation. Default definitions are used for any missing sections in each dialog act definition. Figure 4 shows an example of a dialog act definition, encoding how the user should be prompted to provide the missing value of the *DeliveryAddress* parameter.

5 Demo Outline

We plan to showcase the capabilities of TCP, highlighting in particular the breadth of the platform and the agility of task development.

The platform is capable of executing multiple tasks using the same underlying policy modules, thus allowing for tasks to be developed separately from the policy definition. To this end we will show the platform supporting a conversational agent capable of setting reminders, ordering pizzas, and reserving movie tickets, restaurant tables and taxis (where these scenarios are hooked up to real third party services like Domino's, OpenTable, Uber, *etc.*). Each task is defined by a TaskForm. Users can interact with the system through natural conversation and take initiative at any point, *e.g.* to cancel a task in progress, provide information out of turn, or change previously-provided information.

Many changes to a task can be done simply by manipulating its TaskForm definition. To illustrate this, we will demonstrate some simple modifications to an existing task, such as changing the task triggers, adding a new parameter, modifying some of the conditions set on parameters, and redefining some of the dialog acts used during task execution.

6 Conclusion

We demonstrated the Task Completion Platform, an extensible, mixed-initiative dialogue management platform targeting goal-directed conversations. The platform supports executing multiple tasks. Each task is defined primarily in terms of extensible NLU models and a single configuration file, thus separating task definition from the system-wide dialogue policy. Tasks can be added or modified without requiring a system rebuild. Future work includes extending the platform by allowing multiple tasks to be concurrently in progress, either through nesting or interleaving of tasks, and evaluation of task success and related metrics.

References

A. Bhargava, A. Celikyilmaz, D. Hakkani-Tur, R. Sarikaya, and Z. Feizollahi. 2013. Easy contextual intent prediction and slot detection. In *Proc. ICASSP*, May.

D. Bohus and A. Rudnicky. 2009. The RavenClaw dialog management framework: Architecture and systems. *Computer Speech and Language*.

D. Boies, R. Sarikaya, A. Rochette, Z. Feizollahi, and N. Ramesh. 2016. Using sequence classification to update a partial dialog state (United States patent application 20150095033, filed 2013).

A. Celikyilmaz, Z. Feizollahi, D. Hakkani-Tur, and R. Sarikaya. 2014. Resolving referring expressions in conversational dialogs for natural user interfaces. In *Proc. EMNLP*, October.

A. Celikyilmaz, Z. Feizollahi, D. Hakkani-Tur, and R. Sarikaya. 2015. A universal model for flexible item selection in conversational dialogs. In *Proc. ASRU 2015*, December.

P. A. Crook, J.-P. Robichaud, and R. Sarikaya. 2015. Multi-language hypotheses ranking and domain tracking for open domain dialogue systems. In *Proc. Interspeech*, September.

A. Deoras and R. Sarikaya. 2013. Deep belief network Markov model sequence classification spoken language understanding. In *Proc. Interspeech*, August.

O. Z. Khan, J.-P. Robichaud, P. A. Crook, and R. Sarikaya. 2015. Hypotheses ranking and state tracking for a multi-domain dialog system using ASR results. In *Proc. Interspeech*, September.

C. Liu, P. Xu, and R. Sarikaya. 2015. Deep contextual language understanding in spoken dialogue systems. In *Proc. ASRU*, December.

J.-P. Robichaud, P. A. Crook, P. Xu, O. Z. Khan, and R. Sarikaya. 2014. Hypotheses ranking for robust domain classification and tracking in dialogue systems. In *Proc. Interspeech*, September.

F. Seide and S. McDirmid. 2012. ClippyScript: A programming language for multi-domain dialogue systems. In *Proc. Interspeech*.

VoiceXML. 2000. VoiceXML version 1.0. https://www.w3.org/TR/voicexml/.

Z. Wang, Y. Stylianou, T.-H. Wen, P.-H. Su, and S. Young. 2015. Learning domain-independent dialogue policies via ontology parameterisation. In *Proceedings of SIGdial*.

ILLINOIS MATH SOLVER: Math Reasoning on the Web

Subhro Roy   and   **Dan Roth**
University of Illinois, Urbana Champaign
{sroy9, danr}@illinois.edu

Abstract

There has been a recent interest in understanding text to perform mathematical reasoning. In particular, most of these efforts have focussed on automatically solving school level math word problems. In order to make advancements in this area accessible to people, as well as to facilitate this line of research, we release the ILLINOIS MATH SOLVER, a web based tool that supports performing mathematical reasoning. ILLINOIS MATH SOLVER can answer a wide range of mathematics questions, ranging from compositional operation questions like *"What is the result when 6 is divided by the sum of 7 and 5 ?"* to elementary school level math word problems, like *"I bought 6 apples. I ate 3 of them. How many do I have left ?"*. The web based demo can be used as a tutoring tool for elementary school students, since it not only outputs the final result, but also the mathematical expression to compute it. The tool will allow researchers to understand the capabilities and limitations of a state of the art arithmetic problem solver, and also enable crowd based data acquisition for mathematical reasoning. The system is currently online at `https://cogcomp.cs.illinois.edu/page/demo_view/Math`.

1   Motivation

There has been a lot of interest in understanding text for the purpose of quantitative reasoning. In particular, there has been multiple recent efforts to automatically solve math word problems (Kushman et al., 2014; Hosseini et al., 2014; Roy et al., 2015; Roy and Roth, 2015; Shi et al., 2015; Koncel-Kedziorski et al., 2016). Advancement in this area has great potential to be used as automatic tutoring service for school students. However till date, all the advances in this area are not easily accessible to the general population. ILLINOIS MATH SOLVER addresses this issue by providing a web based platform, where users can type in their math word problem and get the answer. It also outputs the mathematical expression generating the answer, allowing students to understand how to solve the problem. Fig 1 shows a screenshot of the web interface of the ILLINOIS MATH SOLVER.

All systems for math word problem solving are trained and evaluated on datasets created from tutoring websites and textbooks. However the problems from the aforementioned sources tend to have limited variety in problem types and vocabulary. Often these systems are brittle, and make mistakes with slight variation of text. As a result, there is a need for an easy way to analyze the robustness of these systems, as well as extract a wider variety of math word problems not available from textbooks and tutoring websites. ILLINOIS MATH SOLVER solves both these purposes, providing users an easy way to test the robustness of the system, and a tool for crowd based data acquisition. We expect people to query with small edits to math word problem text, to make our system get the wrong answer. This allows for adverserial data acquisition, which can help identify intricacies of mathematical reasoning.

Proceedings of NAACL-HLT 2016 (Demonstrations), pages 52–56,
San Diego, California, June 12-17, 2016. ©2016 Association for Computational Linguistics

Figure 1: Screen Shot of ILLINOIS MATH SOLVER

2 System Description

The ILLINOIS MATH SOLVER consists of two main modules - a context-free grammar (CFG) based semantic parser, and an arithmetic problem solver. We describe each component below.

2.1 CFG Parser

We use a CFG based semantic parser to handle queries asking for operations between numbers. Examples of such queries include *"What is the difference of 22 and 5 ?"* and *"What is the result when 6 is divided by the sum of 7 and 5 ?"*. We refer to such queries as "number queries".

Our parser recognizes the mathematical terms in a number query like "added", "difference", "fraction", etc. It then creates a list of the numbers and math terms mentioned in the query, maintaining the order in which they appear in the query. For the example *"What is the result when 6 is divided by the sum of 7 and 5 ?"*, the parser creates the list $\{6, \text{divided}, \text{sum}, 7, 5\}$.

Next, it tries to parse the list of numbers and the math terms into a mathematical expression, using a list of derivation rules. An example of a derivation rule is as follows:

$$E \rightarrow E_1 \quad \text{divided} \quad E_2$$
$$val(E) \rightarrow val(E_1)/val(E_2)$$

where E, E_1 and E_2 are non-terminals of our CFG representing mathematical expressions. For each such non-terminal, we have an associated function $val(\cdot)$, which computes the numeric value of the mathematical expression represented by that non-terminal. The above rule states that whenever we see the word "divided" between two expressions, we can parse them into a new expression. The value of the new expression will be obtained by dividing the first expression value with the second one. Overall, we have 26 such derivation rules, and we will be augmenting it as we come across more varied number queries. We use CKY algorithm for parsing. The derivation rules naturally capture composition. In the above example, it will first parse $\{$*"sum, 7, 5"*$\}$ into an expression E, and next parse $\{6,$ *divided*, $E\}$.

2.2 General Arithmetic Problem Solver

The second component of our system is the arithmetic word problem solver developed in our previous work (Roy and Roth, 2015). The solver tackles a general class of arithmetic word problems, and achieves state of the art results on several benchmark datasets of arithmetic word problems.

2.2.1 Technical Details

The solver decomposes an input arithmetic problem into several decision problems, and learns predictors for these decision problems. Finally the predictions for the decomposed problems are combined to generate a binary expression tree for the solution mathematical expression. Fig 2 gives an example of an arithmetic word problem coupled with the binary expression tree of the solution.

Problem
Gwen was organizing her book case making sure each of the shelves had exactly 9 books on it. She has 2 types of books - mystery books and picture books. If she had 3 shelves of mystery books and 5 shelves of picture books, how many books did she have total?

Solution	Expression Tree of Solution
$(3 + 5) \times 9 = 72$	

Figure 2: An arithmetic word problem, solution expression and the corresponding expression tree

The arithmetic solver learns classifiers for the following two prediction problems:

1. For every pair of quantities q_i, q_j in a problem P, a classifier is learnt to predict a math operation (one of addition, subtraction, multiplication, division) along with the order of operation (applicable for subtraction and division). This operation is expected to denote the operation at the lowest common ancestor (LCA) node of q_i and q_j in the solution tree. For example, in fig 2, the operation between 3 and 5 is addition, and that between 5 and 9 is multiplication. A multi-class classifier is trained for this prediction task.

   Finally, we define $\text{PAIR}(q_i, q_j, op)$ to denote the likelihood score of op to be the operation at the LCA node of q_i and q_j in the solution expression tree of P. The aforementioned classifier is used to obtain these scores.

2. We also train a classifier to predict whether a quantity q mentioned in a problem P is irrelevant for the solution. For example, in fig 2, the number "2" is irrelevant, whereas all other numbers are relevant. A binary classifier is trained to predict this.

   We define $\text{IRR}(q)$ to denote the likelihood score of quantity q being an irrelevant quantity in P, that is, q is not used in creating the solution. The aforementioned binary classifier is used to obtain these scores.

For an expression E, let $\mathcal{I}(E)$ be the set of all quantities in P which are not used in expression E. Let $\mathcal{T}$ be an expression tree for E. We define $\text{Score}(E)$ of an expression E in terms of the above scoring functions and a scaling parameter w_{IRR} as follows:

$$\text{Score}(E) = w_{\text{IRR}} \sum_{q \in \mathcal{I}(E)} \text{IRR}(q) +$$
$$\sum_{q_i, q_j \notin \mathcal{I}(E)} \text{PAIR}(q_i, q_j, \odot_{LCA}(q_i, q_j, \mathcal{T}))$$

where $\odot_{LCA}(q_i, q_j, \mathcal{T})$ is the operation at the LCA node of q_i and q_j in the expression tree $\mathcal{T}$.

Our search for solution expression tree is also constrained by legitimacy and background knowledge constraints, detailed below.

1. **Positive Answer**: Most arithmetic problems asking for amounts or number of objects usually have a positive number as an answer. Therefore, while searching for the best scoring expression, we reject expressions generating negative answer.

2. **Integral Answer**: Problems with questions such as 'how many" usually expect integral solutions. We only consider integral solutions as legitimate outputs for such problems.

Let $\mathcal{C}$ be the set of valid expressions that can be formed using the quantities in a problem P, and which satisfy the above constraints. The inference algorithm now becomes the following:

$$\arg\max_{E \in \mathcal{C}} \text{Score}(E)$$

2.2.2 Evaluation

We evaluated our arithmetic word problem solver on three publicly available datasets – addition subtraction problems from AI2 dataset (AI2) (Hosseini et al., 2014), single operation problems from Illinois dataset (IL)(Roy et al., 2015), and multi-step problems from commoncore dataset (CC)(Roy and Roth, 2015). We compare against systems which had achieved previously known best scores on these datasets, and show that our system achieves state of the art performance on all the above datasets. Table 1 shows the comparison. Finally, the models of the ILLINOIS MATH SOLVER are trained on the union of the aforementioned datasets.

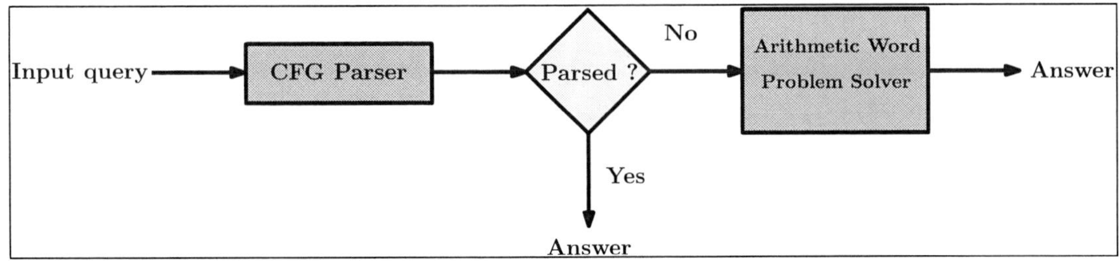

Figure 3: Pipeline of ILLINOIS MATH SOLVER

	AI2	IL	CC
Our system	**78.0**	**73.9**	**45.2**
(Hosseini et al., 2014)	77.7	-	-
(Roy et al., 2015)	-	52.7	-
(Kushman et al., 2014)	64.0	73.7	2.3

Table 1: Accuracy in correctly solving arithmetic problems. We achieve state of the art results in all three datasets.

2.3 Illinois Math Solver pipeline

The pipeline of the ILLINOIS MATH SOLVER is shown in Fig 3. Given input text, we first run the CFG parser, to check whether it is a number query. If our CFG parser can make sense of the query and can generate a mathematical expression from the query, we immediately output it as the answer. Otherwise, the query is fed to the arithmetic problem solver. The output of the solver is then displayed as the result.

3 Related Work

The interface of Wolfram Alpha is probably the closest to ours. However their system is limited to handling mostly number queries, and very simple arithmetic problems. In contrast, our system can solve complicated arithmetic problems described by multiple sentences and requiring multiple operations. There has also been a lot of work in quantitative reasoning. Roy et al. (2015) looks at understanding entailment relations among expressions of quantities in text. There has also been efforts to automatically solve school level math word problems. Hosseini et al. (2014) looks at solving elementary addition subtraction problems, Roy et al. (2015) aims to solve single operation problems and Koncel-Kedziorski et al. (2016) solves single equation problems. The system of Shi et al. (2015) tackles number word

problems by semi-automatically generated parsing rules, and is similar to our CFG parsing approach for tackling number queries. Kushman et al. (2014) proposes a template based approach for solving algebra word problems and finally, our system proposed in Roy and Roth (2015) solves a general class of arithmetic word problems, and achieves state of the art results on multiple arithmetic word problem datasets. This is the solver we use for handling arithmetic problems in ILLINOIS MATH SOLVER.

4 Conclusion and Future Directions

We release ILLINOIS MATH SOLVER, an online tool to automatically solve number queries and arithemtic word problems. It will help elementary school students to self-tutor. In addition, it will be a source of highly varied math queries, which might reveal difficulties of mathematical reasoning, and assist future advancement in the area.

There are various fronts on which we will be improving the system in future. Currently, the arithemetic solver assumes the final solution can be generated by combining the numbers mentioned in the text, and hence, cannot introduce new numbers for the solution. . For example, *"I eat 1 apple each day. How many apples will I eat in 1 week ?"* is currently not handled since it requires knowing that 1 week has 7 days. This will require leveraging a knowledge base to bring in the additional information. We will also try to handle algebra word problems, which involve generating multiple equations with one or more variables, and then solving these equations to generate the answer.

References

[Hosseini et al.2014] M. J. Hosseini, H. Hajishirzi, O. Etzioni, and N. Kushman. 2014. Learning to solve arithmetic word problems with verb categorization. In *Proceedings of the 2014 Conference on Empirical Methods in Natural Language Processing, EMNLP 2014*.

[Koncel-Kedziorski et al.2016] R. Koncel-Kedziorski, H. Hajishirzi, A. Sabharwal, O. Etzioni, and S. Dumas Ang. 2016. Parsing algebraic word problems into equations. In *TACL*.

[Kushman et al.2014] N. Kushman, L. Zettlemoyer, R. Barzilay, and Y. Artzi. 2014. Learning to automatically solve algebra word problems. In *ACL*.

[Roy and Roth2015] S. Roy and D. Roth. 2015. Solving general arithmetic word problems. In *Proc. of the Conference on Empirical Methods in Natural Language Processing (EMNLP)*.

[Roy et al.2015] S. Roy, T. Vieira, and D. Roth. 2015. Reasoning about quantities in natural language. *Transactions of the Association for Computational Linguistics*, 3.

[Shi et al.2015] Shuming Shi, Yuehui Wang, Chin-Yew Lin, Xiaojiang Liu, and Yong Rui. 2015. Automatically solving number word problems by semantic parsing and reasoning. In *Proceedings of the 2015 Conference on Empirical Methods in Natural Language Processing*.

LingoTurk: managing crowdsourced tasks for psycholinguistics

Florian Pusse and **Asad Sayeed** and **Vera Demberg**
Computational Linguistics and Phonetics/M^{2}CI Cluster of Excellence
Saarland University
66123 Saarbrücken, Germany
`{fpusse,asayeed,vera}@coli.uni-saarland.de`

Abstract

LingoTurk is an open-source, freely available crowdsourcing client/server system aimed primarily at psycholinguistic experimentation where custom and specialized user interfaces are required but not supported by popular crowdsourcing task management platforms. LingoTurk enables user-friendly local hosting of experiments as well as condition management and participant exclusion. It is compatible with Amazon Mechanical Turk and Prolific Academic. New experiments can easily be set up via the Play Framework and the LingoTurk API, while multiple experiments can be managed from a single system.

1   Introduction

LingoTurk is a crowdsourced experiment management system aimed at the use case where the experiment user interface must be highly customized. Common web browsers now permit the design of experimental user interfaces with highly sophisticated presentations, allowing crowdsourcing environments to be used as laboratories for psycholinguistic experimentation with paradigms that in the recent past could only be run "in-lab".

Crowdsourcing in language science was originally popularized among researchers for the collection of labelled training data. It has recently gained popularity as a platform for collecting experimental data for cognitive modeling (e.g., Gibson et al., 2013; Kush et al., 2015). Experimenters trade direct control over subject demographics and environment for faster, cheaper experiment completion

with many more subjects. Crowdsourcing can provide experimenters with a way to access populations which are not locally available (e.g., native speakers of a non-local language). Commercial platforms provide micropayment architectures to provide rewards to users. They also manage abuse, track user reliability, track (usually-pseudonymized) identities, and recruit participants.

We designed LingoTurk to handle the condition where the actual experiment must be hosted outside of the "default" systems provided by crowdsourcing platforms. This is motivated by cases in which there is functionality not directly supported by the crowdsourcing platform but can be managed externally, such as the separation of experimental conditions or the storage of specialized data types. Insofar as common crowdsourcing platforms support external interfaces, LingoTurk provides an easily deployed server-side solution to external experiment management. As its administration functions are also web-based, LingoTurk allows for the steering and management of crowdsourcing experiments to be performed without strong technical skills, such as student assistants in non-technical majors.

The source code is made available at `https://github.com/FlorianPusse/ Lingoturk.`

1.1   Crowdsourcing and language science

Crowdsourcing has been a trend in language research for the better part of a decade and has principally been focused on the collection of annotated training data for supervised machine learning in fields like machine translation (Zaidan and Callison-

57

Proceedings of NAACL-HLT 2016 (Demonstrations), pages 57–61,
San Diego, California, June 12-17, 2016. ©2016 Association for Computational Linguistics

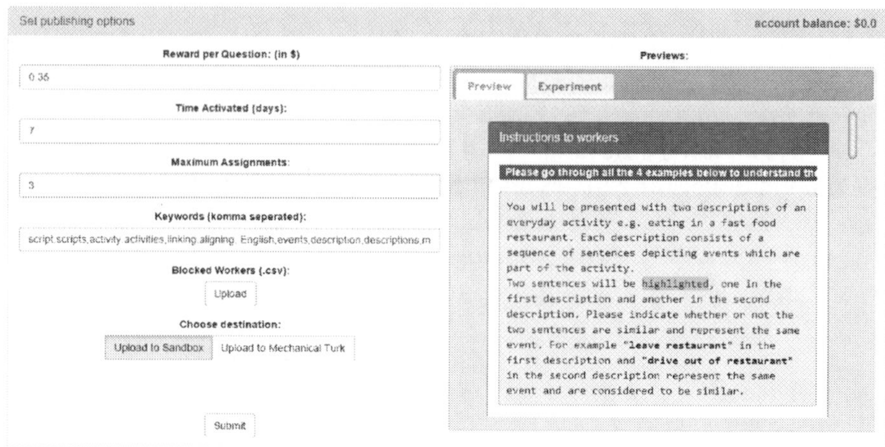

Figure 1: Publishing an experiment to MTurk.

Burch, 2011) and opinion mining (Sayeed et al., 2012). In these areas, the psyche of the annotators is not the principal object of interest.

This has consequences of the relationship of the "requester"—Amazon's term for the task designer—to the crowdsourcing worker. When psycholinguistic experiments are crowdsourced, the objects of interest are no longer directly the "annotations" themselves, but rather what they reveal about the humans who made them. This means that the relationship of the requester to the workers is quite different from what it is in annotation efforts: qualification for the task is replaced by qualification for the study, and annotator reliability is augmented by the need for experimental control.

Psycholinguistic experiments attempt to confirm a hypothesis about the way in which linguistic stimuli are evaluated by the human mind. Experimental items are therefore often separated by condition Normally each subject should only see one item in each condition.

Furthermore, "learning effects" are often a risk in psycholinguistic experiments. Subjects can get used to the experimental paradigm, and as time goes on, their responses can be said to become less and less the spontaneous reaction of linguistic cognition.

Consequently, fine-grained control over condition presentation and worker exclusion are desiderata of a crowdsourcing platform for psycholinguistic experimentation. LingoTurk is designed to address this need via the self-hosting of experiments while offering integration with existing crowdsourcing platforms.

1.2 Crowdsourcing platforms

Amazon Mechanical Turk (MTurk) is the earliest, most widely-used crowdsourcing platform. MTurk provides a set of standard task designs for crowdsourcing as well as the option to create a custom task. Custom tasks can be hosted on an external server, if they are served to Amazon via the MTurk API.

However, MTurk lacks the architecture for experimental exclusion of workers (subjects) by condition. Nevertheless, its API provides the information to construct one server-side, if experimenters host the task on their own server. The MTurk API also permits the experiment interface to appear as a pane inside the MTurk interface, allowing subjects to experience the task seamlessly.

Prolific Academic (PA) is an alternative platform, useful for needs currently unmet by Amazon, particularly a non-US-centric clientele. PA does not provide an API that allows for full external-question integration, but it allows for worker redirection that permits similar server-side participant tracking.

1.3 Comparison to alternative systems

There are other server-side experiment publishing platforms aimed at psychological and psycholinguistic research: for example, Ibex (Drummond, 2013) and PsiTurk (McDonnell et al., 2012). These platforms have functions that overlap with Lingo-

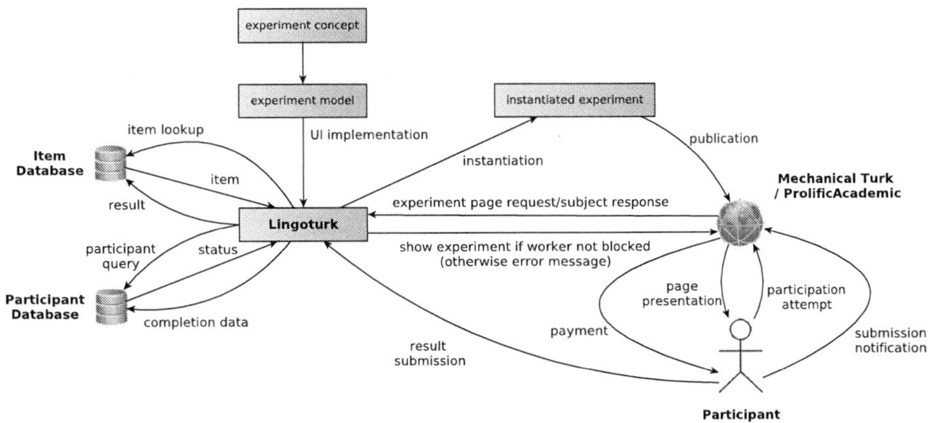

Figure 2: Workflow of crowdsourcing task using LingoTurk.

Turk, but do not cover LingoTurk's full design goals. LingoTurk provides an administration GUI front end for experimenters (figure 1), so that the day-to-day management does not have to be performed via the command line by technically-skilled researchers. LingoTurk is also integrated with the Play Framework, which is intended to accelerate the development of complex, highly scalable web applications using a well-engineered Model-View-Controller (MVC) paradigm in Java and Scala. The MVC paradigm facilitates the development not only of the subject-facing experiment UI, but also user-friendly experiment item entry and testing views for stimulus preparers.

2 Design and workflow

The MVC paradigm combined with database integration makes LingoTurk a platform for reliably engineered experimental interfaces that can handle complex data structures as well as easy object-oriented extensibility. LingoTurk is intended for a self-hosting use case; once a web server has been set up, the Play Framework enables LingoTurk to be a turn-key solution for experiment administration.

Figure 2 shows the design of LingoTurk in terms of its overall workflow. LingoTurk manages communication with the crowdsourcing platform as well as governs interactions with a participant database which keeps track of experimental conditions and exclusions and an item database that keeps track of stimuli and responses. LingoTurk selects the pages to be served to the crowdsourcing platform based on

information provided by the platform. On MTurk, that means that a worker who is ineligible to see an experimental condition will be presented with a page that informs of them of this and asks them to return the task.

Creating a LingoTurk experiment based on an existing interface type (section 3) is done from the graphical administrative console, which is itself a web site. The experimenter instantiates an experiment type and fills the stimuli into web forms that are designed to handle experimental conditions. The experimenter also uses the administrative interface to provide credentials for the crowdsourcing platform as well as to preview and publish the experiment and retrieve the results. Excluded worker IDs (such as those who participated in previous runs of the experiment) can also be uploaded to LingoTurk this way. New experiment designs can be developed and added to the interface using Play Framework-based HTML and Scala templates; common Javascript libraries are provided by default, and an API is provided for server communication.

LingoTurk also allows for the creation of quality control questions that can be used to exclude poorly-performing workers after a threshold of wrong answers is reached. To use this feature, the experimenter must include stimuli with correct or expected responses.

3 Experiment interfaces

LingoTurk has been used for experiments performed by researchers at Saarland University. Here, we

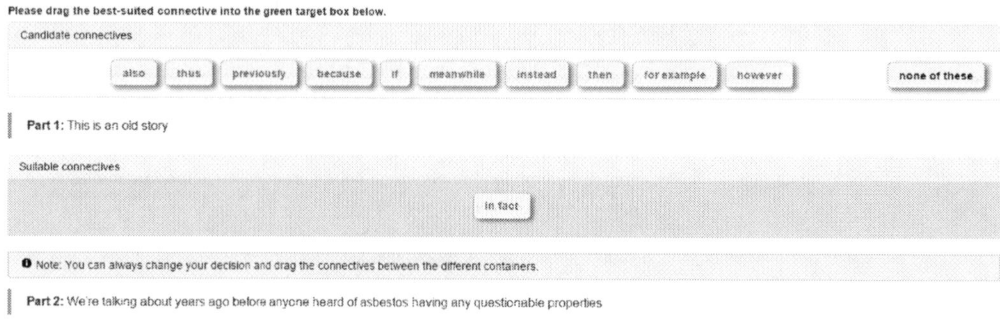

Figure 3: The discourse connective drag-and-drop task.

discuss a couple of examples of interfaces that are included with LingoTurk. We provide other paradigms in the package.

Drag-and-drop discourse connectives Demberg et al. (2015) present the problem of discourse relation prediction: specifically, how do speakers interpret an implicit gap between propositions? They investigated this question through an experiment that allowed subjects to fill in the gap between two sentences, implicitly connected in the Penn Discourse Treebank, with an explicit discourse connective. For this purpose, they used a drag-and-drop paradigm, wherein subjects selected connectives from a set of labelled tiles and dragged them into a target zone (figure 3). They divided this task into phases in order to narrow down the discourse type, with Lingo-Turk presenting a subsidiary tableau of connective phrases depending on the result of the first tableau. The selection of connective tableaux is controlled via the item entry interface on the administrative side of LingoTurk. Data analysis for this task is still on-going.

The advantage of a drag-and-drop paradigm is that it requires the subject to make an explicit choice but also to use a little bit of effort in doing so. This reduces the bias that might be introduced by the least-effort of choosing the first or the last item (Sayeed et al., 2011).

Script alignment by connector drawing Wanzare et al. (2016) use the LingoTurk system to present a task involving the alignment of collected narratives to prepared scripts (e.g., for baking a cake) for an on-going project that is investigating the psycholinguistic aspects of script knowledge as well as developing script corpora. In this paradigm, steps of the narrative (an account of an action collected from subjects during previous research) are presented as tiles in a column on the left side of the window, while steps of the standardized script are presented on the right side. Subjects draw connections between narrative steps and standardized script steps.

4   Demonstration

For our demonstration at the conference, we will bring a computer and present a running instance of the LingoTurk system. We will proceed through the construction of example experiments which will be pushed through to the MTurk Sandbox (MTurk's testing server). We will make use of our built-in experimental paradigms to demonstrate the versatility and convenience of LingoTurk. We will also demonstrate the underlying practical details of developing new experimental paradigms and integrating them into LingoTurk.

5   Future work

There are considerable opportunities to expand the system. One possible direction is integration with other platforms that have been gradually emerging, such as ClickWorker. We are exploring the possibility of integration with the CrowdFlower platform; an important challenge in this case is the integration with CrowdFlower's built-in quality control system. Another direction is increasing the customisability of experiment designs by including a graphical web design tool, reducing the need to interact directly with the Play Framework when developing new experimental paradigms.

References

Demberg, V., Sayeed, A., and Pusse, F. (2015). Discourse annotation via mechanical turk. In *First Action Conference of the TextLink COST Initiative*, Louvain-la-Neuve, Belgium.

Drummond, A. (2013). Ibex farm. *Online server: http://spellout.net/ibexfarm*.

Gibson, E., Bergen, L., and Piantadosi, S. T. (2013). Rational integration of noisy evidence and prior semantic expectations in sentence interpretation. *Proceedings of the National Academy of Sciences*, 110(20):8051–8056.

Kush, D., Lidz, J., and Phillips, C. (2015). Relation-sensitive retrieval: Evidence from bound variable pronouns. *Journal of Memory and Language*, 82:18 – 40.

McDonnell, J., Martin, J., Markant, D., Coenen, A., Rich, A., and Gureckis, T. (2012). psiturk (version 1.02)[software]. new york, ny: New york university.

Sayeed, A. B., Boyd-Graber, J., Rusk, B., and Weinberg, A. (2012). Grammatical structures for word-level sentiment detection. In *Proceedings of the 2012 Conference of the North American Chapter of the Association for Computational Linguistics: Human Language Technologies*, NAACL HLT '12, pages 667–676, Stroudsburg, PA, USA. Association for Computational Linguistics.

Sayeed, A. B., Rusk, B., Petrov, M., Nguyen, H. C., Meyer, T. J., and Weinberg, A. (2011). Crowdsourcing syntactic relatedness judgements for opinion mining in the study of information technology adoption. In *Proceedings of the 5th ACL-HLT Workshop on Language Technology for Cultural Heritage, Social Sciences, and Humanities*, LaTeCH '11, Stroudsburg, PA, USA. Association for Computational Linguistics.

Wanzare, L., Zarcone, A., Thater, S., and Pinkal, M. (to appear 2016). A crowdsourced database of event knowledge sequence descriptions for the acquisition of high-quality script knowledge. In *Language resources and evaluation conference*, Portorož, Slovenia.

Zaidan, O. F. and Callison-Burch, C. (2011). Crowdsourcing translation: Professional quality from non-professionals. In *Proceedings of the 49th Annual Meeting of the Association for Computational Linguistics: Human Language Technologies - Volume 1*, pages 1220–1229, Stroudsburg, PA, USA. Association for Computational Linguistics.

Sentential Paraphrasing as Black-Box Machine Translation

Courtney Napoles[1], **Chris Callison-Burch**[2], and **Matt Post**[3]
[1] Center for Language and Speech Processing, Johns Hopkins University
[2] Computer and Information Science Department, University of Pennsylvania
[3] Human Language Technology Center of Excellence, Johns Hopkins University

Abstract

We present a simple, prepackaged solution to generating paraphrases of English sentences. We use the Paraphrase Database (PPDB) for monolingual sentence rewriting and provide machine translation *language packs:* prepackaged, tuned models that can be downloaded and used to generate paraphrases on a standard Unix environment. The language packs can be treated as a black box or customized to specific tasks. In this demonstration, we will explain how to use the included interactive web-based tool to generate sentential paraphrases.

1 Introduction

Monolingual sentence rewriting encompasses a variety of tasks for which the goal is to generate an output sentence with similar meaning to an input sentence, in the same language. The generated sentences can be called *sentential paraphrases*. Some tasks that generate sentential paraphrases include sentence simplification, compression, grammatical error correction, or expanding multiple reference sets for machine translation. For researchers not focused on these tasks, it can be difficult to develop a one-off system due to resource requirements.

To address this need, we are releasing a black box for generating sentential paraphrases: machine translation language packs. The language packs consist of prepackaged models for the Joshua 6 decoder (Post et al., 2015) and a monolingual "translation" grammar derived from the Paraphrase Database (PPDB) 2.0 (Pavlick et al., 2015). The PPDB provides tremendous coverage over English

text, containing more than 200 million paraphrases extracted from 100 million sentences (Ganitkevitch et al., 2013). For the first time, any researcher with Java 7 and Unix (there are no other dependencies) can generate sentential paraphrases without developing their own system. Additionally, the language packs include a web tool for interactively paraphrasing sentences and adjusting the parameters.

The language packs contain everything needed to generate sentential paraphrases in English:

- a monolingual synchronous grammar,
- a language model,
- a ready-to-use configuration file,
- the Joshua 6 runtime, so that no compilation is necessary,
- a shell script to invoke the Joshua decoder, and
- a web tool for interactive decoding and parameter configuration.

The system is invoked by a single command, either on a batch of sentences or as an interactive server.

Users can choose which size grammar to include in the language pack, corresponding to the PPDB pack sizes (S through XXXL).

In the rest of the paper, we will describe the translation model and grammar, provide examples of output, and explain how the configuration can be adjusted for specific needs.

2 Language pack description

Several different size language packs are available for download.[1] The components of the language packs are described below.

---

[1] `http://joshua-decoder.com/`
`language-packs/paraphrase/`

Proceedings of NAACL-HLT 2016 (Demonstrations), pages 62–66,
San Diego, California, June 12-17, 2016. ©2016 Association for Computational Linguistics

Grammar Our approach to sentential paraphrasing is analogous to machine translation. As a translation grammar, we use PPDB 2.0, which contains 170-million lexical, phrasal, and syntactic paraphrases (Pavlick et al., 2015). Each language pack contains a PPDB grammar that has been packed into a binary form for faster computation (Ganitkevitch et al., 2012), and users can select which size grammar to use. The rules present in each grammar are determined by the PPDB 2.0 score, which indicates the paraphrase quality (as given by a supervised regression model) and correlates strongly with human judgments of paraphrase appropriateness (Pavlick et al., 2015). Grammars of different sizes are created by changing the paraphrase score thresholds; larger grammars therefore contain a wider diversity of paraphrases, but with lower confidences.

Features Each paraphrase in PPDB 2.0 contains 44 features, described in Ganitkevitch and Callison-Burch (2014) and Pavlick et al. (2015). For each paraphrase pair, we call the input the *original* and the new phrase the *candidate*. Features can reflect just the candidate phrase or a relationship between the original and candidate phrases. Each of these features is assigned a weight, which guides the decoder's choice of paraphrases to apply to generate the final candidate sentence. All feature values are pre-calculated in PPDB 2.0.

Decoding The language packs include a compiled Joshua runtime for decoding, a script to invoke it, and configuration files for different tuned models. There is also a web-based tool for interactively querying a server version of the decoder for paraphrases. We include a 5-gram Gigaword v.5 language model for decoding. One or more language-model scores are used to rank translation candidates during decoding. The decoder outputs the n-best candidate paraphrases, ranked by model score.

3 Models

Each language pack has three pre-configured models to use either out of the box or as a starting point for further customization. There are tuned models for (1) sentence compression, (2) text simplification, and (3) a general-purpose model with hand-tuned weights. These models are distinguished only

by the different weight vectors, and are selected by point the Joshua invocation script to the corresponding configuration file.

3.1 Tuned models

We include two models that were tuned for (1) sentence compression and (2) simplification. The compression model is based on the work of Ganitkevitch et al. (2011), and uses the same features, tuning data, and objective function, PRÉCIS. The simplification model is described in Xu et al. (2016), and is optimized to the SARI metric. The system was tuned using the parallel data described therein as well as the Newsela corpus (Xu et al., 2015). There is no specialized grammar for these models; instead, the parameters were tuned to choose appropriate paraphrases from the PPDB.

Sample output generated with these models is shown in Table 1.

3.2 Hand-derived weights

To configure the general-purpose model, which generates paraphrases for no specific task, we examined the output of 100 sentences randomly selected from each of three different domains: newswire (WSJ 0–1 (Marcus et al., 1993)), "simple" English (the Britannica Elementary corpus (Barzilay and Elhadad, 2003)), and general text (the WaCky corpus (Baroni et al., 2009)). We systematically varied the weights of the Gigaword LM and the PPDB 2.0 score features and selected values that yielded the best output as judged by the authors. The parameters selected for the generic language packs are $weight_{\mathrm{lm}} = 10$ and $weight_{\mathrm{ppdb2}} = 15$, with all other weights are set to zero. Example output is shown in Table 1.

4 User customization

The language packs include configuration files with pre-determined weights that can be used on their own or as a jumping-off point for custom configurations. There are weights for each of the 44 PPDB 2.0 features as well as for the language model(s) used by the decoder. We encourage researchers to explore modifications to the model to suit their specific tasks, and we have clearly identified five aspects of the language packs that can be modified:

1. Alternate language models. The decoder can accept multiple LMs, and the packs include LMs es-

Compression
Orig: rice admits mistakes have been made by american administration in rebuilding iraq
Gen: rice admits mistakes <u>were</u> made by american administration in rebuilding iraq
Orig: partisanship is regarded as a crime , and pluralism is rejected , and no one in the shura council would seek to compete with the ruler or distort his image .
Gen: partisanship is regarded as a crime ☐ and pluralism is rejected ☐ and <u>none</u> in the shura council would seek to compete with the ruler or distort his image .
Simplification
Orig: fives is a british sport believed to derive from the same origins as many racquet sports .
Gen: fives is a british sport <u>thought</u> to <u>come</u> from the same <u>source</u> as many racquet sports .
Orig: in the soviet years , the bolsheviks demolished two of rostov 's principal landmarks — st alexander nevsky cathedral (1908) and st george cathedral in nakhichevan (1783-1807) .
Gen: in the soviet years , the bolsheviks <u>destroyed</u> two of rostov 's <u>key</u> landmarks — st alexander nevsky <u>church</u> (1908) and st george <u>church</u> in <u>naxçivan</u> (1783-1807) .
Generic
Orig: because the spaniards had better weapons , cortes and his army took over tenochtitlan by 1521 .
Gen: <u>as</u> the spaniards had better weapons , cortes and his <u>men</u> took over tenochtitlan by 1521 .
Orig: it was eventually abandoned due to resistance from the population .
Gen: it was <u>later</u> abandoned due to <u>opposition</u> from the population .

Table 1: Sample output from the three models. Underlines designate changed spans, and ☐ indicates deletions.

timated over newswire text and "simple" English. Other user-provided LMs can be used for tasks targeting different domains of text.

2. Rank output with a custom metric. The n-best candidate sentences are chosen by their score according to a given metric (LM score for the generic model, and PRÉCIS and SARI for the tuned models), however other metrics can be used instead.

3. Manually adjust parameters. The weights of the features discussed in Section 3 can be adjusted, as well as other PPDB feature weights. The web tool (Figure 1) allows users to select the weights for all of the features and see the top-5 candidates generated with those weights. Some of the more interpretable features to target include the length difference and entailment relations between the phrase original and candidate, as well as formality and complexity scores of the candidate paraphrase.

4. Optimize parameters with parallel data. For tailoring machine translation to a specific task, the weights given to each feature can be optimized to a given metric over a tuning set of parallel data. This metric is commonly BLEU in machine translation, but it can be a custom metric for a specific task, such as PRÉCIS for compression (Ganitkevitch et al., 2011) or SARI for simplification (Xu et al., 2016). The user needs to provide a parallel dataset for tuning, ideally with about 2,000 thousand sentences. The pipeline scripts in the Joshua decoder have options for optimization, with the user specifying the language pack grammar and parallel tuning data. The configuration file included in the language pack can be used as a template for tuning.

5 Interactive tool

Finally, we include a web tool that lets users interact with the decoder and choose custom weights (Figure 1). Once users have downloaded the tool kit, an included script lets them run the decoder as a server, and through the web interface they can type individual sentences and adjust model parameters. The interface includes an input text box (one sentence

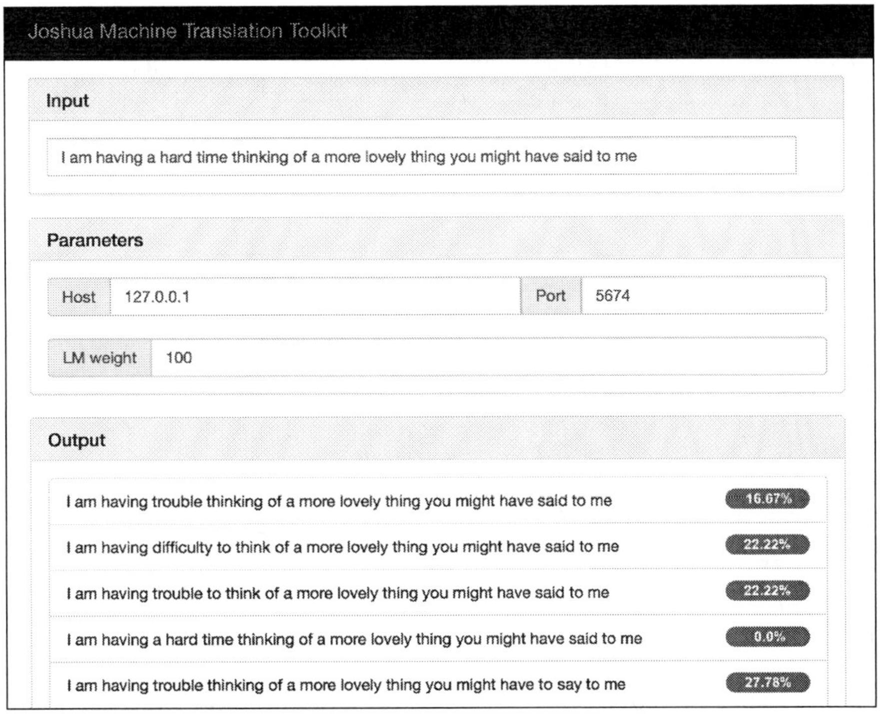

Figure 1: A screen shot of the web tool. The number to the right of each output sentence is the TER.

at a time), and slider bars to change the weights of any of the features used for decoding. Since this model has not been manually evaluated, we favor precision over recall and maintain a relatively conservative level of paraphrasing. The user is shown the top 10 outputs, as ranked by the sentence score. For each output sentence, we report the Translation Edit Rate (TER), which is the number of changes needed to transform the output sentence into the input (Snover et al., 2006).

This tool can be used to demonstrate and test a model or to hand-tune the model in order to determine the parameters for a configuration file to paraphrase a large batch of sentences. Detailed instructions for using the tool and shell scripts, as well as a detailed description of the configuration file, are available at the language pack home page: `http://joshua-decoder.com/language-packs/paraphrase/`

6   Related work

Previous work has applied machine translation techniques to monolingual sentence rewriting tasks. The most closely related works used a monolingual para-phrase grammar for sentence compression (Ganitkevitch et al., 2011) and sentence simplification (Xu et al., 2016), both of which developed custom metrics and task-specific features. Various other MT approaches have been used for generating sentence simplifications, however none of these used a general-purpose paraphrase grammar (Narayan and Gardent, 2014; Wubben et al., 2012, among others). Another application of sentential paraphrases is to expand multiple reference sets for machine translation (Madnani and Dorr, 2010).

PPDB has been used for many tasks, including recognizing textual entailment, question generation, and measuring semantic similarity.

These language packs were inspired by the foreign language packs released with Joshua 6 (Post et al., 2015).

7   Conclusion

We have presented a black box for generating sentential paraphrases: PPDB language packs. The language packs include everything necessary for generation, so that they can be downloaded and invoked with a single command. This toolkit can be used for a variety of tasks: as a helpful tool for writing (what is another way to express a sentence?); generating additional training or tuning data, such as multiple-references for machine translation or other text-to-text rewriting tasks; or for changing the style or tone of a text. We hope their ease-of-use will facilitate future work on text-to-text rewriting tasks.

Acknowledgments

This material is based upon work partially supported by the National Science Foundation Graduate Research Fellowship under Grant No. 1232825. This research was supported by the Human Language Technology Center of Excellence, and by gifts from the Alfred P. Sloan Foundation, Google, and Facebook. This material is based in part on research sponsored by the NSF grant under IIS1249516 and DARPA under number FA8750-13-20017 (the DEFT program). The U.S. Government is authorized to reproduce and distribute reprints for Governmental purposes. The views and conclusions contained in this publication are those of the authors and should not be interpreted as representing official policies or endorsements of DARPA and the U.S. Government.

References

Marco Baroni, Silvia Bernardini, Adriano Ferraresi, and Eros Zanchetta. 2009. The WaCky wide web: a collection of very large linguistically processed web-crawled corpora. *Language resources and evaluation*, 43(3):209–226.

Regina Barzilay and Noemie Elhadad. 2003. Sentence alignment for monolingual comparable corpora. In Michael Collins and Mark Steedman, editors, *Proceedings of the 2003 Conference on Empirical Methods in Natural Language Processing*, pages 25–32.

Juri Ganitkevitch and Chris Callison-Burch. 2014. The multilingual paraphrase database. In *LREC*, pages 4276–4283. Citeseer.

Juri Ganitkevitch, Chris Callison-Burch, Courtney Napoles, and Benjamin Van Durme. 2011. Learning sentential paraphrases from bilingual parallel corpora for text-to-text generation. In *Proceedings of the 2011 Conference on Empirical Methods in Natural Language Processing*, pages 1168–1179, Edinburgh, Scotland, UK., July. Association for Computational Linguistics.

Juri Ganitkevitch, Yuan Cao, Jonathan Weese, Matt Post, and Chris Callison-Burch. 2012. Joshua 4.0: Packing, PRO, and Paraphrases. In *Proceedings of the Seventh Workshop on Statistical Machine Translation*, pages 283–291, Montréal, Canada, June. Association for Computational Linguistics.

Juri Ganitkevitch, Benjamin Van Durme, and Chris Callison-Burch. 2013. PPDB: The paraphrase database. In *HLT-NAACL*, pages 758–764.

Nitin Madnani and Bonnie J. Dorr. 2010. Generating phrasal and sentential paraphrases: A survey of data-driven methods. *Computational Linguistics*, (Early Access):1–47.

Mitchell P Marcus, Mary Ann Marcinkiewicz, and Beatrice Santorini. 1993. Building a large annotated corpus of English: The Penn Treebank. *Computational linguistics*, 19(2):313–330.

Shashi Narayan and Claire Gardent. 2014. Hybrid simplification using deep semantics and machine translation. In *the 52nd Annual Meeting of the Association for Computational Linguistics*, pages 435–445.

Ellie Pavlick, Pushpendre Rastogi, Juri Ganitkevitch, Benjamin Van Durme, and Chris Callison-Burch. 2015. PPDB 2.0: Better paraphrase ranking, fine-grained entailment relations, word embeddings, and style classification. In *Proceedings of the 53rd Annual Meeting of the Association for Computational Linguistics and the 7th International Joint Conference on Natural Language Processing (Volume 2: Short Papers)*, pages 425–430, Beijing, China, July. Association for Computational Linguistics.

Matt Post, Yuan Cao, and Gaurav Kumar. 2015. Joshua 6: A phrase-based and hierarchical statistical machine translation system. *The Prague Bulletin of Mathematical Linguistics*, 104(1):5–16.

Matthew Snover, Bonnie Dorr, Richard Schwartz, Linnea Micciulla, and John Makhoul. 2006. A study of translation edit rate with targeted human annotation. In *Proceedings of Association for Machine Translation in the Americas*, pages 223–231.

Sander Wubben, Antal Van Den Bosch, and Emiel Krahmer. 2012. Sentence simplification by monolingual machine translation. In *Proceedings of the 50th Annual Meeting of the Association for Computational Linguistics: Long Papers-Volume 1*, pages 1015–1024. Association for Computational Linguistics.

Wei Xu, Chris Callison-Burch, and Courtney Napoles. 2015. Problems in current text simplification research: New data can help. *Transactions of the Association for Computational Linguistics*, 3:283–297.

Wei Xu, Courtney Napoles, Ellie Pavlick, Quanze Chen, and Chris Callison-Burch. 2016. Optimizing statistical machine translation for text simplification. *Transactions of the Association for Computational Linguistics*, 4.

A Tag-based English Math Word Problem Solver
with Understanding, Reasoning and Explanation

Chao-Chun Liang, Kuang-Yi Hsu, Chien-Tsung Huang,
Chung-Min Li, Shen-Yu Miao, Keh-Yih Su
Institute of Information Science, Academia Sinica, Taiwan
{ccliang, ianhsu, joecth, cmli, jackymiu, kysu}@iis.sinica.edu.tw

Abstract

This paper presents a tag-based statistical math word problem solver with understanding, reasoning, and explanation. It analyzes the text and transforms both body and question parts into their tag-based logic forms, and then performs inference on them. The proposed tag-based approach provides the flexibility for annotating an extracted math quantity with its associated syntactic and semantic information, which can be used to identify the desired operand and filter out irrelevant quantities. The proposed approach is thus less sensitive to the irrelevant information and could provide the answer more precisely. Also, it can handle much more problem types other than addition and subtraction.

1 Introduction

The math word problem (MWP) (Mukherjee and Garain, 2008) is frequently chosen to study natural language understanding due to the following reasons: (1) Since the answer for the MWP cannot be extracted by simply performing keyword/pattern matching, MWP can clearly show the merits of understanding and inference. (2) As MWP usually possesses less complicated syntax and requires less amount of domain knowledge, it can let the researcher focus on the task of understanding and reasoning. (3) The body part of MWP (which mentions the given information for solving the problem) consists of only a few sentences. The understand-

ing and reasoning procedure could be checked more efficiently. (4) The MWP solver has its own standalone applications such as *Computer Math Tutor* and *Helper for Math in Daily Life*.

Previous English MWP solvers can be classified into three categories. (1) Rule-based approaches with logic inference (Bobrow, 1964; Slagle, 1965), which apply rules to get the answer (via identifying entities, quantities, operations, etc.) with a logic inference engine. (2) Rule-based approaches without logic inference (Charniak, 1968 and 1969; Gelb, 1971; Ballard, 1979; Biermann and Ballard, 1980; Biermann et al., 1982; Fletcher, 1985; Dellarosa, 1986; Bakman, 2007; Liguda and Pfeiffer, 2012; Hosseini et al., 2014), which apply rules (usually defined as schemata) to get the answer without a logic inference engine. (3) Purely statistic-based approaches (Kushman et al., 2014; Roy et al., 2015), which use statistical models to identify entities, quantities, operations, and get the answer without conducting language analysis or inference.

The main problem of the rule-based approaches mentioned above is that the coverage rate problem is serious, as rules with wide coverage are difficult and expensive to construct. Also, it is awkward in resolving ambiguity problems. Besides, most of them only handle *addition and subtraction* these two math operations. On the other hand, the main problem of those approaches without adopting logic inference is that they cannot share the common reasoning part among various problem types. In contrast, the main problems of those purely statistical approaches are that they are sensitive to irrel-

67

Proceedings of NAACL-HLT 2016 (Demonstrations), pages 67–71,
San Diego, California, June 12-17, 2016. ©2016 Association for Computational Linguistics

evant information and that the performance deteriorates significantly when they encounter complicated problems (Hosseini et al., 2014), because the problem is solved without first understanding the text. Besides, they only handle algebra problems.

A *tag-based statistical English MWP solver* is thus proposed to perform understanding and reasoning, and avoid the problems mentioned above. The text of the MWP is first analyzed into its corresponding syntactic tree and then annotated with resolved co-reference chains. Afterwards, it is converted into the logic form via a few mapping rules. The obtained logic form is further mapped into the corresponding domain dependent generic concepts (also expressed in logic form). Finally, the logic inference is performed on those logic statements to get the answer. Various statistical classifiers are applied when there are choices.

Since different questions could be asked for the same given body text, we keep all syntactic relations in the logic form, which are regarded as various tags for selecting the appropriate operands related to the specified question. For example, *"Fred picked 36 limes"* will be converted into *"quan(q1, #, lime)&verb(q1, pick)&nsubj(q1, Fred) = 36"* (where tags are connected with logic *"&"*), in which the quantity *"36"* is identified with a label *"q1"* and attached with its associated tags. The proposed tag provides the flexibility for annotating a given math quantity with associated syntactic and semantic information, which can be used to identify the desired operand and filter out irrelevant quantities. It thus makes our MWP solver less sensitive to the irrelevant information and could provide the answer more precisely.

2 System Framework

The block diagram of proposed math word problem solver is shown in Figure 1. First, each sentence in an MWP is analyzed by the *Language Analyzer* (LA) module. The associated linguistic information is then sent to the *Solution Type Classifier* (STC) to find out the corresponding math operation. Afterwards, they are converted into the logic form by the *Logic Form Converter* (LFC). The *Inference Engine* (IE) then obtains the answer from those obtained logic expressions. Finally, the *Explanation Generator* (EG) module will explain how the answer is obtained according to the given

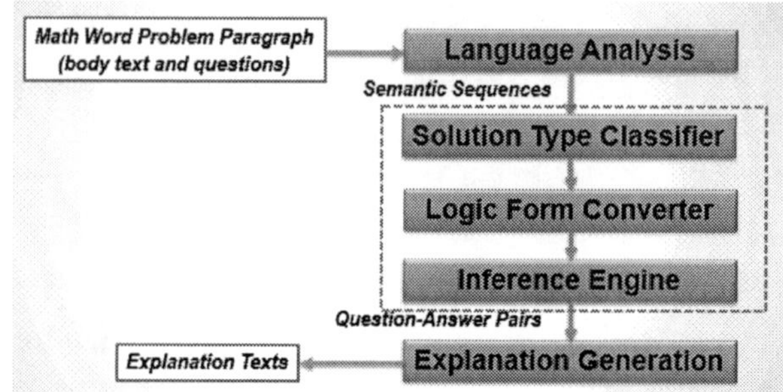

Figure 1: The block diagram of the proposed MWP solver

reasoning chain (Russel and Norvig, 2009).

Among those modules, the STC is responsible for suggesting a way (i.e., a solution type such as addition, subtraction, multiplication, division, etc.) to solve the problem for each question of the MWP. The LFC extracts the related facts from the given linguistic information and then represents those facts as the *first-order logic* (FOL) predicates/functions (Russel and Norvig, 2009). It also transforms each question into a FOL-like utility function according to the suggested solution type. The IE then derives new facts according to inference rules and old facts provided by the LFC. It is also responsible for providing utilities to perform math operations on related facts to get the answer. Detailed description of each module is given below.

2.1 Language Analysis

The Stanford CoreNLP suite (Manning et al., 2014) is adopted as our LA, which enables a list of annotators to generate the necessary linguistic information. The list includes: tokenization, sentence splitting, POS tagging, lemmatization, named entity recognition, parsing and co-reference resolution. The generated linguistic representation mainly depicts the syntactic relations between its words. To solve MWPs, it is crucial to know the relations between various entities. Dependency relation and co-reference resolution will provide such information.

2.2 Solution Type Identification

The STC will select a math operation (that LFC should adopt to solve the problem) based on the global information across various input sentences. Table 1 shows 12 different solution types currently provided. A SVM classifier with linear kernel functions (Chang and Lin, 2011) is used, and it adopted various feature-sets: (1) verb category related features, (2) various keyword indicators, and (3) different pattern-matching indicators for various specified aggregative patterns.

Addition	Multiplication	Surplus
Subtraction	Common-Division	Comparison
Sum	Floor-Division	Algebra
Difference	Ceil-Division	Time Variant

Table 1: Various solution types for solving the MWP

2.3 Logic Form Transformation

A two-stage approach is adopted to transform the linguistic representation of a sentence into its corresponding logic forms. In the first stage, the FOL predicates are generated (via a few deterministic mapping rules) by traversing the input linguistic representation. For example, the sentence *"Fred picks 36 limes"* will be transformed into the following FOL predicates separated by the logic AND operator "&":

$verb(v1,pick)\&nsubj(v1, Fred)\&$
$dobj(v1,n1)\&head(n1, lime)\&nummod(n1, 36)$

All the first arguments of the above FOL predicates (i.e., $v1$ and $n1$) are identifies, and the predicate-names are the domain-independent syntactic dependency relation of the constituents in the dependency structure.

The domain-dependent logic forms are non-deterministically generated in the second stage, which are derived from crucial math facts associated with quantities and relations between quantities. The following FOL function is used to describe the facts about quantities:

$$quan(quan_{id}, unit_{id}, object_{id}) = number \quad (1)$$

For example, *"quan(q1, #, lime)=36"* means *"36 limes"* (the second argument is the unit adopted, and ignored here). Besides domain-dependent facts, some auxiliary domain-independent facts associated with the math fact are also created in this stage to help the IE to find the solutions. For example, *"verb(q1, pick)&nsubj(q1, Fred)"* is the associated auxiliary facts of *"quan(q1, #, lime)=36"*. Those auxiliary facts are our proposed tags to make the system less sensitive to the irrelevant information. They also provide the flexibility of handling various kinds of possible questions.

The questions in the MWP will be transformed into FOL-like utility functions provided by the IE according to the suggested solution type. Take the question *"How many limes were picked in total?"* as an example. The STC will assign the *"Sum"* operation type to it. Based on that, the LFC will generate the FOL function *"Sum(quan(?q, #, limes), verb(?q, pick)"* to search all quantities that are associated with object *"lime"* and also attached with the verb tag *"pick"*.

2.4 Logic Inference

The IE is used to find the solution of an MWP. It is responsible for providing utilities to select desired facts and then obtain the answer by taking math operations on those selected facts. In addition, it is also responsible for using inference rules to derive new facts from those facts which are directly derived from the description of the MWP. Consider the example shown in Figure 2, the IE will first select all qualified quantities which match *"quan(?q, #, lime)"* and with a *"pick"* verb tag, and then perform a *"Sum"* operation on them. The irrelevant quantity *"quan(q4, #, pear)"* in that example is thus pruned out as its verb tag is *"drop"*, not *"pick"*. The answer is then obtained by summing those quantities $q1$, $q2$ and $q3$.

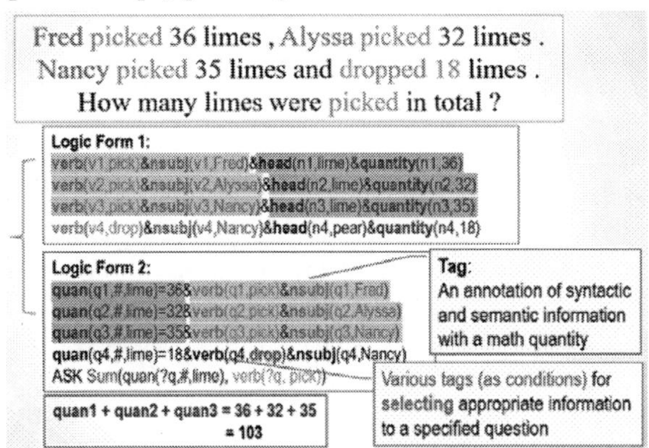

Figure 2: Logic form and logic inference of a *Sum* operation

2.5 Explanation Generation

Based on the reasoning chain generated from the IE (an example is shown in Figure 3), a math operation oriented approach is adopted to explain how the answer is obtained (Huang et al., 2015). A specific template is used to generate the explanation text for each kind of operation. Consider the example given in Figure 2, the template for *"Sum"* operation would be *"Totally **verb Child_1 + Child_2 + Child_3 + ...+ Child_n = Parent**".*. According to that template and the reasoning chain shown in Figure 3, The EG will generate the explanation text *"Totally pick 36 limes + 32 limes + 35 limes = 103 limes"*, which explains that the obtained answer is a summation of *"36 limes"*, *"32 limes"* and *"35 limes"*.

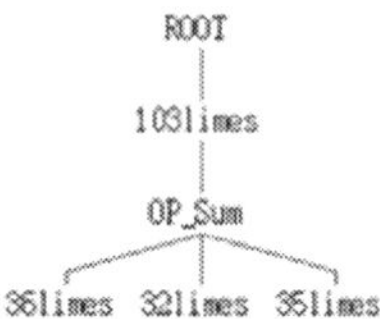

Figure 3: The reasoning Chain from the Inference Engine

3 Demonstration Outline

Examples:
Ex01 **[Addition]** Keith has 20 books . Jason has 21 books . How many books do they have together ?
Ex02 **[Subtraction]** Mary is baking a cake . The recipe wants 8 cups of flour . She already put in 2 cups . How many cups does she need to add ?
Ex03 **[Sum]** Jason picked 46 pears , Keith picked 47 pears , and Mike picked 12 pears from the pear tree . How many pears were picked in total ?
Ex04 **[TVQ-Final]** There are 43 pencils in the drawer and 19 pencils on the desk Dan placed 16 pencils on the desk . How many pencils are now there in total ?
Ex05 **[Irrelevant-Addition]** Joan grew 29 carrots and 14 watermelons . Jessica grew 11 carrots . How many carrots did they grow in all ?
Ex06 **[Irrelevant-Subtraction]** Melanie picked 7 plums and 4 oranges from the orchard . She gave 3 plums to Sam . How many plums does she have now ?
Ex07 **[Irrelevant-TVQ-Final (both Addition and Subtraction)]** Mary had 18 pencils and 6 erasers . Fred gave Mary 26 new pencils . Mary bought 40 pencils . How many pencils does Mary have now ?
Ex08 **[Irrelevant-Sum]** Fred picked 36 limes , Alyssa picked 32 limes . Nancy picked 35 limes and dropped 18 limes . How many limes were picked in total ?

Problem:

Submit

Figure 4: A web interface of the MWP solver

The MWP solver comprises a web user interface and a processing server. The web interface is used to input the problem and display the processing outputs (from each module) of the submitted MWP. The server is responsible to process the submitted problem to get the answer.

The user can use the web interface (Figure 4) to submit various MWPs. After an MWP is submitted, various processing modules will be invoked in a pipelined manner (shown in Figure 1) to solve the given problem. Once the process is finished, the user can browse the outputs generated from each module: (1) Parse Trees, Dependency and Co-Reference chains, which are from the language analyzer. (2) Corresponding linguistic representations, which are converted from the above language analysis result. (3) Suggested solution type, which identifies the desired math operation that the LFC should adopt. (4) Obtained logical forms, which

are transformed from the linguistic representation. (5) Generated reasoning chains and explanation text, which explains how the problem is solved.

An online demo can be found at:
`http://nlul.iis.sinica.edu.tw/Engl ishMathSolver/mathDemo.py`.

4 Experiments

The experiments are performed on the datasets MA1, MA2 and IXL provided by Hosseini et al. (2014), which are the first publically available datasets that can be used to compare various systems. The datasets include 395 problems and 1,483 sentences in total. MA1 covers simple MWPs on addition and subtraction for third, fourth, and fifth graders. Problems in MA2 includes more irrelevant information compared to the other two datasets, and IXL includes more information gaps (Hosseini et al., 2014). The performance of our system is compared with ARIS (Hosseini et al., 2014) which is a rule-based system that changes the entity attribute according to the schema. The result is also compared with KAZB (Kushman et al., 2014), which is a purely statistical approach that aligns the text with various pre-extracted equation templates. We follow the same evaluation setting. Table 2 shows that our system significantly outperforms them in overall performance.

	MA1	IXL	MA2	Total
3-fold Cross validation				
Our System	94.8	71.9	88.4	84.8
ARIS	83.6	75.0	74.4	77.7
KAZB	89.6	51.1	51.2	64.0
Gold Solution Type				
Our System	99.3	97.8	95.0	97.5

Table 2: Performance Comparison

5 Conclusion

A tag-based statistical framework is proposed to perform understanding and reasoning for solving MWPs. The adopted tag can help identify desired operands and filter out irrelevant quantities. Many rule-based approaches only handle addition and subtraction math operations, but we can solve much more problems types, such as Multiplication, Division, Comparison, Algebra, etc.

References

A. Mukherjee, U. Garain. 2008. A review of methods for automatic understanding of natural language mathematical problems, Artif Intell Rev.

D.G. Bobrow. 1964. Natural language input for a computer problem solving system, Ph.D. Dissertation, Massachusetts Institute of Technology.

J.R. Slagle. 1965. Experiments with a deductive question-answering program, J-CACM 8:792-798.

E. Charniak, CARPS. 1968. A program which solves calculus word problems, Report MAC-*TR-51*, Project MAC, MIT.

E. Charniak. 1969. Computer solution of calculus word problems, In Proc. of International Joint Conference on Artificial Intelligence.

D. Dellarosa. 1986. A computer simulation of children's arithmetic word-problem solving, Behavior Research Methods, Instraments, & Computers, 18 147-154.

Y. Bakman. 2007. Robust Understanding of Word Problems With Extraneous Information.

J.P. Gelb. 1971. Experiments with a natural language problem solving system, In Pros. of IJCAI-71.

B. Ballard. A. Biermann. 1979. PROGRAMMING IN NATURAL LANGUAGE : "NLC" AS A PROTO-TYPE, ACM-Webinar.

A.W. Biermann, B.W. Ballard 1980. Toward Natural Language Computation American Journal of Computational Linguistic, 6.

A. Biermann, R. Rodman, B. Ballard, T. Betancourt, G. Bilbro, H. Deas, L. Fineman, P. Fink, K. Gilbert, D. Gregory, F. Heidlage. 1982. INTERACTIVE NATURAL LANGUAGE PROBLEM SOLVING:A PRAGMATIC APPROACH In Pros. of the first conference on applied natural language processing.

C.R. Fletcher. 1985. COMPUTER SIMULATION -- Understanding and solving arithmetic word problems: A computer simulation, Behavior Research Methods, Instruments, & Computers, 17 565-571.

M.J. Hosseini, H. Hajishirzi, O. Etzioni, N. Kushman. 2014. Learning to Solve Arithmetic Word Problems with Verb Categorization, EMNLP.

N. Kushman, Y. Artzi, L. Zettlemoyer, R. Barzilay, 2014. Learning to Automatically Solve Algebra Word Problems, ACL.

C. Liguda, T. Pfeiffer, 2012, Modeling Math Word Problems with Augmented Semantic Networks, NLDB.

S.I. Roy, T.J.H. Vieira, D.I. Roth. 2015. Reasoning about Quantities in Natural Language, TACL, 3 1-13.

S. J. Russell and P. Norvig, 2009. Artificial Intelligence: A Modern Approach (3rd Edition), Prentice Hall.

C.D. Manning, M. Surdeanu, J. Bauer, J. Finkel, S. J. Bethard, and D. McClosky. 2014. The Stanford CoreNLP Natural Language Processing Toolkit In Proceedings of the 52nd Annual Meeting of the Association for Computational Linguistics: System Demonstrations, pp. 55-60.

C.-C. Chang, C.-J. Lin. 2011. LIBSVM: A library for support vector machines. ACM Transactions on Intelligent Systems and Technology.

Y.-C. Lin, C.-C. Liang, K.-Y. Hsu, C.-T. Huang, S.-Y. Miao, W.-Y. Ma, L.-W. Ku, C.-J. Liau, K.-Y. Su. 2015. Designing a Tag-Based Statistical Math Word Problem Solver with Reasoning and Explanation, International Journal of Computational Linguistics and Chinese Language Processing, 20(2), 1-26.

C.-T. Huang, Y.-C. Lin, K.-Y. Su. 2015. Explanation Generation for a Math Word Problem Solver, International Journal of Computational Linguistics and Chinese Language Processing, 20(2), 27-44.

Cross-media Event Extraction and Recommendation

Di Lu[1], Clare R. Voss[2], Fangbo Tao[3], Xiang Ren[3], Rachel Guan[1], Rostyslav Korolov[1],
Tongtao Zhang[1], Dongang Wang[4], Hongzhi Li[4], Taylor Cassidy[2], Heng Ji[1],
Shih-fu Chang[4], Jiawei Han[3], William Wallace[1], James Hendler[1], Mei Si[1], Lance Kaplan[2]

[1] Rensselaer Polytechnic Institute
{lud2,jih}@rpi.edu
[2] Army Research Laboratory, Adelphi, Maryland
{clare.r.voss,taylor.cassidy,lance.m.kaplan}.civ@mail.mil
[3] Computer Science Department, University of Illinois at Urbana-Champaign
hanj@illinois.edu
[4] Electrical Engineering Department, Columbia University
sfchang@ee.columbia.edu

Abstract

The sheer volume of unstructured multimedia data (e.g., texts, images, videos) posted on the Web during events of general interest is overwhelming and difficult to distill if seeking information relevant to a particular concern. We have developed a comprehensive system that searches, identifies, organizes and summarizes complex events from multiple data modalities. It also recommends events related to the user's ongoing search based on previously selected attribute values and dimensions of events being viewed. In this paper we briefly present the algorithms of each component and demonstrate the system's capabilities [1].

1 Introduction

Every day, a vast amount of unstructured data in different modalities (e.g., texts, images and videos) is posted online for ready viewing. Complex event extraction and recommendation is critical for many information distillation tasks, including tracking current events, providing alerts, and predicting possible changes, as related to topics of ongoing concern. State-of-the-art Information Extraction (IE) technologies focus on extracting events from a single data modality and ignore cross-media fusion. More importantly, users are presented with extracted events in a passive way (e.g., in a temporally ordered event chronicle (Ge et al., 2015)). Such technologies do not leverage user behavior to identify the event

properties of interest to them in selecting new scenarios for presentation.

In this paper we present a novel event extraction and recommendation system that incorporates advances in extracting events across multiple sources with data in diverse modalities and so yields a more comprehensive understanding of collective events, their importance, and their inter-connections. The novel capabilities of our system include:

- **Event Extraction, Summarization and Search**: extract concepts, events and their arguments (participants) and implicit attributes, and semantically meaningful visual patterns from multiple data modalities, and organize them into *Event Cubes* (Tao et al., 2013) based on Online Analytical Processing (OLAP). We developed a search interface to these cubes with a novel back-end event summarization component, for users to specify multiple dimensions in a query and receive single-sentence summary responses.

- **Event Recommendation**: recommend related events based on meta-paths derived from event arguments, and automatically adjust the ranking function by updating the weights of dimensions based on user browsing feedback.

2 Overview

2.1 System Architecture

The overall architecture of our system is illustrated in Figure 1. We first extract textual event information, as well as visual concepts, events and patterns from the raw multimedia documents to construct event cubes. Based on the event cubes, the search interface (Figure 2) returns the document that best

---

[1]The system demo is available at: http://nlp.cs.rpi.edu/multimedia/event/navigation_dark.html

72

Proceedings of NAACL-HLT 2016 (Demonstrations), pages 72–76,
San Diego, California, June 12-17, 2016. ©2016 Association for Computational Linguistics

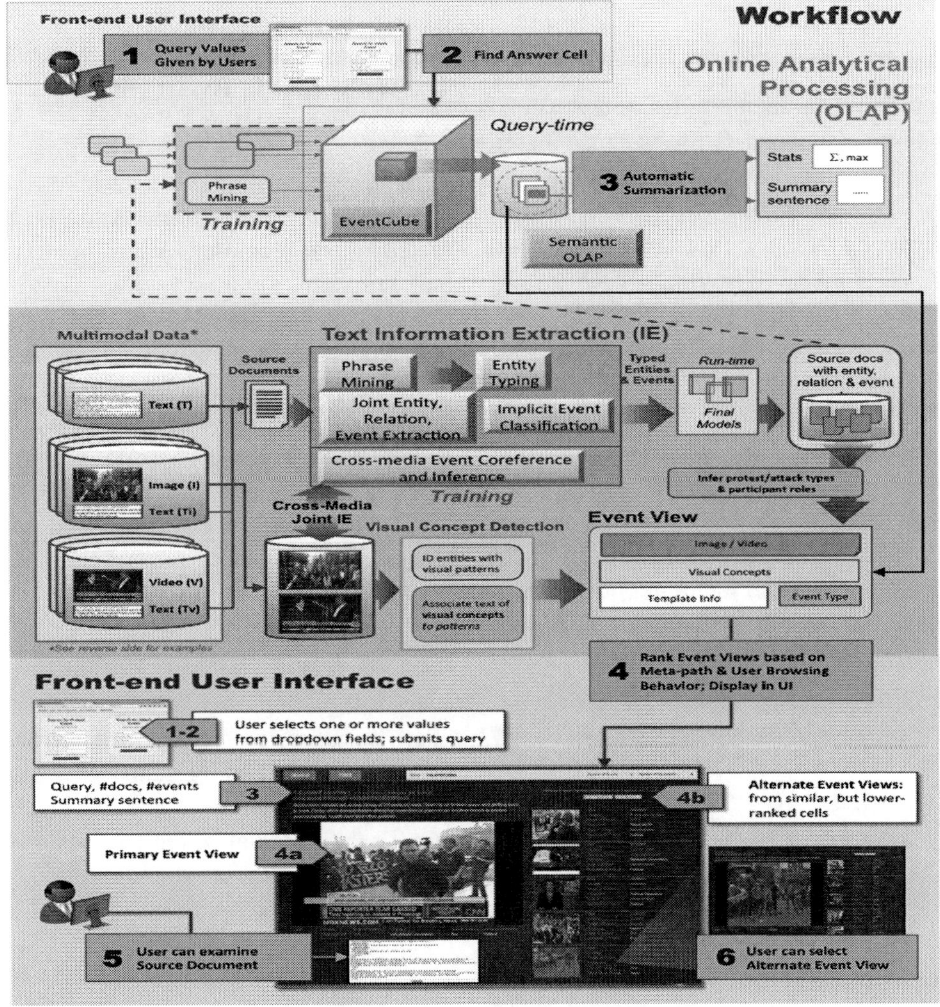

Figure 1: System Workflow.

matches the user's query as the first primary event for display. A query may consist of multiple dimensions. The recommendation interface displays multiple dimensions and rich annotations of the primary event, and recommends similar and dissimilar events to the user.

2.2 Data Sets

To demonstrate the capabilities of our system, we use two event types, *Protest* and *Attack*, as our case studies. We collected the following data sets:

- **Protest**: 59 protest incidents that occurred between January 2009 and December 2010, from 458 text documents, 28 images and 31 videos.
- **Attack**: 52 attack incidents that occurred between January 2014 and December 2015, from 812 text documents, 46 images and 6 videos.

3 Event Cube Construction and Search

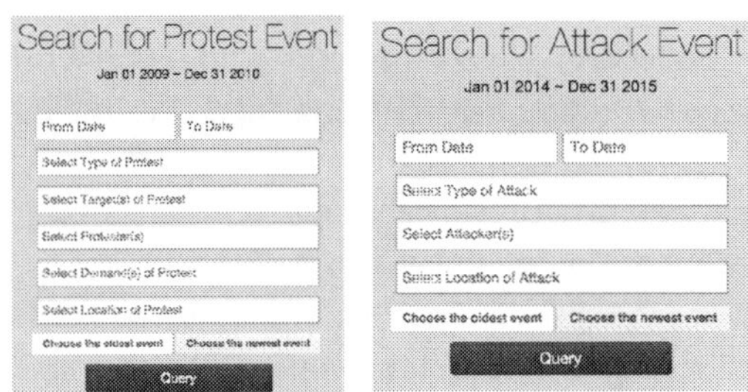

(a) Protest Event   (b) Attack Event

Figure 2: Search Interface.

3.1 Event Extraction

We apply a state-of-the-art English IE system (Li et al., 2014) to jointly extract entities, relations and events from text documents. This system is based on structured perceptron incorporating multiple levels of linguistic features. However, some important event attributes are not expressed by explicit textual clues. To enrich the profile of each protest event, the system identifies two additional implicit attributes that derive from social movement theories (Della Porta and Diani, 2009; Furusawa, 2006; Dalton, 2013):

- **Types of Protest**, including *demonstration, riot, strike, boycott, picket* and *individual protest.*
- **Demands of Protest**, indicating the hidden behavioral intent of protesters, about what they desire to change or preserve, including *pacifist, political, economic, retraction, financial, religious, human rights, race, justice, environmental, sports rivalry* and *social.*

We annotated 92 news documents, 59 of which contained protests, to learn a set of heuristic rules for automatically extracting these implicit attributes from the IE outputs of these documents.

3.2 Event Cube Construction and Search

Event extraction helps in converting unstructured texts into structured arguments and attributes (dimensions). However, a user may still need to "drill down," searching back through many documents and changing query selections before finding an item of interest. We use *EventCube* (Tao et al., 2013) to effectively organize and efficiently search relevant events, and measure event similarity based on multiple dimensions. *EventCube* is a general online analytical processing (OLAP) framework for importing any collection of multi-dimensional text documents and constructing text-rich data cube. *EventCube* differs from traditional search engines in that it returns *Top-Cells*, where relevant documents are aggregated by dimension combinations.

We regard each event as a data point associated with multiple dimension values. After a user inputs a multi-dimensional query in the search interface (Figure 2), we build inverted index upon the dimensions in Event Cube to return related events, which provides much more flexible matching com-

pared to keyword search.

4 Multi-media Event Illustration and Summarization

After the search interface retrieves the most relevant event ('primary event'), the user will be directed to the recommendation interface (Figure 3) and can start exploring various events. The user's initial query is displayed at the top (gray bar) and is updated to capture new user selections. The number of events that match the user's initial query and the number of documents associated with the primary event are displayed in the gray bar, at the far right side. In addition to text IE results, we apply the following multi-media extraction and summarization techniques to illustrate and enrich event profiles.

4.1 Summarization

From each set of relevant documents, we apply a state-of-the-art phrase mining method (Liu et al., 2016) to mine top-k representative phrases. Then we construct an affinity matrix of sentences and apply *spectral clustering* to find several clustering centers (i.e., representative sentences including the most important phrases) as the summary. The user is also provided two options to show the original documents and the document containing the summary.

4.2 Visual Information Extraction

For each event, we retrieve the most representative video/image online using the key-phrases such as date and entities as queries. Videos and images are often more impressive and efficient at conveying information. We first apply a pretrained convolutional neural network (CNN) architecture (Kuznetsova et al., 2012) to extract visual concepts from each video key frame based on the EventNet concept library (Ye et al., 2015). For example, the extracted visual concepts *"crowd on street, riot, demonstration or protest, people marching"* appear when the user's mouse is over the video of the primary event (Figure 3). Then we adopt the approach described in (Li et al., 2015) which applies CNN and association rule mining technique to generate visual patterns and extract semantically meaningful relations between visual and textual information to name the patterns.

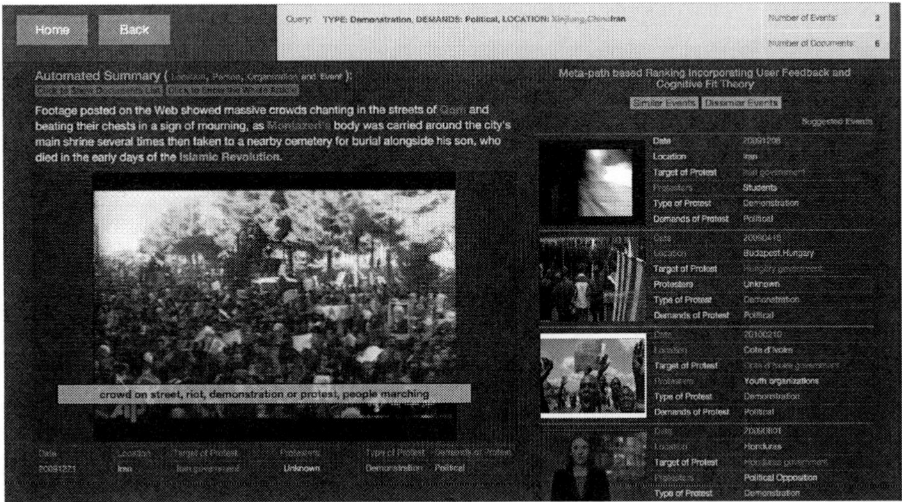

Figure 3: Recommendation Interface.

5   Event Recommendation

We rank and recommend events based on **meta paths** (Sun et al., 2011), by representing the whole data set as a heterogeneous network, that is composed of multi-typed and interconnected objects (e.g., events, location, protesters, target of protesters). A meta path is a sequence of relations defined between different object types. For protest events, we define six meta paths: "event-date-event", "event-location-event", "event-target of protest-event", "event-protesters-event", "event-type of protest-event" and "event-demand of protest-event"; and four meta paths for attack events: "event-date-event", "event-location-event", "event-attackers-event" and "event-type of attack-event".

The similarity between two events is the weighted sum of the six meta path similarities. The weights are assigned dynamically by the user's activity:

- When the user clicks on a certain image/video: assign 1.0 to all meta-path similarities.
- When the user clicks on a certain dimension X: 1.0 for the similarity based on Event-X-Event, and 0.2 to other meta-paths.

To illustrate the meta paths, the dimension names of recommended events are highlighted if they share the same dimensions with the primary event. Moreover, the system is switchable between recommending the most similar and most dissimilar events with a toggle button that the user can click.

6   Conclusions and Future Work

In this paper we present a cross-media event extraction and recommendation system which effectively aggregates and summarizes related complex events, and makes recommendations based on user interests. The current system interface incorporates a medium-level human agency (the capacity of an entity to act) by allowing a human user to provide relevance feedback while driving the browsing interests by multi-dimensional recommendations. We plan to follow the cognitive fit theory (Vessey, 1991) and conduct a series of human utility evaluations to formally quantify the impact of each new component and each data modality on enhancing the speed and quality of aggregating and summarizing event-related knowledge, detecting conflicts and errors, and generating alerts.

Acknowledgments

This work was supported by the U.S. ARL NS-CTA No. W911NF-09-2-0053, DARPA Multimedia Seedling grant, DARPA DEFT No. FA8750-13-2-0041 and NSF CAREER Award IIS-1523198. The views and conclusions contained in this document are those of the authors and should not be interpreted as representing the official policies, either expressed or implied, of the U.S. Government. The U.S. Government is authorized to reproduce and distribute reprints for Government purposes notwithstanding any copyright notation here on.

References

Russell J Dalton. 2013. *Citizen politics: Public opinion and political parties in advanced industrial democracies*. Cq Press.

Donatella Della Porta and Mario Diani. 2009. *Social movements: An introduction*. John Wiley & Sons.

Katsuto Furusawa. 2006. Participation and protest in the european union and the 'outsider'states. *Contemporary politics*, 12(2):207–223.

Tao Ge, Wenzhe Pei, Heng Ji, Sujian Li, Baobao Chang, and Zhifang Sui. 2015. Bring you to the past: Automatic generation of topically relevant event chronicles. In *Proceedings of the 53rd Annual Meeting of the Association for Computational Linguistics (ACL2015)*.

Polina Kuznetsova, Vicente Ordonez, Alexander C Berg, Tamara L Berg, and Yejin Choi. 2012. Collective generation of natural image descriptions. In *Proceedings of the 50th Annual Meeting of the Association for Computational Linguistics: Long Papers-Volume 1*.

Qi Li, Heng Ji, Yu Hong, and Sujian Li. 2014. Constructing information networks using one single model. In *Proceedings of the 2014 Conference of the Empirical Methods on Natural Language Processing (EMNLP2014)*.

Hongzhi Li, Joseph G. Ellis, and Shih-Fu Chang. 2015. Event specific multimodal pattern mining with image-caption pairs. *arXiv preprint arXiv:1601.00022*.

Jialu Liu, Xiang Ren, Jingbo Shang, Taylor Cassidy, Clare Voss, and Jiawei Han. 2016. Representing documents via latent keyphrase inference. In *Proceedings of the 25th international conference on World wide web*.

Yizhou Sun, Jiawei Han, Xifeng Yan, Philip S. Yu, and Tianyi Wu. 2011. Pathsim: Meta path-based top-k similarity search in heterogeneous information networks. In *Proceedings of 2011 Int. Conf. on Very Large Data Bases*.

Fangbo Tao, Kin Hou Lei, Jiawei Han, ChengXiang Zhai, Xiao Cheng, Marina Danilevsky, Nihit Desai, Bolin Ding, Jing Ge Ge, Heng Ji, et al. 2013. Eventcube: multi-dimensional search and mining of structured and text data. In *Proceedings of the 19th ACM SIGKDD international conference on Knowledge discovery and data mining*.

Iris Vessey. 1991. Cognitive fit: A theory-based analysis of the graphs versus tables literature. *Decision Sciences*, 22(2):219–240.

Guangnan Ye, Yitong Li, Hongliang Xu, Dong Liu, and Shih-Fu Chang. 2015. Eventnet: A large scale structured concept library for complex event detection in video. In *Proceedings of the 23rd ACM International Conference on Multimedia*.

SODA : Service Oriented Domain Adaptation Architecture for Microblog Categorization

Himanshu S. Bhatt, Sandipan Dandapat, Peddamuthu Balaji, Shourya Roy, Sharmistha* and Deepali Semwal*

Xerox Research Centre India, Bangalore, INDIA

{Himanshu.Bhatt, Sandipan.Dandapat, Balaji.Peddamuthu2, Shourya.Roy}@xerox.com
†{sharmistha@ssl.serc.iisc.in, semwaldeepali@gmail.com}

Abstract

We demonstrate SODA (Service Oriented Domain Adaptation) for efficient and scalable cross-domain microblog categorization which works on the principle of transfer learning. It is developed on a novel similarity-based iterative domain adaptation algorithm while extended with features such as active learning and interactive GUI to be used by business professionals. SODA demonstrates efficient classification accuracy on new collections while minimizing and sometimes eliminating the need for expensive data labeling efforts. SODA also implements an active learning (AL) technique to select informative instances from the new collection to seek annotations, if a small amount of labeled data is required by the adaptation algorithm.

1 Introduction

Online social media, such as Twitter.com, have become the de facto standard for sharing information, thoughts, ideas, personal feelings, daily happenings *etc.* which essentially led research and development in the field of social media analytics to flourish. Social media analytics provide actionable insights to business by analyzing huge amount of user generated content (UGC) (Sriram et al., 2010; Jo and Oh, 2011; He et al., 2012; Si et al., 2013; Nakov et al., 2013). Sentiment categorization, one of the common social media analytics task, segregates a collection of UGC into different buckets with positive, negative or neutral orientation (Liu and Zhang, 2012;

Thelwall et al., 2011; Bollen et al., 2009). This information is used to aggregate statistics and identify trends which are helpful for many applications viz. *Customer Care*, *Product Marketing*, *User Studies*.

Supervised machine learning (ML) techniques such as *text categorization* have played a key enabler role to classify microblogs into sentiment categories (Pang and Lee, 2008; Tan et al., 2009; Go et al., 2009; Fernández et al., 2014). These are trained on a fraction of annotated data as per client provided label set e.g. {*positive*, *negative*, and *neutral*} for a product/service/domain [1]. One of the obstacles towards rapid adoption of such systems is requirement of labeled tweets for developing ML-based models as it requires extensive human labeling efforts. Additionally, need of manual labeling slows down the process of categorization on high velocity social media which requires fast analytic insights. From our conversations with business professionals, we derived the need of a practical solution which would help them scale up across hundreds of collections and domains without the overhead of annotating data and building models from scratch every time for a new collection.

In this paper, we demonstrate *Service Oriented Domain Adaptation* (SODA) which offers social media analytics as-a-service to the users. Specifically, it provides sentiment categorization as-a-service that allows users to efficiently analyze comments from any new collection without the over-

---

*Work done at Xerox Research Centre India

[1]We use the word *collection* to describe tweets pertaining to a product/service/domain. For example tweets pertaining to *Apple iPhone Maps* and *Samsung S3 Battery* are two different collections. Tweets and comments are used interchangeably.

Proceedings of NAACL-HLT 2016 (Demonstrations), pages 77–81,
San Diego, California, June 12-17, 2016. ©2016 Association for Computational Linguistics

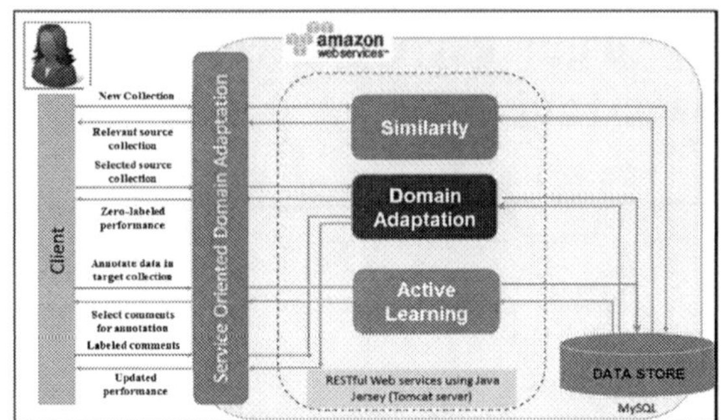

Figure 1: Overall architecture of SODA.

head of manual annotations or re-training models. It thus enables faster wide-scale analysis within and across different domains/industries such as telecom, healthcare, finance etc. SODA is based on an iterative ensemble based adaptation technique (Bhatt et al., 2015) which gradually transfers knowledge from the source to the new target collection while being cognizant of similarity between the two collections. It has been extensively evaluated by business professionals in a user-trial and on a benchmark dataset.

2 SODA Features

Figure 1 illustrates the architecture of SODA comprising three primary modules, 1) similarity, 2) domain adaptation, and 3) active learning. The first two modules use unlabeled data from the new collection while the optional third module helps in creating labeled data for enhanced classification performance. These modules are explained below.

2.1 Similarity

In social media analytics, especially for sentiment categorization, there exist numerous collections about different products or services where labeled data is available and thus can be used to adapt to a new unlabeled collection. Given a target collection, the key question is to identify the best possible source collection to adapt from. The similarity module in SODA identifies the best adaptable source collection based on the similarity between the source and target collections. This is based on the observations from existing literature (Bhatt et al., 2015; Blitzer et al., 2007) which suggest that if the source and target collections are similar, the adaptation performance tends to be better than if the two collections are dissimilar. The similarity module in SODA is capable of computing different kinds of

lexical, syntactic, and semantic similarities between unlabeled target and labeled source collections. For this demonstration on sentiment categorization from social media data, it measures cosine similarity between the comments in each collection and computes sim as the similarity score.

2.2 Domain Adaptation

The heart of SODA is the adaptation module that works on two principles, *generalization* and *adaptation*. During generalization, it learns shared common representation (Blitzer et al., 2007; Ji et al., 2011; Pan et al., 2010) which minimizes the divergence between two collections. We leverage one of the widely used structural correspondence learning (SCL) approach (Blitzer et al., 2007) to compute shared representations. The idea adhered here is that a model learned on the shared feature representation using labeled data from the source collection will also generalize well on the target collection. Towards this, we learn a model (C_S) on the shared feature representation from the source collection, referred to as "source classifier". C_S is then used to predict labels for the pool of unlabeled instances from the target collection, referred to as P_u, using the shared representations. All instances in P_u which are predicted with a confidence (α_1) higher than a predefined threshold (θ_1) are moved to the pool of pseudo-labeled target instances, referred to as P_s. We now learn a target domain model C_T on P_s using the target specific representation, referred to as "target classifier".

C_T captures a separate view of the target instances than the shared representation and hence brings in discriminating target specific information which is useful for categorization in target collection. For further adaptation, the source (C_S) and target (C_T) classifiers are combined in a weighted ensemble (E) with w_s and w_t as the corresponding weights and iterate over the remaining unlabeled instances in P_u. In each iteration, the ensemble processes the remaining instances and iteratively adds confidently predicted instances to P_s which are used to re-train/update C_T. This iterative process continues till all instances in P_u are confidently labeled or a maximum number of iterations is reached. Transfer occurs within the ensemble where the source classifier progressively facilitates the learning of tar-

Algorithm 1 Adaptation Algorithm

Input: $C_s, Q, C_t, P_s, \& P_u$.
Iterate: $l = 0$: till $P_u = \{\phi\}$
Process: Construct ensemble $E \rightarrow w_l^s C_s + w_l^t C_t$. Initialize w_l^s & w_l^t tos 0.5.
  for $i = 1$ **to** n (size of P_u) **do**
    Predict labels: $E(Q\mathbf{x}_i, \mathbf{x}_i) \rightarrow \hat{y}_i$; confidence of prediction: α_i.
    if $\alpha_i > \theta_2$ **then**
      Move i^{th} instance from P_u to P_s with pseudo label $\hat{y}_i$.
    end if.
  end for.
  Re-train C_t & update w_l^s and w_l^t as:
$$w_{(l+1)}^s = \frac{(sim*w_l^s*I(C_s))}{(sim*w_l^s*I(C_s)+(1-sim)*w_l^t*I(C_t))}$$
$$w_{(l+1)}^t = \frac{((1-sim)*w_l^t*I(C_t))}{(sim*w_l^s*I(C_s)+(1-sim)*w_l^t*I(C_t))}$$
end iterate.
Output: Final C_t and updated weights w^s and w^t

get classifier by providing pseudo labeled instances. The weights of the individual classifiers are updated, as a function of error ($I(\cdot)$) and the similarity (sim) between the collections, which gradually shift the emphasis from source to the target classifier. Finally, the ensemble is used to predict labels for future unseen instances in the target collection. Algorithm 1 summarizes our approach (refer (Bhatt et al., 2015) for more details).

2.3 Active Learning

SODA also implements an active learning module to allow users to annotate a few selected informative comments from the target collection. These comments are selected using cross entropy difference (CED) (Axelrod et al., 2011) such that the difference with source collection and the similarity with target collection is maximized. It selects comment(s) from target collection that have low CED score i.e. comments that have high entropy with respect to source $H_S(\cdot)$ and low entropy with respect to target collection $H_T(\cdot)$ as in Equation (1).

$$CED(s) = H_T(s) - H_S(s) \qquad (1)$$

Note, this active learning module is optional and should be used when the adaptation performance with unlabeled instances is not satisfactory. More and more instances can be annotated in multiple rounds till a satisfactory performance is achieved. These annotated instances are used to build a stronger target classifier for the ensemble based adaptation algorithm.

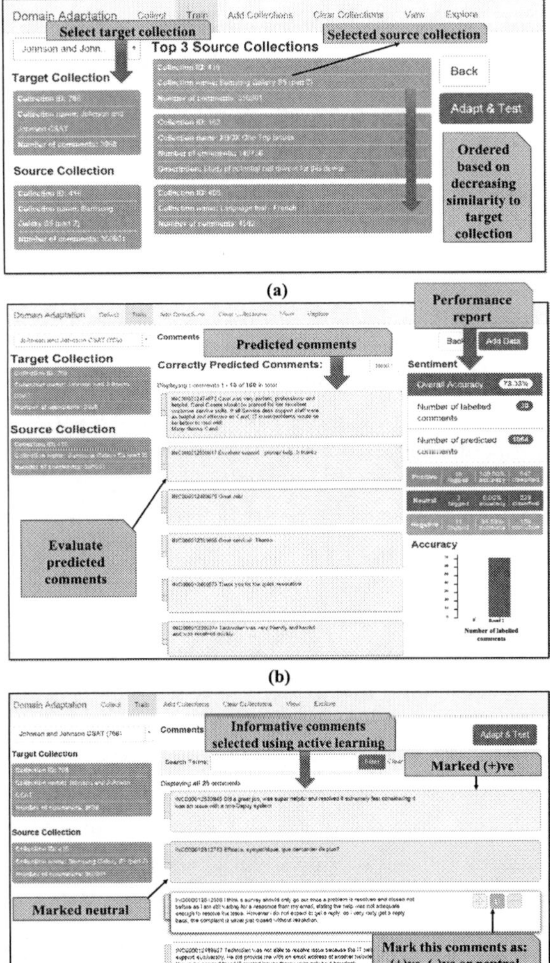

Figure 2: Interactive GUI of service oriented domain adaptation (SODA) (best viewed in color).

3 Design and Internals

Figure 2(a) illustrates the interactive user interface (UI) of SODA where one can select a new target collection for the analysis task (i.e. sentiment categorization). For a new target collection, it identifies relevant adaptable source collections based on their similarity. One can select any of the candidate source collections (selected collection highlighted in Figure 2(a)) and adapt. Figure 2(b) shows the performance report along with the predicted comments from the target collection. User evaluates the adaptation performance in unlabeled target collection by analyzing the predicted comments and decides whether to annotate additional comments in

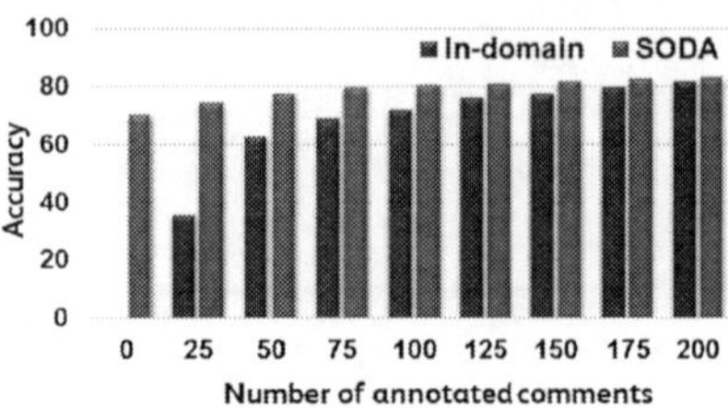

Figure 3: The effect of labeled comments on the performance while adapting from Coll-1 → Coll-6.

target collection? If yes, Figure 2(c) lists a few informative comments selected using the active learning module to seek annotations. One can mark these comments as positive, negative or neutral and subsequently adapt using these labeled instances from the target collection. Figure 2(b) also shows the adaptation performance with a few labeled instances in the target collection. One can continue annotating more instances in the target collection until satisfactory performance is achieved. For more detailed demonstration, please refer to the video.[2]

The interactive UI of SODA is developed using Ruby on Rails framework. All collections are managed in MySQL server. All three modules in SODA fetch data from the server and write the output back to the server. All modules work in real time enabling the system to be highly responsive to the user. The application is hosted on Amazon AWS as RESTful web services using Java Jersey (Tomcat server) that act as a bridge between the UI and back end.

4   User Trial & Experimental Results

To evaluate the overall experience, a user trial was conducted where several business professionals provided feedback on SODA. The objective was to evaluate the overall usability, reduction in required efforts, and the performance on the new target collections. The overall evaluation rated SODA 5 on usability and 4 for reduction in efforts (1 being worst & 5 being the best). Table 1 reports the classification accuracy of SODA with few labeled comments from the target collection (ranging from 0 to 100). It also reports the performance of the in-domain classifier which is trained and tested on data from the same collection. *Coll-1* to *Coll-8* refer to collections pertaining to *marketing & sales, comcast support,*

[2]https://www.youtube.com/watch?v=
zKnP5QEHVAE

Table 1: User-trial results on social media data.

Source	Target	Accuracy with annotations					In-domain
		0	25	50	75	100	
Coll-1	Coll-6	70	74	77	79	**80**	71.7
Col-2	Coll-8	73	45	71	73	**79**	74.5
Coll-3	Coll-5	87	94	94	93	**95**	92.0
Coll-4	Coll-7	83	84	94	96	**96**	85.7

Table 2: Results on the Amazon review dataset.

Target	Source	BL	SCL	SODA	In-domain
B	E	61.5	76.1	78.9	**80.4**
	K	68.4	66.2	74.8	
	D	60.1	77.6	80.0	
E	B	68.2	77.8	80.3	84.4
	D	61.5	74.1	76.4	
	K	76.2	83.1	**85.2**	
K	B	71.7	78.8	80.1	87.7
	D	60.3	79.4	82.0	
	E	73.2	83.8	**87.9**	
D	B	63.5	74.2	81.9	**82.4**
	E	62.3	74.8	80.1	
	K	67.4	76.5	78.8	

DirectTV support, ASUS, Johnson & Johnson CSAT, Apple iPhone6, and *HUWAEI* respectively. Figure 3 compares the effect of adding labeled comments in batches of 25 comments at-a-time. When there is no labeled data in the target collection, in-domain classifier can not be applied while SODA still yields good classification accuracy. Moreover, SODA consistently performs better than the in-domain classifier with same amount of labeled data.

We also evaluated the performance of domain adaptation (DA) module of SODA on the Amazon review dataset (Blitzer et al., 2007) which is a benchmark dataset for sentiment categorization. It has 4 domains, namely, books(**B**), dvds(**D**), electronics(**E**), and kitchen(**K**) each with 2000 reviews divided equally into positive and negative reviews. Table 2 shows that DA module of SODA outperforms 1) a widely used domain adaptation technique , namely, structural correspondence learning (SCL) (Blitzer et al., 2007; Blitzer et al., 2006), 2) the baseline (**BL**) where a classifier trained on one domain is applied on another domain, and 3) the in-domain classifier. Note that in Table 2, the performance of DA module of SODA is reported when it does not use any labeled instances from the target domain.

5   Conclusion

We demonstrated SODA for efficient microblog categorization on new social media collections with minimum (or sometimes no) need of manual annotations; thus, enabling faster and efficient analytics.

References

Amittai Axelrod, Xiaodong He, and Jianfeng Gao. 2011. Domain adaptation via pseudo in-domain data selection. In *Proceedings of the Conference on Empirical Methods in Natural Language Processing*, pages 355–362.

Himanshu Sharad Bhatt, Deepali Semwal, and Shourya Roy. 2015. An iterative similarity based adaptation technique for cross-domain text classification. In *Proceedings of Conference on Computational Natural Language Learning*.

John Blitzer, Ryan McDonald, and Fernando Pereira. 2006. Domain adaptation with structural correspondence learning. In *Proceedings of Conference on Empirical Methods in Natural Language Processing*, pages 120–128.

John Blitzer, Mark Dredze, and Fernando Pereira. 2007. Biographies, bollywood, boomboxes and blenders: Domain adaptation for sentiment classification. In *Proceedings of Association for Computational Linguistics*, pages 187–205.

Johan Bollen, Alberto Pepe, and Huina Mao. 2009. Modeling public mood and emotion: Twitter sentiment and socio-economic phenomena. *CoRR*.

Javi Fernández, Yoan Gutiérrez, José M Gómez, and Patricio Martınez-Barco. 2014. Gplsi: Supervised sentiment analysis in twitter using skipgrams. In *Proceedings of International Workshop on Semantic Evaluation (SemEval)*, pages 294–299.

Alec Go, Richa Bhayani, and Lei Huang. 2009. Twitter sentiment classification using distant supervision. *CS224N Project Report, Stanford*, 1:12.

Yulan He, Chenghua Lin, Wei Gao, and Kam-Fai Wong. 2012. Tracking sentiment and topic dynamics from social media. In *Proceedings of International AAAI Conference on Weblogs and Social Media*.

Yang-Sheng Ji, Jia-Jun Chen, Gang Niu, Lin Shang, and Xin-Yu Dai. 2011. Transfer learning via multi-view principal component analysis. *Journal of Computer Science and Technology*, 26(1):81–98.

Yohan Jo and Alice H Oh. 2011. Aspect and sentiment unification model for online review analysis. In *Proceedings of International Conference on Web Search and Data Mining*, pages 815–824.

Bing Liu and Lei Zhang. 2012. A survey of opinion mining and sentiment analysis. In *Mining Text Data*, pages 415–463.

Preslav Nakov, Zornitsa Kozareva, Alan Ritter, Sara Rosenthal, Veselin Stoyanov, and Theresa Wilson. 2013. Semeval-2013 task 2: Sentiment analysis in twitter.

Sinno Jialin Pan, Xiaochuan Ni, Jian-Tao Sun, Qiang Yang, and Zheng Chen. 2010. Cross-domain sentiment classification via spectral feature alignment. In *Proceedings International Conference on World Wide Web*, pages 751–760.

Bo Pang and Lillian Lee. 2008. Opinion mining and sentiment analysis. *Foundations and trends in information retrieval*, 2(1-2):1–135.

Jianfeng Si, Arjun Mukherjee, Bing Liu, Qing Li, Huayi Li, and Xiaotie Deng. 2013. Exploiting topic based twitter sentiment for stock prediction. In *Proceedings of Association for Computational Linguistics*, volume 2013, pages 24–29.

Bharath Sriram, Dave Fuhry, Engin Demir, Hakan Ferhatosmanoglu, and Murat Demirbas. 2010. Short text classification in twitter to improve information filtering. In *Proceedings of International ACM SIGIR conference on Research and Development in Information Retrieval*, pages 841–842.

Songbo Tan, Xueqi Cheng, Yuefen Wang, and Hongbo Xu. 2009. Adapting naive bayes to domain adaptation for sentiment analysis. In *Advances in Information Retrieval*, pages 337–349.

Mike Thelwall, Kevan Buckley, and Georgios Paltoglou. 2011. Sentiment in twitter events. *Journal of the American Society for Information Science and Technology*, 62(2):406–418.

Lecture Translator
Speech translation framework for simultaneous lecture translation

Markus Müller, Thai Son Nguyen, Jan Niehues, Eunah Cho, Bastian Krüger
Thanh-Le Ha, Kevin Kilgour, Matthias Sperber, Mohammed Mediani
Sebastian Stüker, Alex Waibel
Institute for Anthropomatics and Robotics
Karlsruhe Institute of Technology
Adenauerring 2, 76131 Karlsruhe, Germany
m.mueller@kit.edu

Abstract

Foreign students at German universities often have difficulties following lectures as they are often held in German. Since human interpreters are too expensive for universities we are addressing this problem via speech translation technology deployed in KIT's lecture halls. Our simultaneous lecture translation system automatically translates lectures from German to English in real-time. Other supported language directions are English to Spanish, English to French, English to German and German to French. Automatic simultaneous translation is more than just the concatenation of automatic speech recognition and machine translation technology, as the input is an unsegmented, practically infinite stream of spontaneous speech. The lack of segmentation and the spontaneous nature of the speech makes it especially difficult to recognize and translate it with sufficient quality. In addition to quality, speed and latency are of the utmost importance in order for the system to enable students to follow lectures. In this paper we present our system that performs the task of simultaneous speech translation of university lectures by performing speech translation on a stream of audio in real-time and with low latency. The system features several techniques beyond the basic speech translation task, that make it fit for real-world use. Examples of these features are a continuous stream speech recognition without any prior segmentation of the input audio, punctuation prediction, run-on decoding and run-on translation with continuously updating displays in order to keep the latency as low as possible.

1 Introduction

The rapid development of communication technology nowadays makes it easier than ever before to communicate with other people independent of distance. With distances becoming irrelevant, one of the last barriers that hinders communications are different languages. Although English has become a lingua franca in large parts of the world, in many situations and for many people it is not an option. The different languages in the world also carry cultural heritage that needs to be protected. Forcing people to speak the same language will lead to a sever loss of cultural diversity.

There exist multiple possibilities to overcome this language divide. One possibility is to use interpreters for simultaneous interpretation. But since this is a very costly method, it is only possible in certain areas. One example is the European Parliament, where the demand for translation services is met by human interpreters.

Another area that can benefit from translation services are universities in non English speaking countries. Looking at the statistics, universities in English speaking countries have on average a higher percentage of students from abroad. One reason for this difference is the language barrier. While offering lectures in English might increase a university's attractiveness towards foreign students it is not desirable due to the loss in cultural identity and intellectual diversity that occurs when universities around the world stop teaching in their native language. Unlike the European Parliament, universities do not have the funds to employ sufficient amounts of human interpreters to simultaneously translate their

Proceedings of NAACL-HLT 2016 (Demonstrations), pages 82–86,
San Diego, California, June 12-17, 2016. ©2016 Association for Computational Linguistics

lectures. Therefore, we developed a fully automatic translation solution that fits a university's budget and deployed it within the Karlsruhe Institute of Technology (KIT). By combining state-of-the-art automatic speech recognition (ASR) and machine translation (MT) with auxiliary technologies, such as re-segmentation, punctuation prediction, and unsupervised speaker and domain adaptation we created a system that performs this task.

Developing systems for simultaneous translation poses several challenges. While the output should be of reasonable quality in order to being useful, the system is required to produce it in a timely fashion. Interactive scenarios like university lectures demand low latency. The delay of the output should be as low as possible in order to match the slides and the lecturers gestures. Due to reasons, such as multimodal channels for the consumer and the lack of a need of additional technology in the lecture hall, we display the translation result as captions in a web browser that students can view on their own devices, such as laptops, tablets and smart phones. Preliminary studies have shown that textual output is easier to digest than synthesized speech, especially if it does contain errors. Lately, we introduced various improvements in our setup to decrease the latency, e.g., by outputting preliminary captions fast and, if necessary, updating parts as both the transcription and translation hypotheses stabilize over time as more context is becoming available.

2 Related Work

The development of systems for speech translation started in the 90s. First systems were able to translate very domain specific and formalized dialogues. Later, systems supported greater variety in language, but were still built for specific domains (Stüker et al., 2007).

Despite a difference in the overall quality of the translations, MT systems suffer from not being able to anticipate context like human interpreters. MT systems are unable to do so because of the lack of background and context knowledge. This results in a higher delay of the translation. But there has been some research towards the reduction of the latency and the translation of incomplete utterances (Fügen and Kolss, 2007), (Sridhar et al., 2013), (Oda et al., 2015). The goal is to find the optimal threshold between quality and latency (Shavarani et al., 2015), (Yarmohammadi et al., 2013), (Oda et al., 2014).

With ongoing research and development, the systems have matured over the years. In order to assess whether our system helps students to better understand lectures, we have conducted a user study (Müller et al., 2016) (to appear). The outcome was that students actually benefit from our system.

3 Speech Translation Framework

The Speech Translation Framework used for the lecture translation system is a component based architecture. It is designed to be flexible and distributed. There are 3 types of components: A central server, called the "mediator", "workers" for performing different tasks and clients that request certain services. Our setup has 3 different kinds of workers: ASR systems, punctuation predictors and MT systems. But the communication protocol itself does not distinguish between these different types and does not limit the types of work be to performed.

Each worker registers on the central mediator, providing a "fingerprint" and a name the mediator. The fingerprint tells the mediator which type of service the worker provides. Based on these fingerprints, the mediator selects the appropriate chain of workers to perform the requested task. E.g., if a client asks for a Spanish transcription of English audio, the mediator would first select an English ASR worker and would then route the output through a segmenter for English Text and finally run the output through the MT to translate the English text into Spanish.

4 Lecture Translator

4.1 System Description

The Lecture Translator (LT) at KIT was implemented based on the speech translation framework described above (Cho et al., 2013). We developed all workers in-house. The audio is being transcribed using the Janus Recognition Toolkit (JRTk) (Woszczyna et al., 1994), which features the IBIS single-pass decoder (Soltau et al., 2001). The acoustic model was trained using several hundred hours of recordings from lectures and talks.

Figure 1: *User interface of the Lecture Translator showing an ongoing session*

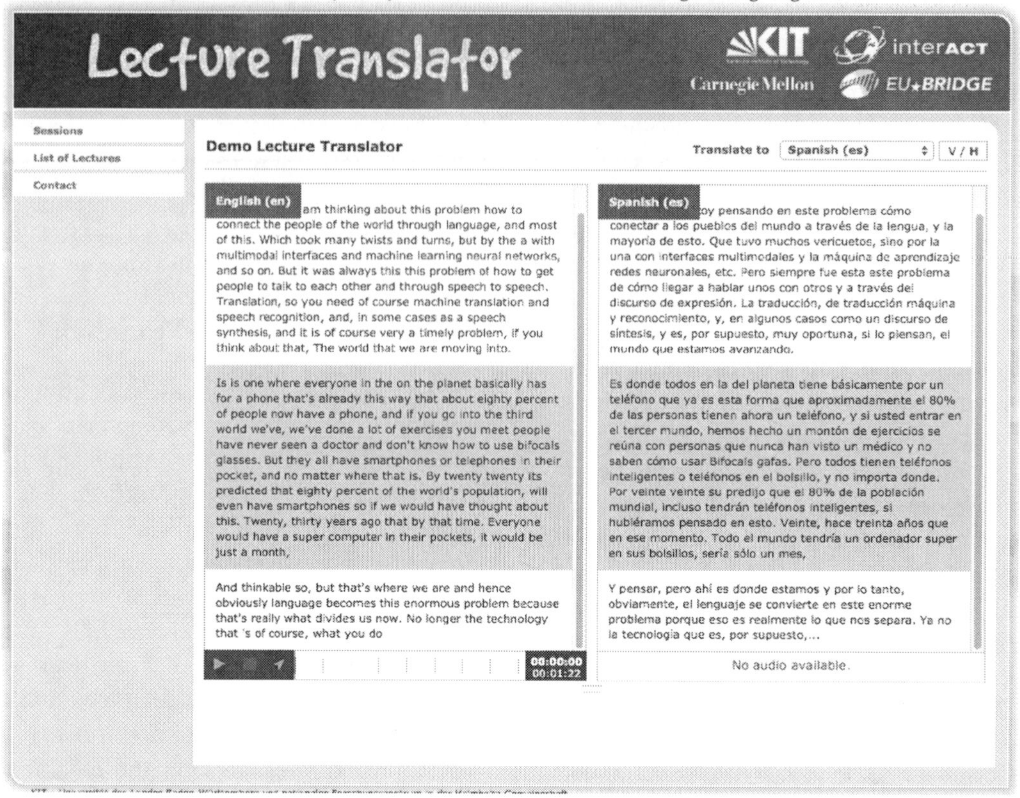

For translation, we used a phrase-based decoder (Vogel, 2003). It uses advanced models for domain adaptation, bilingual and cluster language models in addition to Discriminative Word Lexica for producing the translation. We use POS-based word reordering (Rottmann and Vogel, 2007; Niehues and Kolss, 2009). The translation model was trained on 1.8 million sentences of parallel data. It includes data from various sources and in-domain data.

4.2 System Operation

The LT is in regular use for multiple years now and currently translates approx. 10 different lectures per term. We have installed this system in multiple lecture halls, among them KIT's largest hall, called "Audimax".

In each hall, the system is tightly integrated in the PA to ensure smooth operation. The audio is captured via the PA from the microphone that the lecturer uses to address the audience. The operation of the system itself is time controlled: It starts at the time when the lecture begins and runs until the lecture is finished. The workers of the system run distributed over multiple servers. This ensures overall system stability as it allows for fail-overs in case of server failure. There are multiple instances of each worker running in order to translate multiple lectures in parallel.

During the every day operation the LT does not require any special preparations from the lecturer prior to each lecture because of the integration into the PA and the time controlled operation. But the quality of the output can be improved if slides or lecture notes are being made available beforehand. This way, the system is able to adapt to the specific domain of a lecture by covering any terms or named entities special to this lecture. The second advantage that we use is that the same lectures are usually given repeatedly in different terms. This way, we can use several iterations of the same lecture to improve the performance. Using the collected data, we adapt the ASR to certain speakers and ASR and MT to certain topics.

As the goal is to provide the service as cost efficient as possible, we decided to use the devices that the students already own to display the output. The Lecture Translator is therefore a web based service. Listeners wanting to see the transcription can go to the website of the service[1] to see a list of currently running sessions. Depending on the permissions from the lecturer, the output can be displayed either only to people who know the password or viewers from within KIT or globally. A screen-shot from the user interface running an active session is shown in Figure 1. The transcription is displayed on the left part of the window while the translation is shown on the right. The user has the choice of various target languages, depending on the source language.

Our system currently supports the translation from German audio into English and French text. Using English as input language, the system is able to produce French, German and Spanish output.

5 Intermediate Output

One of the main problems of earlier versions of our speech translation framework was the latency of the system. Since machine translation systems are usually trained on sentence level, the translation can only be displayed if the whole sentence is recognized. In order to overcome this drawback, we extended our framework to handle intermediate outputs. This allows us to display a translation of a partly recognized sentence and later update it with the translation of the whole sentence. The same technique is also be applied to the to display intermediate hypotheses from the speech recognition that are later updated.

In the framework, each message has properties defining the time span to which its content relates. For example, if the MT component generates a new translation, it will generate a message with the start and end time of the translation and the translation itself. In the baseline system, the start time has to be equal or greater than the end time of all previous messages.

In order to limit the complexity, we only allow to update the most recent messages. Every time a message with a new starting time is received, this implicitly will mark all messages prior to this starting time as final and no updates to the content of these

---

messages is allowed. Allowing updates for every message would be too complex, as we also allow to change the time span of the updated messages. This would lead to difficulties for all messages except the most recent one. Furthermore, in this case the different components would need to store information about the whole session instead of only information about the non-final sections.

In order to facilitate the new possibilities of the framework, each component was extended in order to handle intermediate output and input. On the input side, the content of the new message can no longer be simply attached to the previous output, but it might also overwrite part of the stored content. Therefore, additional bookkeeping is necessary. On the output side, we can now already output preliminary results and later update them with better hypotheses.

When generating new messages we have to make sure that we do not mark content as final by using a new start time for the next message although the input for this text has not been marked final by the previous component.

6 Conclusion

In this paper we presented our automatic simultaneous translation system for university lectures. The lecture translator is installed in four lecture halls at KIT and has been running for several years now. The system features several techniques that are specifically tailored at the needs of a simultaneous system processing an unsegmented stream of continuous speech. Feedback from the students and a systematic user study have shown that the system helps students to better follow the lectures if they are not (yet) completely fluent in German. Currently we are increasing the number of lecture halls at KIT that the system is installed in and are working with other universities that are also interested in deploying the system.

References

Eunah Cho, Christian Fügen, Teresa Herrmann, Kevin Kilgour, Mohammed Mediani, Christian Mohr, Jan Niehues, Kay Rottmann, Christian Saam, Sebastian Stüker, et al. 2013. A real-world system for simul-

---

¹http://lecture-translator.kit.edu

taneous translation of german lectures. In *INTER-SPEECH*, pages 3473–3477.

Christian Fügen and Muntsin Kolss. 2007. The influence of utterance chunking on machine translation performance. In *Proceedings of the eighth Annual Conference of the International Speech Communication Association (INTERSPEECH 2007)*, pages 2837–2840, Antwerp, Belgium.

Markus Müller, Sarah Fünfer, Sebastian Stüker, and Alex Waibel. 2016. Evaluation of the KIT Lecture Translation System. In *Language Resources and Evaluation Conference (LREC)*, Portoroz, Slovenia, May.

Jan Niehues and Muntsin Kolss. 2009. A POS-Based Model for Long-Range Reorderings in SMT. In *Proceedings of the Workshop on Statistical Machine Translation*, WMT 2009, Athens, Greece.

Yusuke Oda, Graham Neubig, Sakriani Sakti, Tomoki Toda, and Satoshi Nakamura. 2014. Optimizing segmentation strategies for simultaneous speech translation. In *Proceedings of the 52nd Annual Meeting of the Association for Computational Linguistics (ACL 2014)*, Baltimore, Maryland, USA.

Yusuke Oda, Graham Neubig, Sakriani Sakti, Tomoki Toda, and Satoshi Nakamura. 2015. Syntax-based simultaneous translation through prediction of unseen syntactic constituents. In *The 53rd Annual Meeting of the Association for Computational Linguistics (ACL)*, Beijing, China, July.

Kay Rottmann and Stephan Vogel. 2007. Word Reordering in Statistical Machine Translation with a POS-Based Distortion Model. In *Proceedings of the International Conference on Theoretical and Methodological Issues in Machine Translation (TMI 2007)*, Skövde, Sweden.

Hassan S. Shavarani, Maryam Siahbani, Rantim M. Seraj, and Anoop Sarkar. 2015. Learning segmentations that balance latency versus quality in spoken language translation. In *Proceedings of the Eleventh International Workshop on Spoken Language Translation (IWSLT 2015)*, Da Nang, Vietnam.

Hagen Soltau, Florian Metze, Christian Fugen, and Alex Waibel. 2001. A one-pass decoder based on polymorphic linguistic context assignment. In *Automatic Speech Recognition and Understanding, 2001. ASRU'01. IEEE Workshop on*, pages 214–217. IEEE.

Vivek Kumar Rangarajan Sridhar, John Chen, Srinivas Bangalore, Andrej Ljolje, and Rathinavelu Chengalvarayan. 2013. Segmentation strategies for streaming speech translation. In *Proceedings of the Conference of the North American Chapter of the Association for Computational Linguistics: Human Language Technologies (NAACL-HLT 2013)*, pages 230–238, Atlanta, Georgia, USA.

Sebastian Stüker, Christian Fügen, Florian Kraft, and Matthias Wölfel. 2007. The isl 2007 english speech transcription system for european parliament speeches. In *INTERSPEECH*, pages 2609–2612.

Stephan Vogel. 2003. SMT Decoder Dissected: Word Reordering. In *Proceedings of the International Conference on Natural Language Processing and Knowledge Engineering*, Beijing, China.

Monika Woszczyna, N. Aoki-Waibel, Finn Dag Buø, Noah Coccaro, Keiko Horiguchi, Thomas Kemp, Alon Lavie, Arthur McNair, Thomas Polzin, Ivica Rogina, Carolyn Rose, Tanja Schultz, Bernhard Suhm, M. Tomita, and Alex Waibel. 1994. Janus 93: Towards spontaneous speech translation. In *International Conference on Acoustics, Speech, and Signal Processing 1994*, Adelaide, Australia.

Mahsa Yarmohammadi, Vivek Kumar Rangarajan Sridhar, Srinivas Bangalore, and Baskaran Sankaran. 2013. Incremental segmentation and decoding strategies for simultaneous translation. In *IJCNLP*, pages 1032–1036.

Zara The Supergirl: An Empathetic Personality Recognition System

Pascale Fung, Anik Dey, Farhad Bin Siddique,
Ruixi Lin, Yang Yang, Wan Yan, Ricky Chan Ho Yin
Human Language Technology Center
Department of Electronic and Computer Engineering
Hong Kong University of Science and Technology, Hong Kong
`pascale@ece.ust.hk, adey@connect.ust.hk, fsiddique@connect.ust.hk,`
`rlinab@connect.ust.hk, yyangag@connect.ust.hk,`
`ywanad@connect.ust.hk, eehychan@ust.hk`

Abstract

Zara the Supergirl is an interactive system that, while having a conversation with a user, uses its built in sentiment analysis, emotion recognition, facial and speech recognition modules, to exhibit the human-like response of sharing emotions. In addition, at the end of a 5-10 minute conversation with the user, it can give a comprehensive personality analysis based on the user's interaction with Zara. This is a first prototype that has incorporated a full empathy module, the recognition and response of human emotions, into a spoken language interactive system that enhances human-robot understanding. Zara was shown at the World Economic Forum in Dalian in September 2015.

1 Introduction

"Sorry I didn't hear you" maybe the first empathetic utterance by a commercial machine. Since the late 1990s when the Boston company SpeechWorks International began providing their customer-service software to other numerous companies, which was programmed to use different phrases, people have gotten used to speaking to machines. As people interact more often by voice and gesture, they expect the machines to have more emotional intelligence, and understand other high level communication features such as humor, sarcasm and intention. In order to make such communication possible, the machines need an empathy module in them, which is a software system that can extract emotions from human speech and facial expressions, and can accordingly decide the correct response of the robot. Al-

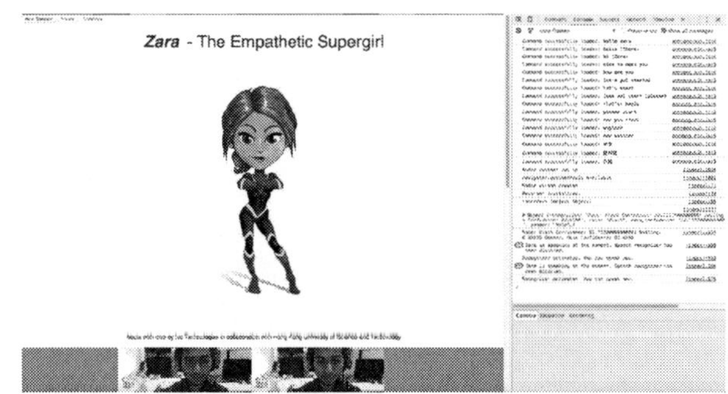

Figure 1: Screenshot of Zara

though research on empathetic robots is still in the primary stage, current methods involve using signal processing techniques, sentiment analysis and machine learning algorithms to make robots that can 'understand' human emotion (Fung, 2015).

We propose Zara the Supergirl as a prototype system. It is a web program running on a server in the cloud. It is basically a virtual robot, with an animated cartoon character to present itself on the screen. Along the way it will get 'smarter' and more empathetic, by having machine learning algorithms, and gathering more data and learning from it. Later stage would involve installing the program into a humanoid robot, and therefore give Zara a physical body.

2 System Description

2.1 Design and Training

Zara's current task is a conversational MBTI personality assessor and we designed 6 categories of personality-assessing questions, each named as a 'state', in attempts to assess the user's personal-

87

Proceedings of NAACL-HLT 2016 (Demonstrations), pages 87–91,
San Diego, California, June 12-17, 2016. ©2016 Association for Computational Linguistics

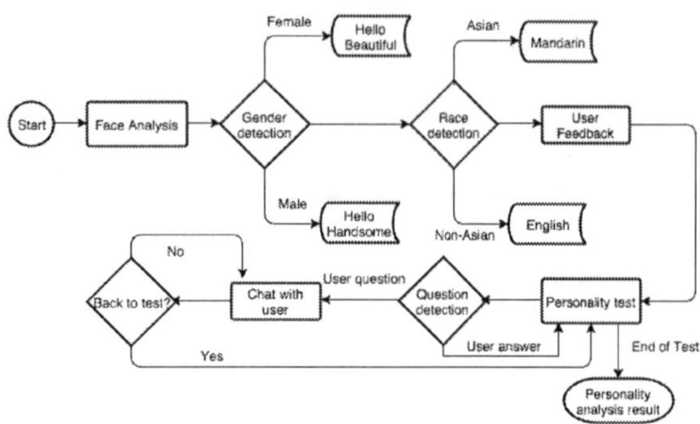

Figure 2: System state diagram

ity (Polzehl et al., 2010). These 6 states inquire about the user's earliest childhood memory, his or her last vacation, challenges at work, creative story-telling, friendship, and affinity toward human-robot conversations. Each state comprises of a series of questions, beginning with one opening inquiry with follow-up questions depending on the length of the user's preceding response. Each user is allocated 5-6 minutes to complete the personality assessment (approx. 1-2 minutes per question). The tests are conducted independently using url link rendered on a browser using built-in microphone and camera on Macs and PCs.

A dialog management system with different states is designed to control the flow of the conversation, which consists of one part machine-initiative questions from Zara and answers from human users, and another part user-initiative questions and challenges to Zara.

2.2 Facial and Speech Recognition

At the beginning of the conversation with the user, the program waits until a face is detected. The face recognition algorithm analyses the image captured by the computer's webcam to guess a possible gender and ethnicity.

For our speech recognition module, we use English audio data with 1385hrs from LDC corpora and public domain corpora for acoustic model training. We train our acoustic models by Kaldi speech recognition toolkit (Povey et al., 2011). We train deep neural network (DNN) HMMs with 6 hidden layers. The DNN is initialized with stacked restricted Boltzmann machines (RBMs) which are pre-trained in a greedy layerwise fashion. Cross-

entropy (CE) criterion DNN training is first applied on the state alignments produced by discriminative trained GMM-HMMs. State alignment is then reproduced with DNN-HMMs, and DNN training with CE criterion is done again. Finally, sequence discriminative training on DNN-HMMs with state level minimum Bayes risk (sMBR) criterion is applied.

Our text data contains 88.6M sentences. It comprises acoustic training transcriptions, web crawled news and book data, Cantab filtering sentences on Google 1 billion word LM benchmark, weather domain queries, music domain queries and common chat queries. We train witten-bell smoothing interpolated trigram language model (LM) and CE based recurrent neural network (RNN) LM using the SRI-LM toolkit (Stolcke and others, 2002) and CUED-RNNLM toolkit (Chen et al., 2016) respectively. The ASR decoder performs search on weighted finite state transducer (WFST) graph for trigram LM and generates lattice, and then performs lattice rescoring with RNN LM. The decoder is designed for input audio data that is streamed from TCP/IP or HTTP protocol, and performs decoding in real time. The decoder supports simultaneous users by multiple threads and user queue. The ASR system achieves 7.6% word error rate on our clean speech test data.

2.3 Audio features for emotion recognition

The dataset we used for training speech emotion recognition is from the Emotional Prosody Speech and Transcripts, Linguistic Data Consortium (LDC) catalog number LDC2002S28[1] and ISBN 1-58563-237-6 (Liberman et al., 2002). The recordings contain audio and transcripts, which consist of professional actors reading a series of semantically neutral utterances (dates and numbers). There are 15 sentiments, 7 subjects and a total number of 2445 utterances. Each subject reads around 3,000 seconds.

We use openSMILE (Eyben et al., 2010) to extract features from LDC dataset. The features are calculated based on the INTERSPEECH 2009 Emotion Challenge feature set for emotion recognition. The final features are computed from a series of input frames and output a single static summary vector, e.g, the smooth methods, maximum and min-

---

[1] https://catalog.ldc.upenn.edu/LDC2002S28

Anxiety	Interest	Shame	Sadness	Pride	Elation
66.2	67.6	62.9	67.7	53.2	59.1
Neural	Despair	Hot anger	Disgust	Boredom	Happy
87.5	58.4	75.0	50.0	63.0	69.9
Panic	Contempt	Cold anger			
65.5	74.7	56.9			

Figure 3: Binary classification accuracy in percentage for each sentiment

imum value, mean value of the features from the frames (Liscombe et al., 2003).

For each sentiment, there are around 170 utterances. We implement an SVM learning method on the binary classification. We first construct a balanced dataset for each sentiment by choosing the same number of utterances per sentiment. Then we split the data into three categories, i.e. training, developing and testing parts in the ratio 6:2:2. We train the SVM with linear kernel and the maximum iteration time is 5,000. The development set is used to tune the number of iteration times. The model is chosen from the highest accuracy results from the development set (results given in figure 3).

2.4 Language understanding for sentiment analysis

In the first version of Zara, sentiment analysis is based on natural language understanding of lexical features. We look for keyword matches from a pool of positive and negative emotion lexicons from LIWC[2] dictionary. The positive lexicons have positive scores, and the negative lexicons have negative scores (Pennebaker et al., 2015). Moreover, when a *negate* word ('do not', 'cannot', etc) is present along with the emotion words, then the score is adjusted accordingly (for example, "I am not at all happy" would have a negative score, even though 'happy' is a positive emotion lexicon).

If there are more than five words in a sentence, then a n-gram model is used containing a number of 5 grams, which is then further analysed to give a total sentiment score across all the 5-grams. This tends to perform better than non n-gram methods in the case for long sentences.

2.5 Personality Analysis

We designed a set of personal questions in six different domains in order to classify user personal-

---

[2] http://liwc.wpengine.com/

Level	Introvert	Extravert
Conversational behaviour	Listen Less back-channel behaviour	Initiate conversation More back-channel behaviour
Topic selection	Self-focused Problem talk, dissatisfaction Strict selection Single topic Few semantic errors Few self-references	Not self-focused* Pleasure talk, agreement, compliment Think out loud* Many topics Many semantic errors Many self-references
Style	Formal Many hedges (tentative words)	Informal Few hedges (tentative words)
Syntax	Many nouns, adjectives, prepositions (explicit) Elaborated constructions Many words per sentence Many articles Many negations	Many verbs, adverbs, pronouns (implicit) Simple constructions* Few words per sentence Few articles Few negations
Lexicon	Correct Rich High diversity Many exclusive and inclusive words Few social words Few positive emotion words Many negative emotion words	Loose* Poor Low diversity Few exclusive and inclusive words Many social words Many positive emotion words Few negative emotion words
Speech	Received accent Slow speech rate Few disfluencies Many unfilled pauses Long response latency Quiet Low voice quality Non-nasal voice Low frequency variability	Local accent* High speech rate Many disfluencies* Few unfilled pauses Short response latency Loud High voice quality Nasal voice High frequency variability

Figure 4: Summary of identified language cues for extraversion and various production levels (Mairesse et al., 2007)

ity from among sixteen different MBTI personality types[3]. The original MBTI test questionnaire contains about 70 questions. We asked a group of training users to answer this questionnaire but also answer questions from Zara. The personality type generated by the MBTI questionnaire is used as the gold standard label for training the Zara system. Based on user answers to Zara's questions, scores are calculated in four dimensions (namely Introversion - Extroversion, Intuitive - Sensing, Thinking - Feeling, Judging - Perceiving).

We use the output of the sentiment analysis from language and emotion recognition from speech as linguistic and speech cues to calculate the score for each personality dimension based on previous research (Mairesse et al., 2007). For each response, the individual score for each of the four dimensions is calculated and updated, and the final score in each dimension is the group average of all the responses.

3 Handling user challenges

The personality test consists mostly of machine-initiative questions from Zara and human answers. However, as described in the user analysis section below, there are scenarios where the user does not respond to questions from Zara directly. 24.62% of the users who tried Zara exhibited some form of verbal challenge in their responses during the dialogue conversation, of which 37.5% of users evade the questions with an irrelevant answer. 12.5% of

---

[3] https://www.personalitypage.com/html/high-level.html

users challenged Zara's ability more directly with questions unrelated to the personality test.

Challenge here refers to user responses that were difficult to handle and impeded the flow of conversation with Zara. They include the following 6 types: 1. Seeking disclosure reciprocity; 2. Asking for clarification; 3. Avoidance of topic; 4. Deliberate challenge of Zara's ability; 5. Abusive language; 6. Garbage.

Several of the above categories can be observed in human-human interactions. For instance, seeking disclosure reciprocity is not uncommon in human conversations (Wheeless and Grotz, 1977).

Responses that revealed some form of avoidance of topic was the largest response group. Avoidance in psychology is viewed as a coping mechanism in response to stress, fear, discomfort, or anxiety (Roth and Cohen, 1986). In the dataset collected, two types of avoidance were observed. Users who actively avoid the topic specifically reveal their unwillingness to continue the conversation ("I dont want to talk about it", "I am in no mood to tell you a story Zara") while users who adopts a more passive strategy had the intent to discontinue the conversation implied ("Let's continue.", "Make it a quick one", "You know...").

Abusive language includes foul, obscene, culturally and socially inappropriate remarks and the like. Currently collected data revealed surprisingly few inappropriate comments such as "get lost now" and "None of your business". These challenges are comparatively mild. Owing to the context of Zara's role as a personality assessor, the reasons here for abuse could be the need to trust the robotic assessor and feeling of discomfort instead of the common enjoyment or group thinking reasons (Nomura et al., 2015).

Asking for clarification examples included "Can you repeat?" and "Can you say it again?". Clarification questions observed in this dataset are primarily non- reprise questions as a request to repeat a previous utterance (Purver, 2004).

Deliberate challenge of a robot's ability was also observed. This took the form of direct requests ("Can I change a topic?", "Why can't you speak English?" in the Chinese mode), or statements unrelated to the questions asked ("Which one is 72.1 percent?").

Zara is programmed with a gentle but witty personality to handle different user challenges. For example, when abusive language is repeatedly used against her, she would ask for an apology after expressing concern for the user's level of stress. If the user asks a general domain question unrelated to the personality test (e.g. "What is the population of Hong Kong"), Zara will try to entertain the question with an answer from a general knowledge database using a search engine API[4], much like Siri or Cortana. However, unlike these other systems, Zara will not chat indefinitely with the user but will remind the user of their task at hand, namely the personality test.

4 Future Work

We are also working on a second approach for the audio emotion recognition. This uses a deep neural network framework, with raw audio data from TED[5] audio database as training data. A total of around 200 hours of TED audio data was used, and was labelled in 13-second frames. This labelled data was used to train a binary classifier of 11 different mood categories.

An FFmpeg command-line software is used to extract the envelop of the raw audio input. Each value is a 16-bit integer. Since the sample rate is 8 kHz and each training sample is around 10 seconds in length, the input dimension should be 80,000. We set 5 ms (40 integers) as the window size and 3.25 ms (26 integers) as the moving step for the first convolutional layer. The regional max-pooling layer takes 40 vectors each time. The window size of the second convolutional layer is 26 which is slightly smaller than the first one. The moving step is 1. We execute the maximum function over all the vectors of the outputs of the second pooling layer.

There are two convolutional, two max-pooling and one embedding layers in the CNN model. The first convolutional layer accepts a short period of audio as input. Then the model moves to convolute the adjacent period of audio with fixed overlap of last period, and the vector input is converted into a matrix. The next layer, max-pooling layer, is a form of non-linear down-sampling. It partitions the

---

[4]https://www.houndify.com//
[5]https://www.ted.com/talks

input matrix into a set of non-overlapping smaller matrices. For each sub-region, it outputs the entry-wise maximum value in one dimension. The second max-pooling layer is to output the entry-wise maximum on the entire matrix instead of sub-regions, which outputs a vector. The embedding layer performs similar function as that of a multi layer perceptron, which maps the vector into a probabilistic distribution over all categories (Palaz and Collobert, 2015) (Golik et al., 2015).

5 Conclusion

We have demonstrated a prototype system of an empathetic virtual robot that can recognize user personalities from speech, language and facial cues. It is too early to say that the time of empathetic and friendly robots has arrived. We have so far developed only the most primary tools that future emotionally intelligent robots would need. The empathetic robots including Zara that are there currently, and the ones that will be there in the near future, might not be completely perfect. However, the most significant step is to make robots to be more human like in their interactions. This means it will have flaws, just like humans do. If this is done right, then future machines and robots will be empathetic and less likely to commit harm in their interactions with humans. They will be able to get us, understand our emotions, and more than anything, they will be our teachers, our caregivers, and our friends.

Acknowledgments

This work was funded by grant #16214415 of the Hong Kong Research Grants Council.

References

Xie Chen, Xunying Liu, Yanmin Qian, Mark JF Gales, Philip Woodland, et al. 2016. Cued-rnnlm–an open-source toolkit for efficient training and evaluation of recurrent neural network language models.

F. Eyben, M. Wollmer, and B. Schuller. 2010. opensmile - the munich versatile and fast open-source audio feature extractor. *ACM MM, Florence, Italy*, pages 1459–1462.

Pascale Fung. 2015. Robots with heart. *Scientific American*, pages 60–63.

P. Golik, Z. Tuske, R. Schluter, and H. Ney. 2015. Convolutional neural networks for acoustic modelling of raw time signal in lvcsr. *Sixteenth Annual Conference of the International Speech Communication Association*.

Mark Liberman, Kelly Davis, Murray Grossman, Nii Martey, and John Bell. 2002. Emotional prosody speech and transcripts ldc2002s28. *Philadelphia:Linguistic Data Consortium*.

J. Liscombe, J. Venditti, and J.B. Hirschberg. 2003. Classifying subject ratings of emotional speech using acoustic features. *Columbia University Academic Commons*.

Francois Mairesse, Marilyn A. Walker, Matthias R. Mehl, and Roger K. Moore. 2007. Using linguistic cues for the automatic recognition of personality in conversation and text. *Journal of Artificial Intelligence Research*, pages 457–500.

T. Nomura, T. Uratani, T. Kanda, Matsumoto K., Kidokoro H., Y. Suehiro, and S. Yamada. 2015. Why do children abuse robots? *In Proceedings of the Tenth Annual ACM/IEEE International Conference on Human-Robot Interaction Extended Abstracts*, pages 63–64.

Dimitri Palaz and Ronan Collobert. 2015. Analysis of cnn based speech recognition system using raw speech as input. *Interspeech*, (EPFL-CONF-210029).

J.W. Pennebaker, R.J. Booth, R.L. Boyd, and M.E. Francis. 2015. Linguistic inquiry and word count: Liwc2015. *Austin, TX: Pennebaker Conglomerates*.

T. Polzehl, S. Moller, and F. Metze. 2010. Automatically assessing personality from speech. *In Semantic Computing (ICSC), 2010 IEEE Fourth International Conference*, pages 134–140.

Daniel Povey, Arnab Ghoshal, Gilles Boulianne, Lukas Burget, Ondrej Glembek, Nagendra Goel, Mirko Hannemann, Petr Motlicek, Yanmin Qian, Petr Schwarz, et al. 2011. The kaldi speech recognition toolkit. In *IEEE 2011 workshop on automatic speech recognition and understanding*, number EPFL-CONF-192584. IEEE Signal Processing Society.

M. Purver. 2004. The theory and use of clarification requests in dialogue. *Unpublished doctoral dissertation, University of London*.

S. Roth and L.J. Cohen. 1986. Approach, avoidance, and coping with stress. *American psychologist*, 41(7):813.

Andreas Stolcke et al. 2002. Srilm-an extensible language modeling toolkit. In *INTERSPEECH*.

L. R. Wheeless and J. Grotz. 1977. The measurement of trust and its relationship to self-disclosure. *Human Communication Research*, 3(3):250–257.

Kathaa: A Visual Programming Framework for NLP Applications

Sharada Prasanna Mohanty, Nehal J Wani, Manish Srivastava, Dipti Misra Sharma
Language Technology Research Center
International Institute of Information Technology, Hyderabad
{spmohanty, nehal.wani}@research.iiit.ac.in, {m.shrivastava, dipti}@iiit.ac.in

Abstract

In this paper, we present Kathaa[1], an open source web based Visual Programming Framework for NLP applications. It supports design, execution and analysis of complex NLP systems by choosing and visually connecting NLP modules from an already available and easily extensible Module library. It models NLP systems as a Directed Acyclic Graph of optionally parallalized information flow, and lets the user choose and use available modules in their NLP applications irrespective of their technical proficiency. Kathaa exposes a precise Module definition API to allow easy integration of external NLP components (along with their associated services as docker containers), it allows everyone to *publish* their services in a standardized format for everyone else to use it out of the box.

1 Introduction

Natural Language Processing systems are inherently very complex, and their design is heavily tied up with their implementation. There is a huge diversity in the way the individual components of the complex system consume, process and spit out information. Apart from that, many of the components also have associated services which in many cases are really hard to replicate and/or setup. Hence, most researchers end up writing their own in-house methods for gluing the components together, and in some cases, own in-house re-implementations of the individual components, often inefficient re-implementations. And on top of that, most of the

---

[1]https://github.com/kathaa/kathaa

popular NLP components make many assumptions about the technical proficiency of the user who will be using those components. All of these factors clubbed together shut many potential users out of the whole ecosystem of NLP systems, and hence many potentially creative applications of these components. With Kathaa, we aim to separate the design and implementation layers of Natural Language Processing systems, and efficiently pack every component into consistent and reusable black-boxes which can be made to interface with each other through an intuitive visual interface, irrespective of the software environment in which the components reside, and irrespective of the technical proficiency of the user using the system. Kathaa builds on top of numerous ideas explored in the academia around Visual Programming Languages in general(Green and Petre, 1996) (Shu, 1988) (Myers, 1990), and also on Visual Programming Languages in the context of NLP (Cunningham et al., 1997).

2 Kathaa Modules

Kathaa Modules are the basic units of computation in the proposed Visual Programming Framework. They consume the input(s) across multiple input channels, process them, and finally pass on their output(s) across the many output channels they might have. The user has access to a whole array of such modules with different utilities via the Kathaa Module Library. The user can connect together these modules in any combination as he pleases, as long as the modules are compatible with each other. The user also has the ability to tinker with the functionality of a particular module in real time by using an

Proceedings of NAACL-HLT 2016 (Demonstrations), pages 92–96,
San Diego, California, June 12-17, 2016. ©2016 Association for Computational Linguistics

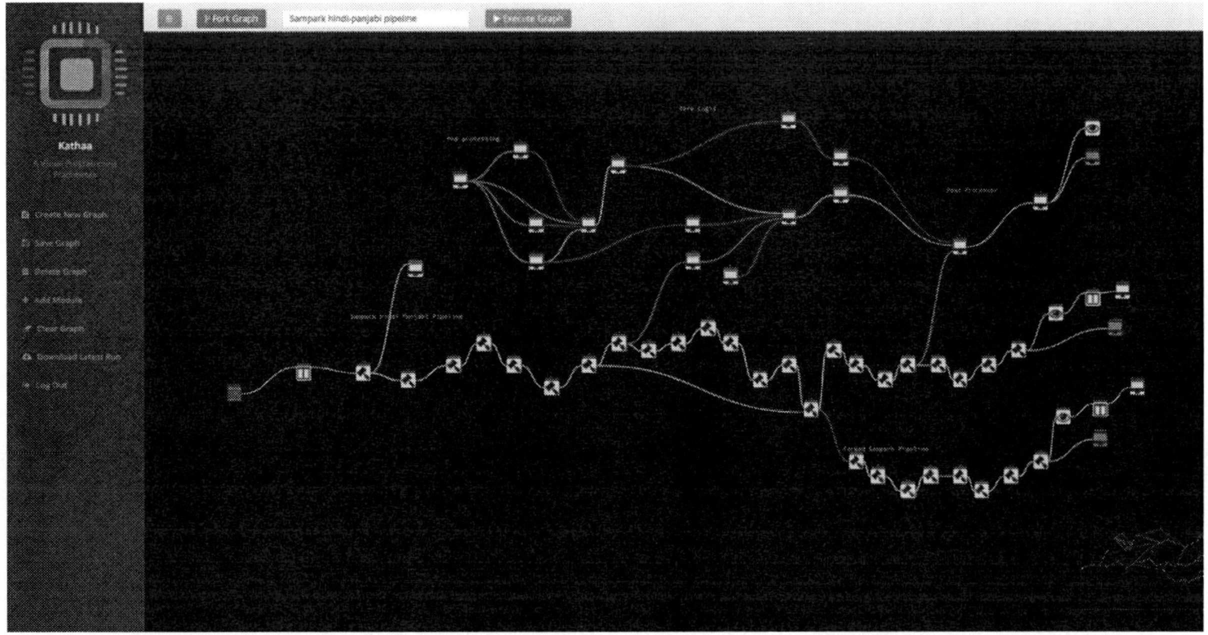

Figure 1: Example of a Hindi-Panjabi Machine Translation System, visually implemented using Kathaa.

embedded code editor in the Kathaa Web Interface during or before the execution of the Kathaa Graph.

2.1 Kathaa Data Blobs

Every module receives inputs across multiple channels, or ports. Every input channel receives the data in the form of a series of **kathaa-data-blobs**, and all the input channels have the exact same number of kathaa-data-blobs. Data blobs are processed in parallel by different instances of the same module during execution, and most modules generate the same number of data blobs across all their output channels. The concept of numerous data blobs spread across multiple input channels enables us to efficiently empower module writers to leverage from the inherent parallelizability in tasks performed by numerous NLP components. For example, some modules might work at the level of sentences, so if we have multiple sentences as inputs to this module, all of them are passed as different kathaa-data-blobs so that the framework can efficiently parallelize their processing depending, of course, on the availability of resources. Similarly, other modules could expect parallelizability at the level of words, or phrases or even a whole discourse. The kathaa-data-blobs were very much inspired by the data-blobs used in Caffe. (Jia et al., 2014)

2.2 Types of Kathaa Modules

2.2.1 Kathaa General Modules

As mentioned previously, most modules produce the exact same number of kathaa-data-blobs as they receive across their input channels. This can be guaranteed because during execution, all the parallel instances of the module are provided only a single kathaa-data-blob in each of their input channels, and when they are done processing, they write a single kathaa-data-blob across their output channels. The *kathaa-orchestrator* deals with the separation of the blobs before passing the inputs to the module instance, and the aggregation of the blobs after each instance of the module has finished processing their corresponding kathaa-data-blobs. These type of modules can be basically called as the **Kathaa General Modules**. To illustrate the above described concepts we implement a very simple Echo module[2], which simply takes in a few data blobs across a single channel, and spits out the same into a single output channel. We also have a very flexible implementation of a Custom Module[3] which can act as a quick starting point when defining Kathaa General Modules.

---

[2]https://git.io/vV4RA
[3]https://git.io/vV4Rp

2.2.2 Kathaa Blob Adapters

Kathaa Blob Adapters, on the other hand are a class of Kathaa Modules, which are provided with all the blobs across all their input channels at the same time, and they have the ability to modify the number of blobs and pass it over to their output channels. They can be used in giving the user a more fine grained control over the parallalizability of different parts of their Kathaa graphs by using kathaa-data-blobs. For example, a graph which receives a whole discourse as a single blob, might want to process the sentences parallely, and they could use a line-splitter[4] to split the whole discourse represented as a single kathaa-data-blob into multiple kathaa-data-blobs each representing a single sentence, and when finally the user desired processing of the individual sentences are complete, a line-aggregator[5] could be used to aggregate the processed sentences again into a single kathaa-data-blob. Similar kathaa-blob-adapters could be implemented to deal with splitting and aggregation of kathaa-data-blobs at the level of words, phrases, or even some custom logic. Kathaa Blob Adapters will be crucial in exercising the control over the inherent parallalisation support in Kathaa Orchestrator. For example, in contrast to the example cited above, if we are dealing certain language processing tasks which are inherently not parallalizable after a certain level of granularity, like say Anaphora Resolution, Multi Document Summarisation, etc, the user will have to use an appropriate Kathaa Blob Adapter, to make sure that all the information that is required for the particular language processing task is available as a single blob to be passed onto the module. In the case of Anaphora Resolution, a single Kathaa Blob will contain a string of N sentences, and in the case of Multi Document Summarisation, a single Kathaa Blob will contain a string of M Documents. In both the previous cases, the module can receive multiple such Kathaa Blobs, which can then be processed parallely based on the availability of resources.

2.2.3 Kathaa User Intervention Module

In some NLP systems, the overall execution of the system might have to halt for some kind of user feedback. Like in the case of resource creation, where

for example, you start with a bunch of sentences, parse them using an available parser module, and then you would want to add Anaphora annotations by a human annotator (Sangal and Sharma, 2001). In that case, a **Kathaa User Intervention** Module could be used, where the overall execution at the particular node in the graph halts till the user modifies the kathaa-data-blobs as he pleases and resumes the execution at the said node. Kathaa core implements a Kathaa User Intervention[6] module for reference.

2.2.4 Kathaa Resource Module

Kathaa Resource Modules are the class of Kathaa Modules which do not do any processing of the data, but instead they store and provide a corpus of text which can be used by any of the modules in the whole graph during execution.

2.2.5 Kathaa Evaluation Module

The aim of Kathaa is to provide an intuitive environment for not only prototyping and deployment but also debugging and analysis of NLP system. Hence, we include a class of modules called as **Kathaa Evaluation Modules** which very much like Kathaa Blob Adapters receive all the blobs across all the input channels, and do some analysis and spit out the results into the output channels. While in principle this a subset of Kathaa Blob Adapters, these modules enjoy a separate category among Kathaa Modules because of their utility in designing complex NLP systems. We implement a sample classification evaluator[7] to help researchers quickly come up with easy to visualize confusion matrices to aid them in evaluating the performance of any of their subsystems. This could act as a starting point for easily implementing any other Evaluation modules.

2.3 Kathaa Module Services

Most popular NLP Components work in completely different software environments, and hence standardizing the interaction between all of them is a highly challenging task. Kathaa allows every module to define an optional service by referencing a publicly available *docker container* in the module definition. Kathaa deals with the life-cycle management of the referenced containers on a config-

---

[4]https://git.io/vV4Rj
[5]https://git.io/vV40v

[6]https://git.io/vV40U
[7]https://git.io/vV40f

urable set of Host Machines. The corresponding kathaa-modules function definition then acts as a light weight wrapper around this service. This finally enables different research groups to **publish their service** in a consistent and reusable way, such that it fits nicely in the Kathaa Module ecosystem.

2.4 Kathaa Module Packaging and Distribution

Kathaa Modules reside as a collection of Kathaa Module Groups in a publicly accessible `git` Repository. Each of these modules have a specification definition file called as `package.json`, where the author of the module has to specify the basic metadata about the module like the name, version, input channels, output channels, etc. The user has the option to reference the corresponding Kathaa-Service by referencing the Docker container in this file. The *type* of the input and output channels can also be specified to mark compatibility of different modules with each other. A sample example of a Kathaa module template can be seen in the case of the custom module[8]. All the supported Module Groups for a particular Kathaa Instance can be referenced directly by their publicly available links on the Kathaa Server, and under the hood, Kathaa deals with the dependency resolution of the modules, downloading of all the modules, instantiation of the associated Docker Container if any, etc.

2.5 Kathaa Interface

Kathaa Interface lets the user design any complex NLP system as a Directed Acyclic Graph with the Kathaa Modules as nodes, and edges being the flow of kathaa-data-blobs between them. Users have the option to not only execute any such graph, but also interact with it in real time by changing both the state and functionality of any of the module right from within the interface. It can be a really useful aid in debugging complex systems, as it lets the User easily visualize and modify the flow of kathaa-data-blobs across the whole Kathaa Graph. Apart from that, it also encourages code-reuse by lettings users "Fork" a graph, or "remix" the designs of NLP systems to come up with better and adapted versions of the same systems.

2.6 Kathaa Orchestrator

Kathaa Orchestrator is at the core of the whole Visual Programming Framework. Kathaa Orchestrator obtains the structure of the Kathaa Graph and the initial state of the execution initiator modules from the Kathaa Interface, and then it goes on to efficiently orchestrate the execution of the graph depending on the nature and state of the modules, while dealing with process parallelisms, module dependencies, etc under the hood.

3 Use Cases

Kathaa, as a Visual Programming Framework was developed with Sampark Machine Translation System as a use case. We ported all the modules of the Hindi-Panjabi[9] and Hindi-Urdu[10] Translation Pipelines of Sampark Machine Translation System into Kathaa (SAM, 2016). We then demonstrated the use of Kathaa in creation of NLP Resources by the use of Kathaa User Intervention modules, and also moved on to demonstrate visual analysis of different classification approaches by using the Kathaa-Classification-Evaluation module. We are currently also exploring the use of Kathaa in classrooms to help students interact with and design complex NLP systems with a much lower barrier to entry. All these example Kathaa Graphs are the seed Graphs that are included in the repository, and can be used out of the box. It is important to note that these use cases that we managed to explore are only the tip of the iceberg when it comes to what is possible using a framework like Kathaa. One of the key features in Kathaa which enables for it to be used in a whole range of use cases is the easy extensibility. The Kathaa Module Definition API, enables the user of the system to theoretically define any function as a Kathaa Module. Also, Kathaa internally works using event triggers, hence making it a practical possibility to define modules which may run for days or weeks, quite helpful when exploring Kathaa for use cases where the user might want to define a Kathaa Module which trains a model based on some pre-processed data. The NPM(Tilkov and Vinoski, 2010) inspired packag-

---

[8]`https://git.io/vV40J`

[9]`https://github.com/kathaa/hindi-panjabi-modules`

[10]`https://github.com/kathaa/hindi-urdu-modules`

ing system, is again something which we believe can help with large scale adoption of a system like Kathaa. It paves the way for a public contributed repository of NLP components, all of which can be mashed together in any desired combination. The ability to optionally package individual services using Docker Containers also helps make a strong case when pitching for the possibility of a large public contributed repository of NLP components. These are a few things which set Kathaa apart from already existing systems like LAPPS Grid(Ide et al., 2014), ALVEO(Cassidy et al., 2014) where the easy extensibility of the system is a major bottleneck in its large scale adoption. The interoperability between existing systems is also of key importance, and the design of Kathaa accommodates for its easy adaptation to be used along with other similar system. The assumption, of course, is that a wrapper Kathaa Module has to be designed for each target system using the Kathaa Module Definition API. The wrapper modules would be completely decoupled from the Kathaa Core codebase, and hence can be designed and implemented by anyone just like any other Kathaa Module.

A demonstration video of many features and use cases of Kathaa is also available to view at :

https://youtu.be/woK5x0NmrUA

4   Conclusion

We demonstrate an open source web based Visual Programming Framework for NLP Systems, and make it available for everyone to use under a MIT License. We hope our efforts can in some way catalyze more new and creative applications of NLP components, and enables an increased number of researchers to more comfortably tinker with and modify complex NLP Systems.

Acknowledgments

The first real world implementation of a Kathaa Graph was achieved by porting numerous modules from Sampark MT system developed during the "Indian Language to India Language Machine translation" (ILMT) consortium project funded by the TDIL program of Department of Electronics and Information Technology (DeitY), Govt. of India. Kathaa is built with numerous open source tools and libraries, an (almost) exhaustive list of which is available in the Github Repository of the project, and we would like to thank each and every contributor to all those projects.

References

[Cassidy et al.2014] Steve Cassidy, Dominique Estival, Tim Jones, Peter Sefton, Denis Burnham, Jared Burghold, et al. 2014. The alveo virtual laboratory: A web based repository api.

[Cunningham et al.1997] Hamish Cunningham, Kevin Humphreys, Robert Gaizauskas, and Yorick Wilks. 1997. Gate - a general architecture for text engineering. In *Proceedings of the Fifth Conference on Applied Natural Language Processing: Descriptions of System Demonstrations and Videos*, pages 29–30, Washington, DC, USA, March. Association for Computational Linguistics.

[Green and Petre1996] Thomas R. G. Green and Marian Petre. 1996. Usability analysis of visual programming environments: A 'cognitive dimensions' framework. *J. Vis. Lang. Comput.*, 7(2):131–174.

[Ide et al.2014] Nancy Ide, James Pustejovsky, Christopher Cieri, Eric Nyberg, Di Wang, Keith Suderman, Marc Verhagen, and Jonathan Wright. 2014. The language application grid. In *LREC*, pages 22–30.

[Jia et al.2014] Yangqing Jia, Evan Shelhamer, Jeff Donahue, Sergey Karayev, Jonathan Long, Ross Girshick, Sergio Guadarrama, and Trevor Darrell. 2014. Caffe: Convolutional architecture for fast feature embedding. In *Proceedings of the 22Nd ACM International Conference on Multimedia*, MM '14, pages 675–678, New York, NY, USA. ACM.

[Myers1990] Brad A. Myers. 1990. Taxonomies of visual programming and program visualization. *J. Vis. Lang. Comput.*, 1(1):97–123.

[SAM2016] 2016. Sampark: Machine translation among indian languages. http://sampark.iiit.ac.in/sampark/web/index.php/content. Accessed: 2016-02-10.

[Sangal and Sharma2001] Rajeev Sangal and Dipti Misra Sharma. 2001. Creating language resources for nlp in indian languages 1. background.

[Shu1988] Nan C Shu. 1988. *Visual programming*. Van Nostrand Reinhold.

[Tilkov and Vinoski2010] Stefan Tilkov and Steve Vinoski. 2010. Node. js: Using javascript to build high-performance network programs. *IEEE Internet Computing*, 14(6):80.

"Why Should I Trust You?"
Explaining the Predictions of Any Classifier

Marco Tulio Ribeiro
University of Washington
Seattle, WA 98105, USA
`marcotcr@cs.uw.edu`

Sameer Singh
University of Washington
Seattle, WA 98105, USA
`sameer@cs.uw.edu`

Carlos Guestrin
University of Washington
Seattle, WA 98105, USA
`guestrin@cs.uw.edu`

Abstract

Despite widespread adoption in NLP, machine learning models remain mostly black boxes. Understanding the reasons behind predictions is, however, quite important in assessing trust in a model. Trust is fundamental if one plans to take action based on a prediction, or when choosing whether or not to deploy a new model. In this work, we describe LIME, a novel explanation technique that explains the predictions of any classifier in an interpretable and faithful manner. We further present a method to explain models by presenting representative individual predictions and their explanations in a non-redundant manner. We propose a demonstration of these ideas on different NLP tasks such as document classification, politeness detection, and sentiment analysis, with classifiers like neural networks and SVMs. The user interactions include explanations of free-form text, challenging users to identify the better classifier from a pair, and perform basic feature engineering to improve the classifiers.

1 Introduction

Machine learning is at the core of many recent advances in natural language processing. Unfortunately, the important role of humans is an oft-overlooked aspect in the field. Whether humans are directly using machine learning classifiers as tools, or are deploying models into products that need to be shipped, a vital concern remains: *if the users do not trust a model or a prediction, they will not use it.* It is important to differentiate between two different (but related) definitions of trust: (1) *trusting a prediction*, i.e. whether a user trusts an individual prediction sufficiently to take some action based on it, and (2) *trusting a model*, i.e. whether the user trusts a model to behave in reasonable ways if deployed "in the wild". Both are directly impacted by how much the human understands a model's behavior, as opposed to seeing it as a black box. Recent resurgence of neural networks has resulted in state-of-art models whose working is quite opaque to the user, exacerbating this problem.

A common surrogate for ascertaining trust in a model is to evaluate accuracy on held-out annotated data. However, there are several ways this evaluation can go wrong. Data leakage, for example, defined as the unintentional leakage of signal into the training (and validation) data that would not occur in the wild (Kaufman et al., 2011), potentially increases accuracy. Practitioners are also known to overestimate the accuracy of their models based on cross validation (Patel et al., 2008), as real-world data is often significantly different. Another particularly hard to detect problem is dataset shift (Candela et al., 2009), where training data is different than test data. Further, there is frequently a mismatch between that metrics that we can compute and optimize (e.g. accuracy) and the actual metrics of interest such as user engagement and retention. A practitioner may wish to choose a less accurate model for content recommendation that does not place high importance in features related to "clickbait" articles (which may hurt user retention), even if exploiting such features increases the accuracy of the model in cross validation.

In this paper, we describe a system that *explains* why a classifier made a prediction by identifying useful portions of the input. It has been observed

Proceedings of NAACL-HLT 2016 (Demonstrations), pages 97–101,
San Diego, California, June 12-17, 2016. ©2016 Association for Computational Linguistics

that providing an explanation can increase the acceptance of computer-generated movie recommendations (Herlocker et al., 2000) and other automated systems (Dzindolet et al., 2003), and we explore their utility for NLP. Specifically, we present:

- LIME, an algorithm that can explain the predictions of *any* classifier, by approximating it locally with an interpretable model.

- SP-LIME, a method that selects a set of representative explanations to address the "trusting the model" problem, via submodular optimization.

- A demonstration designed to present the benefits of these explanation methods, on multiple NLP classification applications, classifier algorithms, and trust-related tasks.

2 Explaining Predictions and Models

By "explaining a prediction", we mean presenting visual artifacts that provide qualitative understanding of the relationship between the instance's components (e.g. words in text) and the model's prediction. Explaining predictions is an important aspect in getting humans to trust and use machine learning effectively, provided the explanations are faithful and intelligible. We summarize the techniques here; further details and experiments are available in Ribeiro et al. (2016).

Local Interpretable Model-Agnostic Explanations

We present Local Interpretable Model-agnostic Explanations (**LIME**). The overall goal of LIME is to identify an **interpretable** model over the *interpretable representation* that is **locally faithful** to predictions of **any classifier**. It is important to distinguish between features and interpretable data representations, the latter is a representation that is understandable to humans, regardless of the actual features used by the model. A possible *interpretable representation* for text is a binary vector indicating the presence or absence of a word, even though the classifier may use more complex (and incomprehensible) features such as word embeddings. We denote $x \in \mathbb{R}^d$ as the original instance, and $x' \in \{0,1\}^{d'}$ to denote a binary vector for its interpretable representation.

Formally, we define an explanation as a model $g \in G$, where G is the class of linear models,

such that $g(z') = w_g \cdot z'$ Note that g acts over absence/presence of the *interpretable components*, i.e. we can readily present it to the user with visual artifacts. We let $\Omega(g)$ be a measure of *complexity* (as opposed to *interpretability*) of the explanation $g \in G$. For text classification, we set a limit K on the number of words included, i.e. $\Omega(g) = \infty \mathbb{1}[\|w_g\|_0 > K]$.

Let the model being explained be denoted f, i.e. $f(x)$ is the probability (or a binary indicator) that x belongs to a certain class. We further use $\Pi_x(z)$ as a proximity measure between an instance z to x, so as to define locality around x. Finally, let $\mathcal{L}(f, g, \Pi_x)$ be a measure of how unfaithful g is in approximating f in the locality defined by Π_x. We use the locally weighted square loss as $\mathcal{L}$, as defined in Eq. (1), where we let $\Pi_x(z) = exp(-D(x,z)^2/\sigma^2)$ be an exponential kernel on cosine distance D.

$$\mathcal{L}(f, g, \Pi_x) = \sum_{z,z' \in \mathcal{Z}} \Pi_x(z) \left(f(z) - g(z') \right)^2 \quad (1)$$

In order to ensure both **interpretability** and **local fidelity**, we minimize $\mathcal{L}(f, g, \Pi_x)$ while having $\Omega(g)$ be low enough to be interpretable by humans.

$$\xi(x) = \operatorname{argmin}_{g \in G} \ \mathcal{L}(f, g, \Pi_x) + \Omega(g) \quad (2)$$

We approximate $\mathcal{L}(f, g, \Pi_x)$ by drawing samples, weighted by Π_x. Given a sample $z' \in \{0,1\}^{d'}$ (which contains a fraction of the nonzero elements of x'), we recover the sample in the original representation $z \in R^d$ and obtain $f(z)$, which is used as a *label* for the explanation model. Given this dataset $\mathcal{Z}$ of perturbed samples with the associated labels, we optimize Eq. (2) to get an explanation $\xi(x)$ by first selecting K features with Lasso (Efron et al., 2004), forward selection or some other method, and then learning the weights via least squares.

Submodular Pick for Explaining Models

Although an explanation of a single prediction provides some understanding into the reliability of the classifier to the user, it is not sufficient to evaluate and assess trust in the model as a whole. We propose to give a global understanding of the model by explaining a set of individual instances. Even though explanations of multiple instances can be insightful, these instances need to be selected judiciously, since users may not have the time to examine a large number of explanations. We represent the number of explanations humans are willing to look at a budget B, i.e. given a set of instances X, we select B explanations for the user to inspect. We construct an $n \times d'$ *explanation matrix* $\mathcal{W}$ that represents the local importance of the interpretable components for each instance, i.e. for an instance x_i and explanation $g_i = \xi(x_i)$, we set $\mathcal{W}_i = |w_{g_i}|$. Further, for each component j in $\mathcal{W}$, we let I_j denote the *global* importance, $I_j = \sqrt{\sum_{i=1}^{n} \mathcal{W}_{ij}}$.

While we want to pick instances that cover the important components, the set of explanations must not be redundant in the components they show the users, i.e. avoid selecting instances with similar explanations. We formalize this non-redundant coverage intuition in Eq. (3), where coverage $\mathcal{C}$, given $\mathcal{W}$ and I, computes the total importance of the features that appear in at least one instance in a set V.

$$\mathcal{C}(V, \mathcal{W}, I) = \sum_{j=1}^{d'} \mathbb{1}_{[\exists i \in V : \mathcal{W}_{ij} > 0]} I_j \qquad (3)$$

The pick problem thus consists of finding the set $V, |V| \leq B$ that achieves highest coverage.

$$Pick(\mathcal{W}, I) = \operatorname{argmax}_{V, |V| \leq B} \mathcal{C}(V, \mathcal{W}, I) \qquad (4)$$

The problem in Eq. (4) is maximizing a weighted coverage function, and is NP-hard (Feige, 1998). Due to submodularity, a greedy algorithm that iteratively adds the instance with the highest coverage gain offers a constant-factor approximation guarantee of $1 - 1/e$ to the optimum (Krause and Golovin, 2014).

3 Demo Outline

Using this explanation system that is capable of providing visual explanations for predictions of any classifier, we present an outline for a demonstration using different NLP tasks, models, and user interactions. The complete source code and documentation for installing and running the demonstration is available at `https://github.com/uw-mode/naacl16-demo`, which uses the code for explaining classifiers available as an open-source python implementation at `https://github.com/marcotcr/lime`.

Applications

We explore three NLP classification tasks, which differ in the types of text they apply to and predicted cat-

egories: politeness detection for sentences (Danescu-Niculescu-Mizil et al., 2013), multi-class content classification for documents (20 newsgroups data), and sentiment analysis of sentences from movie reviews (Socher et al., 2013). We explore classifiers for these tasks that vary considerably in their underlying representation, such as LSTMs (Wieting et al., 2015), SVMs, and random forests, trained on bag of words or on word embeddings.

We will outline the specific user interactions using a running example of the 20 newsgroups dataset, and the interfaces for the other applications will look similar. In particular, we focus on differentiating between "Christianity" from "Atheism", and use an SVM with an RBF kernel here. Although this classifier achieves 94% held-out accuracy, and one would be tempted to trust it based on this, the explanation for an instance shows that predictions are made for quite arbitrary reasons (words "Posting", "Host" and "Re" have no connection to either Christianity or Atheism).

3.1 Explaining Individual Predictions

The first part of the demo focuses on explaining individual predictions. Given an instance that the user either selects from the dataset or writes their own piece of text, we provide the set of words that are important for the prediction according to the classifier of their choosing. The interface for the user is shown in Figure 1, which embedded in an iPython notebook. For most datasets and classifiers, our current system can produce an explanation in under three seconds, and some simple further optimizations can be used to produce near-instant explanations.

3.2 Explaining and Comparing Models

For the second part of the demonstration, we provide explanations of different models in order to compare them, based on explanations of a few selected instances. The interface presents the explanations one at a time, similar to that in Figure 1. By default the instances are selected using our submodular approach (SP-lime), however we also allow users to write their own text as well, and produce explanations for the classifiers for comparison.

3.3 Improving Classifiers

As the final demonstration, we consider a simple version of feature engineering. Specifically, we initiate

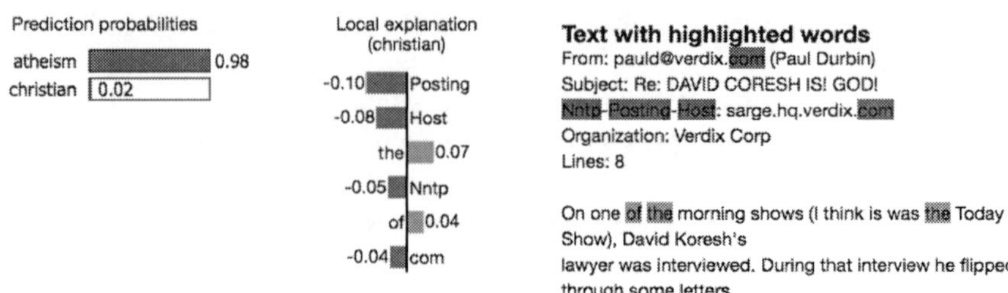

Figure 1: Example explanation for an instance of document classification. The bar chart represents the importance given to the most relevant words by the classifier, also highlighted in the text. Color indicates which class the word is important for (orange for "Christianity", blue for "Atheism").

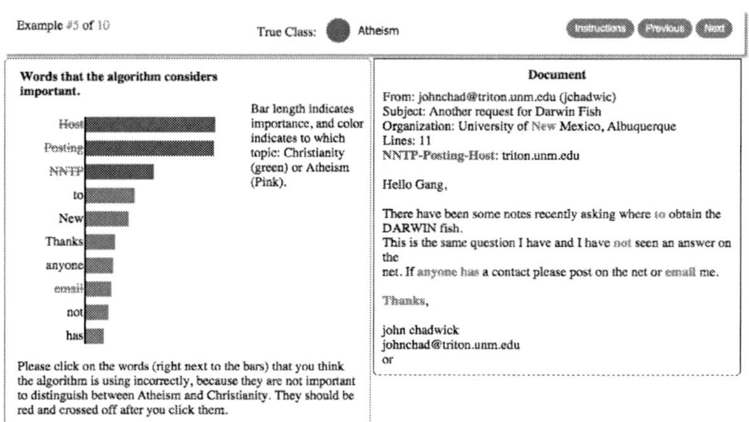

Figure 2: Interface for *feature cleaning*, a simple version of feature engineering where users select words to remove from the model by clicking on them (indicated by red, struck-out text). Here, green bars indicate importance of the word for "Christianity", and magenta "Atheism".

each user with a classifier trained using *all* features, including both noisy and correct ones. We then show explanations of the classifier to the users, and ask them to select which words to remove from the classifier (see Figure 2 for the interface). Given this feedback, we retrain the classifier and provide the users with a score of how well their classifier performed on a hidden set, along with a *leader board* of the accuracy of all the participants.

4 Conclusions

We argue that trust is crucial for effective human interaction with machine learning based NLP systems, and that explaining individual predictions is important in assessing trust. We present a demonstration for LIME, a modular and extensible approach to faithfully explain the predictions of *any* model in an interpretable manner, and SP-LIME, a method to select representative and non-redundant explanations, providing a global view of the model to users. The user interactions on multiple applications and classifiers span a variety of trust-related tasks: getting insights into predictions, deciding between models, and improving untrustworthy models.

Acknowledgments

We would like to thank Kevin Gimpel, John Wieting, and Cristian Danescu-Niculescu-Mizil for making their classifiers and datasets available for use. This work was supported in part by the TerraSwarm Research Center, one of six centers supported by the STARnet phase of the Focus Center Research Program (FCRP) a Semiconductor Research Corporation program sponsored by MARCO and DARPA.

References

J. Quiñonero Candela, M. Sugiyama, A. Schwaighofer, and N. D. Lawrence. 2009. *Dataset Shift in Machine Learning*. MIT.

Cristian Danescu-Niculescu-Mizil, Moritz Sudhof, Dan Jurafsky, Jure Leskovec, and Christopher Potts. 2013. A computational approach to politeness with application to social factors. In *Proceedings of ACL*.

Mary T. Dzindolet, Scott A. Peterson, Regina A. Pomranky, Linda G. Pierce, and Hall P. Beck. 2003. The role of trust in automation reliance. *Int. J. Hum.-Comput. Stud.*, 58(6).

Bradley Efron, Trevor Hastie, Iain Johnstone, and Robert Tibshirani. 2004. Least angle regression. *Annals of Statistics*, 32:407–499.

Uriel Feige. 1998. A threshold of ln n for approximating set cover. *J. ACM*, 45(4), July.

Jonathan L. Herlocker, Joseph A. Konstan, and John Riedl. 2000. Explaining collaborative filtering recommendations. In *Conference on Computer Supported Cooperative Work (CSCW)*.

Shachar Kaufman, Saharon Rosset, and Claudia Perlich. 2011. Leakage in data mining: Formulation, detection, and avoidance. In *Knowledge Discovery and Data Mining (KDD)*.

Andreas Krause and Daniel Golovin. 2014. Submodular function maximization. In *Tractability: Practical Approaches to Hard Problems*. Cambridge University Press, February.

Kayur Patel, James Fogarty, James A. Landay, and Beverly Harrison. 2008. Investigating statistical machine learning as a tool for software development. In *Human Factors in Computing Systems (CHI)*.

Marco Tulio Ribeiro, Sameer Singh, and Carlos Guestrin. 2016. "Why should I trust you?": Explaining the predictions of any classifier. *CoRR*, abs/1602.04938.

Richard Socher, Alex Perelygin, Jean Wu, Jason Chuang, Christopher D. Manning, Andrew Y. Ng, and Christopher Potts. 2013. Recursive deep models for semantic compositionality over a sentiment treebank. In *Proceedings of the 2013 Conference on Empirical Methods in Natural Language Processing*, pages 1631–1642, Stroudsburg, PA, October. Association for Computational Linguistics.

John Wieting, Mohit Bansal, Kevin Gimpel, and Karen Livescu. 2015. Towards universal paraphrastic sentence embeddings. *CoRR*, abs/1511.08198.

Association for Computational Linguistics
209 N. Eighth Street
Stroudsburg, Pennsylvania 18360

ISBN 978-1-5108-2513-0